When The Ground Shifts:

How to Thrive in the Age of AI Job Displacement with the Haversack Method

by

Phil Finane

The examples and case studies in this book are composite representations based on patterns observed across multiple professional contexts. They are designed to illustrate common challenges whilst protecting individual privacy. Any resemblance to specific individuals or organisations beyond publicly referenced information is coincidental.

The information and perspectives in this book are intended for general guidance only. While the author has made every effort to ensure accuracy, no guarantees are given regarding completeness or applicability to individual circumstances. The author and publisher accept no responsibility for any loss or damage arising from reliance on the content of this book.

First published in 2025
Publisher: Monard X Publishing
Cork, Ireland

ISBN (Paperback): 978-1-9194174-0-0

Printed and distributed by print-on-demand services. Also available on eBook.

For Claire,

Always rock solid when the ground shifts.

Table of Contents

Foreword

When people ask me where we are with AI and jobs, I tell them we're in transition. Not at the beginning, where it all felt like a curiosity, and not at the end, where whole industries have been reshaped. We're somewhere in between, watching the changes accelerate.

The early phase came quietly. Automated systems slipped into call centres, translation apps took hold, and software helped speed up processes that used to need clerks or assistants. No one felt their job disappear, but the edges of work began to change.

The acceleration phase followed. AI writing assistants and coding tools moved from experimental to everyday. Suddenly, the first draft of a report, a marketing campaign, or even a chunk of computer code could be generated in seconds. The job was not gone, but the work inside the job was different.

That's where we live now. Generative AI is mainstream. The productivity gains are real, the time savings are measurable, and the unease is widespread. You can sense both the opportunity and the threat at the same time.

Some argue we are in an AI bubble, that the hype exceeds reality, that market corrections will follow. They might be right. The Dotcom bubble was real, and it burst spectacularly. But the internet didn't go away; if anything, it accelerated. The bubble question misses the point. Whether AI development follows a straight line or experiences setbacks, the work you're doing today looks different from the work you did last year. That change is real, bubble or not. And it's here to stay.

The hardest phase is still to come. Companies are only beginning to ask the structural question: if AI can produce most of the output, why maintain the same headcount? That's when displacement moves from tasks to roles. History shows us that organisations are slower to change than technology itself, but once the logic clicks, restructuring follows fast.

So, from a job perspective, we are not at the start of this story, and we're nowhere near the end. We're in the transition. Some sectors are already feeling it. Most others remain busy but uneasy, aware that what feels solid today may not hold tomorrow.

This book will not try to predict which jobs survive or tell you how much time you have. What it will attempt to give you is a method that works when predictions fail. A way to notice what matters in your specific context, build skills that create immediate value, and help you move faster than the disruption around you. It is called the Haversack Method, and it's designed for exactly this: staying capable when the definitions keep changing.

Introduction

Let us be honest about something. If you have picked up this book, chances are your work life feels a bit wobbly at the moment. Maybe you've watched colleagues disappear into redundancy whilst their tasks get handled by some clever bit of software. Perhaps you've seen job adverts that read like science fiction compared to what you do now. Or you're one of the growing number of people who've been told their role is being "restructured" in ways that sound suspiciously like being automated out of existence.

You are not imagining it, and you're definitely not alone.

I started thinking about this problem when my own work began changing in ways I hadn't expected. Like many people, I found myself in that uncomfortable position of watching familiar tasks become automated whilst trying to work out what that meant for my future. The standard advice about upskilling and pivoting sounded sensible enough, but it didn't seem to match the reality of trying to learn new things whilst everything around me was shifting.

That disconnect between advice and reality got me thinking about whether there might be different approaches. Not the grand career reinvention that sounds impressive but feels overwhelming, and not the head-in-the-sand approach that ignores change altogether. Something more practical, more sustainable, more human.

What I've worked out over the past couple of years is an approach I call Temperance Learning, combined with something I term the Haversack Method. These aren't revolutionary concepts or proprietary systems. They're simply practical ways of thinking about learning and career development that seem to work better when circumstances won't stay predictable.

Throughout this book, you'll find composite examples based on workplace conversations, industry observations, and patterns I've seen repeated across different fields. These scenarios combine elements from various real situations to illustrate common challenges whilst protecting individual privacy. They're meant to feel familiar rather than provide formal case studies.

The approach isn't complicated, and it doesn't require expensive courses or dramatic lifestyle changes. It focuses on finding sustainable ways to keep learning, adapting and remaining professionally relevant when traditional career advice no longer seems to fit our changing reality.

This book exists because I think we need better ways to navigate uncertainty. Not methods that promise to eliminate unpredictability (that's impossible) but approaches that help the reader function effectively despite ambiguous circumstances. Approaches that work when you don't have perfect information about what comes next.

The Challenge We're Actually Facing

Before we dive into solutions, it's worth being clear about what we're dealing with. The current wave of workplace disruption isn't like previous technological shifts. It's faster, broader, and more unpredictable.

When computers started showing up in offices back in the 1980s and 1990s, most jobs changed gradually. You swapped your typewriter for word processing, traded ledger books for spreadsheets, replaced filing cabinets with databases. Your core skills still mattered, you just used different tools to apply them. And you had time to figure it all out.

Artificial Intelligence (AI) displacement is different. It doesn't just change your tools; it can eliminate entire categories of work. Legal research that once required trained professionals can now be handled by AI systems. Customer service enquiries that needed human empathy can now be managed by chatbots. Financial analysis that took experienced professionals' hours to reconcile can now be completed by algorithms in minutes.

This isn't scaremongering. Walk into any office building and you'll find people dealing with this reality right now. The speed of change means that by the time you've noticed the trend, it's often quite advanced.

The challenge this creates isn't just practical (how do you pay the bills?) but psychological. Who are you professionally if your expertise becomes less relevant? Many people facing AI displacement describe feeling not just unemployed but somehow made invisible, as if their years of experience suddenly don't count for anything.

That psychological dimension matters because it affects how people respond. Some freeze, hoping their particular role will somehow be spared. Others panic, frantically trying to learn everything at once. Both responses are understandable, and both tend to make things worse.

Why Traditional Advice Doesn't Work

The standard response to technological displacement has always been "upskill yourself." Learn new technologies, get additional qualifications, move into areas that computers can't handle. This advice isn't wrong exactly, but it misses crucial realities about how most people actually live and work.

It assumes you have time and resources most people don't have. It assumes you can predict which skills will remain valuable when AI capabilities are expanding so rapidly. And it often ignores the expertise you've already built, suggesting you abandon years of professional experience in favour of starting completely fresh.

When change is constant and unpredictable, you need an approach to professional development that's sustainable and adaptable, not just comprehensive.

We'll explore these challenges in more detail in Section One, where Chapter 1 examines exactly why traditional approaches break down under AI displacement.

A Different Approach

The approach I outline in this book starts from a different premise. I do not try to guess what will happen in the future or put all my eggs in one basket when it comes to certain skills. Instead, the focus is on developing adaptability itself. Not just learning new things but developing the ability to learn in a world where the ground keeps shifting.

This means building systems and habits that work regardless of which particular technology comes next. It means extracting maximum value from what you already know whilst gradually expanding into new areas. Most importantly, it means doing all of this in a way that does not burn you out or overwhelm you.

The practical core of this approach is something I call the *Haversack Method.* It's a portable system for building adaptive capability when you can't predict which specific skills will matter next. You'll learn to notice useful fragments of knowledge as you encounter them, save the valuable ones as scraps, spot patterns when scraps cluster around similar themes, then systematically build Minimum Viable Skills that create immediate value whilst preparing you for whatever comes next.

But the method only works when you understand what's broken about traditional approaches and what philosophy should replace them. Context before tools. That's why the book builds carefully from problem to philosophy to practice.

The people who navigate AI displacement most successfully tend to share certain characteristics. They are curious without being scattered. They experiment without losing focus. They build new capabilities whilst maintaining confidence in their existing strengths. They adapt their professional identity without losing their sense of self.

These characteristics are not innate gifts, but they can be developed. The following chapters will show you how, starting with understanding exactly what we're up against.

What You'll Find Here

This book takes you on a journey from understanding the problem to building sustainable solutions. We'll start by examining exactly why everything feels so uncertain right now, then develop the mindset and tools needed to help navigate that uncertainty effectively.

In Section One we will explore why the ground feels so unstable and why many traditional approaches to professional development have quietly stopped working. You'll understand what makes this disruption different from previous technological shifts and why clinging to old strategies often makes things worse.

In Section Two we'll meet the philosophy of temperance learning which focuses on finding balance between doing nothing and trying to do everything. This isn't about perfect planning or comprehensive knowledge.

It's about sustainable approaches that work when you can't predict what's coming next.

The Haversack Method comes in Section Three - a simple system for collecting, organising, and using knowledge fragments as you encounter them. Think of it as building a portable toolkit that travels with you regardless of what job you are doing. You'll put these ideas into practice through focused learning projects, proof creation, and real-world application. Turning scattered information into demonstrable skills whilst building confidence in your ability to adapt to whatever changes emerge.

Section Four will show you how to integrate these approaches into your daily work and life, building habits that support continuous adaptation without overwhelming your other responsibilities. We'll explore what this means for your long-term professional development as you move from crisis response to confident navigation of an uncertain world.

Who This Is For

This book is written for people who are dealing with AI displacement in practical, immediate ways. You might be someone who's already lost their job to artificial intelligence. You might be watching parts of your role get automated whilst wondering what comes next. You might be in an industry that is obviously heading for AI-related disruption and want to prepare before it hits.

The approach works regardless of your technical background, age, or industry. The examples draw from fields as diverse as customer service and software engineering, legal research, and financial planning, but the principles apply broadly. What matters is not your starting point but your willingness to try a different approach to professional development.

The book assumes you are dealing with real constraints. Limited time, financial pressure, family responsibilities, and the stress that comes with professional uncertainty. The strategies here are designed to work within these constraints, not to ignore them.

What This Book Is Not

This book will not tell you which specific skills to learn or which industries to move into. Those decisions depend on your particular situation, interests, and circumstances. Instead, it gives you a framework for making those decisions and the tools to act on them effectively.

It's not a promise that following this approach will guarantee employment or solve all career problems. AI displacement is real, and its effects can be severe. What this book offers is a way to respond that maximises your chances whilst preserving your sanity and self-respect.

It is also not anti-technology or anti AI. I am not interested in fighting against technological progress or sticking my head in the ground, pretending it isn't happening. The goal is to find ways for humans to adapt and remain useful in the workplace alongside these changes. Some of the most successful adaptations involve working with AI tools rather than competing against them.

How to Use This Book

You do not need to read this book sequentially, though you can. Each section builds on earlier ones, but individual chapters stand alone. If you're dealing with immediate pressure, you might start with the practical sections. If you want to understand the bigger picture first, begin with the problem analysis.

Think of this book as your first haversack item. Use it. Mark it up. Dog-ear pages. Spill coffee on it. It is meant to be a working document, not a coffee table decoration.

Most importantly, start small. The temptation when facing professional disruption is to try to fix everything at once. That rarely works. Instead, pick one small thing from what you read here and try it. Then pick another. The cumulative effect of small, consistent changes is far more powerful than grand gestures that burn you out.

The professional world is changing faster than most of us expected. But that does not mean we have to panic or give up. With the right approach, the right tools, and a sustainable pace, it is possible to not just survive these changes but to build something better on the other side.

The journey starts here, but the destination is entirely up to you.

Let us begin.

Section One: The Shaky Ground

Why the world feels unstable and why many traditional learning models no longer cut it.

The first step in adapting to any change is understanding what you are dealing with. This section examines the current wave of workplace disruption in detail, not to alarm you but to give you a clear picture of the landscape. Grasping why the workplace feels so unstable helps you stop wasting energy fighting the wrong battles and start focusing on responses that will actually work.

We will explore what makes AI displacement different from previous technological shifts, why it affects people's professional identity so deeply, and why the comfortable assumption that you could learn once and coast forever has become dangerous. Most importantly, we'll look at why clinging to old approaches to professional development not only doesn't help but can make things worse.

This is not about catastrophe peddling. It's about clarity. The next four chapters examine the mechanics of disruption: how fast it's happening, how broadly it's spreading, and why it feels so impossible to predict. Once you understand what's happening and why it feels so destabilising, you can stop being surprised by it and start working with reality instead of against it.

Chapter 1: The Ground is Moving

Jobs vanish, roles morph, and skills date faster than milk. The world isn't ending, but you need a new way to stay upright.

I remember the exact moment I realised the ground had shifted under my feet. It was not dramatic or sudden. Rather more like that uncomfortable sensation you get when you are walking and realise the pavement isn't quite where you thought it was. I was reading an industry newsletter, scanning through the usual updates about new technologies and market trends, when I came across an article about a company that had automated away an entire department. Not gradually, not with months of consultation and retraining. Just gone, replaced by software that could do the job faster and cheaper.

What got to me was not just that it had happened. What really unsettled me was realising that the work they'd automated was remarkably like work I had been doing for years. Tasks I was good at. A career I'd spent years building.

If you are reading this book, maybe you have had a similar moment. Maybe you watched a colleague's job disappear into an "efficiency improvement." Perhaps you have seen those job adverts that require skills you have never heard of for roles that sound like yours, but somehow, are now completely different. Or maybe you are one of the growing number of people who have had that awkward conversation about how your role is about to be "restructured" in ways that sound suspiciously like being phased out.

The thing is you are not imagining this. The ground really is moving.

Why Everything Feels Wobbly

Look, everyone knows work does not feel as stable as it used to, but most of us don't like talking about it. The old assumptions about career progression, skills development, and job security have been quietly evaporating whilst most of us were just trying to get on with our jobs.

Think about how careers worked for earlier generations. You learnt a trade or profession, got good at it, and could reasonably expect that expertise to carry you through decades of employment. A carpenter stayed a carpenter. An accountant stayed an accountant. A lawyer stayed a lawyer. The tools might change, new regulations might appear, but the fundamental skills remained consistent and had value.

That predictability is largely gone now. The half-life of professional skills has shortened dramatically. What you learn this year might be automated next year. The capabilities you have spent your career building and perfecting might become less relevant in the coming months rather than decades.

I am not trying to be alarmist here. I'm trying to be realistic. Because once you accept that the ground is moving, you can stop wasting energy being surprised by it and start figuring out how to walk on unstable terrain.

The Speed Problem

Previous technological shifts gave people time to adapt. When manufacturing moved from handcraft to assembly lines, workers had decades to transition. When telephones replaced telegraph operators, the change rolled out city by city over years. Even when email began replacing fax machines, offices adopted it gradually, often running both systems side by side for ages.

AI displacement is different. A recruitment agency can deploy AI screening software over a weekend and potentially eliminate three junior positions by the following Tuesday. A law firm can implement document review AI software and discover that work which previously took a team of paralegals a week to complete now takes one person just an afternoon. A marketing department can start using AI content tools and suddenly only need half the copywriters they employed the previous month.

This creates a particular kind of stress. When change happens faster than you can adapt to it, specialist knowledge becomes a liability rather than an asset. The more specialised your capabilities, the more vulnerable you become when that specialisation gets automated.

I know someone who worked in Big Pharma procurement. She spent fifteen years learning supplier relationships, contract negotiations, the subtle art of reading between the lines in vendor proposals. Then her company deployed an AI system that could analyse supplier performance, predict delivery issues, and even negotiate basic contract terms. Within six months, what had been a team of five became a team of two, with the AI handling everything except the most complex strategic relationships.

"The weird thing," she told me, "wasn't losing colleagues. It was watching the AI make decisions I would have made, but faster and with better data than I could access. I felt simultaneously vindicated (on one hand my approach was right) but on the other, completely replaceable."

The speed also makes traditional career planning nearly impossible. Why train for roles that might not exist by the time you're qualified? How do you build towards senior positions when the ladder itself is disappearing rung by rung?

The Scope and Unpredictability Problem

Then there's the breadth of change. Previous technological waves usually affected particular industries or specific types of work. Factory automation hit manufacturing. Computers changed office work. The internet disrupted media and retail. Each wave was significant, but most people could see it coming and had some idea of where the safe ground might be.

AI is different because it potentially affects almost any role that involves information processing, pattern recognition, or communication. That covers an enormous range of work. Legal research, medical diagnosis, financial analysis, content creation, customer service, translation, design: these are all areas where AI tools are becoming increasingly capable and cheap to deploy.

There's no obvious safe haven to retreat to. Even those roles that would traditionally seem inherently human (like counselling or creative work) are seeing AI applications that would have been unthinkable just a few short years ago.

This breadth means that traditional advice about "moving into tech" or "focusing on human skills" doesn't necessarily provide the security it once promised. Tech roles are being automated and many human skills are being replicated by increasingly sophisticated AI systems.

Perhaps the most unsettling aspect of the current changes is how unpredictable they are. With previous technological shifts, you could usually tell which jobs were vulnerable and which were protected. Physical jobs seemed safer than routine office work. Creative roles seemed more secure than data processing. Jobs requiring human interaction looked protected.

AI has scrambled these assumptions completely. It can generate marketing campaigns, diagnose medical conditions, create detailed financial reports, and even provide emotional support in some contexts. The boundary between "work only humans can do" and "work AI can handle" keeps shifting in unexpected directions.

What makes this unpredictability maddening is that it makes it increasingly difficult to plan conventional career moves. How do you decide which skills to develop when you can't predict which skills will remain valuable? How do you choose which industry to move into when AI capabilities are expanding so rapidly?

The Fragmentation of Work

Another way AI is changing employment is by breaking traditional job roles into smaller, more specific tasks. Instead of replacing entire jobs overnight, AI often starts by handling particular components of a role, leaving humans to manage the parts that still require human judgement or creativity.

This fragmentation can be disorienting. Instead of having a clear, coherent professional identity, you might find yourself eventually only managing a collection of tasks that don't necessarily add up to a traditional job description.

Think about what's happened to many marketing roles. Traditional marketing jobs involved writing copy, managing campaigns, analysing performance, and coordinating with other teams. AI tools can now handle much of the copy writing, automate campaign management, and provide sophisticated performance analytics. The human marketer becomes someone who manages AI outputs, handles complex strategic decisions, and deals with situations that require human judgement.

This isn't necessarily worse than traditional work, but it's different in ways that can be challenging. When your job becomes a collection of disparate tasks like managing AI outputs, handling exceptions, strategic thinking, and whatever else needs doing - it becomes harder to know what skills to develop or how to explain the value you are bringing to your next potential employer.

Why Common Responses Fail

When people realise their careers are being disrupted, the standard advice is usually rolled out. Upskill yourself. Learn new technologies, get additional qualifications, move into areas that machines can't handle.

This advice isn't necessarily wrong, but it assumes the ground will stay still long enough for you to build new foundations. Upskilling advice worked in a world where you could predict which skills would remain valuable and where you had time to develop them properly. But when the landscape keeps changing due to AI displacement, those assumptions break down in damaging ways.

Firstly, it assumes you have the time and resources that most people facing disruption don't have. When job pathways were steady, it made sense to suggest someone spend two years learning data science. But when you need to pay your bills next month and can't be sure data science will still be useful by the time you finish your course, that advice stops making sense.

Secondly, it ignores the reality that you can't build lasting capabilities in an unstable environment. The people who pivoted to social media marketing five years ago are now watching AI tools handle content creation and campaign management. What seemed like future-proof skills turned out to be temporary refuges.

Thirdly, traditional upskilling advice often undervalues what you already know. It focuses so heavily on acquiring new capabilities that it overlooks how existing expertise might transfer or adapt. This creates the impression that years of professional experience have become suddenly irrelevant, which is both wasteful and psychologically brutal. Your accumulated knowledge doesn't become worthless overnight, even if the technical aspects of your role change.

One common response to AI displacement is the search for so-called "AI-proof" jobs. The thinking goes that if you can identify roles AI will never handle, you can upskill for those positions and achieve long-term security.

This leads to familiar advice: learn a trade because AI can't do physical work, go into healthcare because AI can't replace human compassion, pursue creative fields because AI can't truly be creative, or focus on leadership because AI can't manage people.

There's some truth in those suggestions, but they're incomplete. AI doesn't need to completely replace human work to reshape employment. It only needs to increase productivity enough that fewer humans are required.

Take the role of an electrician, often cited as AI-proof because it requires physical skill and problem-solving in unpredictable environments. Even here, technology is changing the profession. Smart diagnostic tools can identify electrical faults remotely. AI-powered scheduling systems optimise routes and predict which jobs will take longest. Augmented reality can guide apprentices through complex wiring tasks that previously required years of experience. The electrician isn't replaced, but the work becomes more efficient. One experienced electrician with AI support can now handle diagnostic work that used to take several site visits or the supervision of apprentices on jobs they wouldn't have been ready for before.

The same pattern appears across other supposedly safe industries. Accounting was considered stable and human-dependent, but AI can now handle routine bookkeeping, expense categorisation, and even basic tax filing. Retail management seemed safe because it relied on human judgement about customers and staff, but AI systems can now predict inventory needs, optimise schedules, analyse behaviour patterns, and robotically pick and ship goods, reducing the number of humans required in the workflow process.

The search for AI-proof jobs misses the deeper point. The problem isn't finding work that AI will never affect. The problem is learning to adapt as AI changes whatever field you're in.

I'm not arguing against learning new things. What I challenge is the assumption that simply learning more is the solution to AI displacement. When change is constant and unpredictable, you need a development approach that's sustainable and adaptable, not just ambitious.

Before exploring what that different approach looks like (we'll get to that in Section Two), we need to understand exactly what's happening in workplaces right now. The abstract concept of "AI displacement" becomes clearer when you see its early signs in real working environments.

Early Signs and Tremors

Most people don't wake up one morning to find their job has been automated overnight. Instead, the changes happen gradually, often in ways that are easy to miss until they're quite advanced. Learning to recognise the early warning signs can give you time to adapt before you're forced into reactive mode.

Your work is becoming more routine and standardised. If your job has become increasingly procedural, with more clearly defined processes and less room for individual judgement, it's probably becoming more automatable. Tasks that follow predictable patterns are prime candidates for AI replacement.

New tools are being introduced that handle parts of your role. Pay attention when management introduces "helpful" AI tools or software that automates routine tasks. These are often pilot programmes for more comprehensive automation. The tool that helps you write reports today might write all the reports tomorrow.

Your industry publications are focusing heavily on AI and automation. When professional journals and trade websites start running frequent articles about AI applications in your field, it usually means the technology is moving from experimental to practical.

Clients or customers are asking about AI capabilities. If the people you serve are inquiring whether your company uses automated systems or suggesting that machine learning might handle their needs, it's a sign they're aware of alternatives to your services.

Your company is talking about "digital transformation" or "operational efficiency." These phrases often mean "we're going to automate as much as possible to reduce costs." If your organisation is focused on digital transformation, assume your role will be affected and start preparing accordingly.

You're spending more time managing AI outputs rather than creating original work. If an increasing portion of your day involves reviewing, editing, or approving AI-generated content rather than creating content yourself, your role is already being transformed by artificial intelligence.

What Adaptation Actually Looks Like

The people who navigate technological disruption successfully tend to share certain characteristics that have little to do with intelligence or technical background. They don't panic and try to learn everything at once. Instead of freezing and hoping the changes will pass them by, they find ways to adapt steadily and sustainably.

They build on their existing strengths rather than abandoning them. They learn to work with new technologies rather than compete against them. Most importantly, they move at a pace they can sustain without burning out or losing direction.

One of the hardest parts of adapting is learning to function despite uncertainty about what comes next. Traditional career planning assumed a predictable future. You could look at senior people in your field and imagine a similar path for yourself. If that predictability hasn't already gone, believe me, it's going. The jobs available in five years will not look the same as those available today, and the skills that matter most might not be the ones that seem important right now.

This type of uncertainty can easily turn into paralysis if you let it. Yet that same uncertainty also creates opportunity, though it rarely feels that way when you're in the middle of it. When established career paths become unstable, there is more room for unconventional approaches. When traditional qualifications become less reliable as a measure of capability, there is more scope to show your value in different ways.

The key is learning to take action despite not having full clarity. That does not mean making reckless decisions. It means accepting that progress will often happen with incomplete information and moving forward anyway.

Adaptation of this kind is rarely dramatic. It does not make for viral posts about transformation or grand reinvention. It is quieter, more gradual, and more human. It is also far more effective over time.

Beyond the practical problems, there's something harder to talk about. When what you're good at becomes less relevant, it's not just your income that takes a hit. Your sense of who you are professionally gets shaken too.

I've had conversations with people who've told me their years of experience feel like they suddenly count for nothing. A financial analyst who spent a decade learning to read market data, then watched AI systems do the same work in minutes. A graphic designer who built real skills in layout and visual communication, now competing with AI tools that generate professional designs from text prompts. A legal researcher who mastered finding relevant case precedents, now watching AI systems scan thousands of documents and pull key cases in seconds.

These people haven't necessarily lost their jobs. But they're asking themselves whether their professional identity still makes sense. When the thing you built your career around gets automated, who are you at work?

The emotional responses are predictable: anger at the unfairness, fear about keeping up, shame about not seeing it coming, grief over lost plans. These feelings are real and valid. They're also potentially paralysing if you let them drive your response to change.

I get it. These responses are completely human and understandable. But they don't help you move forward.

So recognising that change is constant does not solve the problem of AI displacement, but it changes how you respond to it. Once you accept that the old ideas of career security no longer hold, you can stop wasting energy trying to preserve them and start focusing on approaches that fit the world as it is now.

That does not mean abandoning everything you know or starting over. It means building on your existing knowledge while developing new capabilities that complement rather than compete with technology. It means learning to work with ambiguity rather than waiting for certainty. And it means developing patterns of continuous learning that you can maintain without exhaustion.

The old model of "learn once, apply for decades" no longer works. The new reality is "learn continuously, adapt constantly". That might sound tiring, but it does not have to be. With the right rhythm, learning can be steady, enjoyable, and part of ordinary working life.

What matters most is balance. Not the frantic scramble to learn everything at once, and not the paralysis that comes from feeling overwhelmed.

That is what the rest of this book is about, developing tools and techniques that help you stay steady when circumstances shift. Not so you can predict exactly what comes next, but so you can stay upright and ready for whatever does.

The ground will keep shifting. That is not going to stop. But you do not have to fall.

The next chapter explores why the old model of professional development felt so reassuring, and why holding onto it now can make genuine adaptation harder. Understanding what you are leaving behind is just as important as knowing what you are moving towards.

Chapter 2: The Myth of Mastery

The old idea of "get qualified once, coast forever" is gone. Skills now expire. The trick is to adapt before panic sets in.

There is a comforting story most of us carry around about how careers are supposed to unfold. You study hard, get the right qualifications, build expertise in your chosen field, and then (this is the crucial bit) you reach a point where you are sorted. A point where you know your stuff well enough that you can coast on that knowledge for the rest of your working life.

Most people have believed this story for longer than they care to admit. It made sense of all the effort that goes into building a career. Why would anyone spend years learning if that learning were not going to provide lasting security? The entire system seemed designed around the promise that expertise, once acquired, would remain valuable.

While the knowledge remains valuable, that promise of career security has quietly expired whilst most of us were not paying attention.

In the last chapter we saw the ground moving beneath your work. This chapter explores what happens when even mastery offers no solid footing.

I remember having a conversation with someone a few years older than me who had built a successful career in graphic design. We were talking about how the field had changed, and he mentioned that he'd essentially had to relearn his entire profession three times: once when computers replaced traditional design tools, again when the internet changed how design worked, and a third time when mobile devices reshaped everything.

"The frustrating thing," he said, "is that each time I thought I'd finally mastered it. I'd spend years getting really good at something, feeling confident and competent, and then the whole landscape would shift, and I'd be back to feeling like a beginner again."

His experience is not unusual anymore. It is becoming the norm across an ever-growing number of fields. The comfortable plateau of mastery that earlier generations could reach and maintain simply does not exist in the same way.

The Appeal of Mastery (And Why It Broke Down)

To understand why letting go of traditional mastery feels so difficult, you first need to recognise what made it appealing. Mastery offered us several things that made career planning manageable and mentally satisfying.

It offered a clear endpoint. You could see a finish line ahead where you would have learnt enough to feel secure. All the effort needed to build expertise felt worthwhile because you could see where it led: lasting competence, professional security, and the confidence that came from being genuinely good at what you did.

It offered identity and status. Being recognised as an expert in your field gave you social recognition and professional credibility. You could introduce yourself at social gatherings knowing that people understood what you did and why it mattered.

It offered the efficiency promise. Once you'd learnt something thoroughly, you could apply that knowledge repeatedly without having to relearn it. The investment in developing expertise would pay dividends for decades to come.

Most importantly, it offered psychological security. Knowing that you were genuinely competent at something valuable gave you confidence about your future prospects. You had something real to offer, something that couldn't easily be taken away.

All of these benefits were genuine when change happened slowly enough for expertise to remain relevant for extended periods. When the tools, techniques, and requirements of a profession stayed relatively stable, mastery was both achievable and valuable.

The problem isn't that expertise has become worthless. The issue is that the timeframe for keeping it relevant has shortened dramatically whilst the complexity of staying current has increased. Look at what's happened to software development over the past decade or so.

A programmer who mastered Java in 2010 would have found that knowledge steadily losing value as new frameworks, languages, and paradigms emerged. React, Node.js, Python for data science, mobile development, cloud computing, machine learning, containerisation. Each one demanded significant learning investment that hadn't seemed necessary when Java expertise felt like enough.

And this isn't limited to technology. You see the same pattern almost everywhere. Accountants now need to understand increasingly complex regulations, master new accountancy packages and platforms, and work alongside systems that automate reconciliation and reporting. Marketing professionals need to understand social media algorithms, content creation automation, and data analytics platforms. Even fields once considered stable, like manufacturing, face rapid change in production monitoring, quality control, and supply chain tools.

In the era of AI displacement, mastery has become a moving target. By the time you've achieved deep expertise in something, there's often a time lag before you realise the landscape has shifted. Your knowledge remains valuable, but it needs significant updating to stay relevant.

This creates what you might call the mastery trap. You invest time, money, and energy in developing expertise, which makes you reluctant to admit when it needs updating. That emotional investment makes it harder to see when your expertise has fallen too far behind current requirements.

The Productivity Paradox

Here's where things get particularly tricky. In many cases, new technologies don't make human expertise worthless; they make it incredibly more productive. One person using AI tools might be able to accomplish what previously required a team of experts. This sounds positive, but it creates what economists call a productivity paradox: productivity rises for individuals using the technology, but the system's capacity to develop future expertise collapses.

If one person can now do the work that previously needed five people, what happens to the other four? They don't necessarily become unemployed immediately, but the demand for their expertise decreases dramatically. Goldman Sachs estimates that up to 300 million full-time jobs globally are exposed to AI automation, particularly in administrative, legal, and basic technical roles.

This is happening across many industries. Automated customer service systems can handle routine inquiries much faster than human agents, so call centres no longer need as many customer representatives. Machine learning tools can flag suspicious transactions and identify patterns in financial data more quickly than manual reviewers, so banks no longer need as many compliance analysts. Intelligent content generation tools can produce marketing copy more efficiently than human writers, so companies no longer need as many copywriters.

The remaining professionals often end up doing more complex, strategic work (which, on the surface, sounds like a positive development). Companies gain immediate efficiency. Individual senior staff become more productive. The quarterly numbers look good. But the long-term cost is invisible: the development pathway that created those senior staff is disappearing. You can't learn to be a strategic thinker by spending years on routine tasks if those tasks are being automated away.

What we're seeing is a fundamental gap in professional development that's emerging faster than most organisations can respond to. Harvard Business Review recently published research warning that 50-60% of typical junior tasks can already be executed by AI, whilst Wharton Business School is questioning whether AI is pushing us to break the talent pipeline entirely, highlighting how junior employees are losing opportunities to develop skills as companies rely on AI for entry-level tasks. This isn't just about individual careers. It's a systemic problem most companies aren't considering, and the impact is already measurable: a recent Indeed and Harris Poll survey found that 49% of Gen Z job seekers believe AI has specifically made their degrees less valuable in the job market.

Think about what happens when you rely on your phone for everything. You stop developing handwriting. You lose the ability to remember phone numbers. Navigation skills atrophy. You cheat at pub quizzes. Worse still, you can become uncomfortable with face-to-face conversation when you're used to typing everything out.

The same thing is happening with professional development, but the stakes are higher. When you automate away entry-level work, you eliminate the apprenticeship that creates expertise. Estimates suggest nearly 30% of work could be automated by generative AI by 2030. Meanwhile, the World

Economic Forum reports that 60% of workers will require training before 2027, yet only half have access to adequate training opportunities. Junior lawyers never learn to spot patterns by reviewing thousands of documents. Junior analysts never develop intuition by building hundreds of models. Junior designers never understand fundamentals by doing layout after layout.

The pipeline breaks. You can't have senior strategic thinkers if nobody goes through the experiences that build that thinking.

We're creating a future where we'll need strategic experts but are eliminating the very experiences that create them. How do you develop judgement and expertise when the entry-level work that used to provide that development experience no longer exists?

Later, (in Chapter 4), we will dig deeper into the challenges presented when career ladders and learning pathways disappear.

The Shelf-Life Problem

Not all knowledge ages at the same rate and understanding this matters more now than it ever has.

Some things you learn stay useful for decades. Understanding how people make decisions, the basics of clear communication, fundamental maths, core business principles - these weather technological storms because they're about humans and systems, not tools. They get applied differently as the world changes, but the underlying concepts hold.

Then there's the middle ground: industry-specific expertise, particular business models, regulatory frameworks. These have a shelf life measured in years or decades. They don't expire quickly, but they need regular updates to stay current. What worked in retail logistics in 2015 needs adjusting for 2025, but the foundations still matter.

And then there's the stuff that goes stale fast. Specific software skills, current best practices in rapidly changing fields, knowledge of particular tools and platforms. This knowledge can become outdated within months, not years. Master a specific AI tool in January, and by June there might be three better alternatives that work completely differently.

Here's the problem: traditional professional development treats all learning as equally permanent. Spend four years getting a degree, and the assumption is that investment pays off for decades. Take a certification course, and you're told it's a credential that proves lasting competence. But when half of what you're learning might be obsolete before you've even finished the course, that model stops making sense.

The result? People over-invest in knowledge that won't last (spending months mastering tools that will change) whilst under-investing in the foundational understanding that transfers across changes. They chase credentials in rapidly shifting fields whilst neglecting the deeper patterns that would help them adapt when those fields transform.

AI has made this problem urgent. As the pace of change accelerates, the shelf life of technical knowledge grows ever shorter. Skills that once defined a career may now lose their value within just a few years.

You can't plan professional development the same way anymore. The question isn't just "what should I learn?" It's "how long will this actually matter, and what happens when it doesn't?"

The Confidence Problem

Traditional mastery provided a particular type of confidence that came from knowing you were genuinely good at something valuable. This confidence was important not just for psychological well-being, but for professional effectiveness. When you know you can handle whatever comes up in your field, you can take on challenging projects, make decisions under pressure, and provide leadership when needed.

When expertise becomes unstable, this confidence can erode in damaging ways. If you aren't sure whether your knowledge is current or relevant, you might become hesitant to take on challenging work or reluctant to make important decisions. This hesitation can become self-reinforcing, leading to professional stagnation even when adaptation is possible.

The challenge is rebuilding confidence in an environment where expertise is fluid. This requires a different kind of self-assurance; not certainty in specific knowledge, but trust in your ability to learn and adapt as needed.

This meta-confidence is harder to develop than traditional expertise-based certainty, but it's more robust in uncertain environments. Instead of "I know how to handle this situation," it becomes "I can figure out what to do next."

What Replaces Mastery?

So if the old model is broken, what actually works?

The answer isn't to abandon expertise. It's to change how you build it. The goal now is to develop capability as you need it, not to spend years chasing a fixed qualification that might be outdated by the time you finish studying and pass your exams. In a world shaped by AI displacement, the value of learning lies in timing and adaptability.

Rather than aiming for some final state of mastery, the focus shifts to sustainable fluency. You learn enough to work effectively, stay curious enough to spot what's changing, and keep developing as the landscape moves. Fluency has movement built in. It's about keeping your footing while the ground keeps shifting.

One of the most overlooked challenges in making this shift is figuring out which bits of your expertise actually transfer to new contexts and which don't. When technology makes specific skills obsolete, it's tempting to think years of professional development have been wasted. But that's rarely true.

Understanding how customers make decisions, knowing how to manage complex projects, developing judgement about which information matters and which doesn't. These capabilities often remain valuable even when the specific technical skills become irrelevant. The hard part is learning to recognise what transfers and what doesn't. This requires thinking about professional knowledge differently - not as a collection of specific skills you've mastered, but as principles, patterns, and judgement you can apply across different contexts when things shift.

This recognition changes how you approach professional development. Rather than narrow specialisation, you move toward connected competence. Not becoming a shallow generalist, but building a portfolio of related abilities that can evolve together. The people adapting best to AI disruption aren't the ones who know everything about one thing. They're the ones who can draw connections between capabilities that used to sit in separate boxes.

This portfolio approach isn't new. Versions of it have existed since the 1990s, often describing people who built careers from a mix of roles or income streams. But in the age of AI, it's becoming essential as a way to learn and adapt. It means developing working knowledge across multiple areas instead of chasing mastery in just one. Staying current with trends across your wider field, not just your narrow specialisation. Building relationships and understanding across teams and disciplines, instead of staying boxed into a single professional silo.

The portfolio approach requires a different learning strategy than the old mastery model. Rather than deep and exhaustive study of one subject, it focuses on broader exposure, pattern recognition, and the ability to develop working knowledge in new areas as needed. It can feel less satisfying than traditional mastery because you rarely reach the same depth in any one area. But it offers far greater security in unpredictable times, because you're not betting your whole future on one skillset staying relevant.

Learning itself becomes continuous. It's no longer a four-year sprint followed by decades of application. It's a rhythm you build into your working life. You learn, apply, adapt, repeat. And the source of security changes too. It's no longer about being irreplaceable in a single role. It's about being able to create value in multiple ways when your environment changes.

That's not an easy adjustment for anyone raised on the promise of stability through mastery. It means letting go of the comfort that came from deep specialisation and learning to stay steady in motion. But it's far more realistic than clinging to a model that no longer fits how work actually operates.

The Continuous Learning Challenge (And Making Peace with It)

If expertise is no longer a permanent asset, then learning becomes a continuous requirement rather than a front-loaded investment. This creates both practical and psychological challenges that most people aren't prepared for.

On the practical side, you need to build learning into your ongoing routine rather than treating it as something you do between jobs or careers. That means developing systems for staying current with developments in your field, experimenting with new tools and techniques, and regularly updating your skills.

Mentally, you have to accept that you'll often feel less than fully competent, that you'll frequently be learning things you don't immediately need, and that much of what you learn may become outdated before you've fully mastered it.

This continuous learning requirement can be exhausting if approached the wrong way. The key is finding sustainable approaches that don't burn you out whilst keeping you sufficiently current to remain relevant.

Perhaps more important than any specific learning strategy is making peace with the impermanence of professional knowledge itself. This isn't about giving up on learning or settling for mediocrity. What it means is developing a relationship with expertise that bends instead of breaks.

The shift looks something like this. Obsolescence stops being failure and becomes part of how professional development works. Knowledge that's becoming irrelevant? You let it go without the drama, extracting whatever still transfers to new contexts. The security you used to get from permanent expertise will get replaced by confidence in your ability to adapt when things inevitably change.

This psychological adjustment matters more than any particular learning tactic you might choose. Once you've accepted that change isn't stopping and adaptation isn't optional, you can put your energy into building systems that actually work within that reality instead of pretending it isn't happening.

The myth of mastery is hard to let go of because it promised something real. Security through expertise. That promise made sense for decades. But when expertise has a shelf life you can measure in years rather than careers, holding onto that old promise can leave you worse off, not better. You end up defending something that no longer really serves you.

The alternative isn't abandoning competence or expertise. It's building a more fluid relationship with professional knowledge, one that acknowledges continuous change whilst still giving you the capability and confidence you need to do work that matters.

Understanding what needs to replace mastery is one thing. Actually building sustainable approaches that work whilst you're still doing your job? That's where most people struggle.

The continuous learning requirement can exhaust you if approached the wrong way. Trying to stay current with everything, chasing every new development, treating adaptation like a second full-time job - that path leads to burnout, not capability. The key is finding approaches that keep you sufficiently current without consuming all your energy.

Section Two introduces a different philosophy about learning and adaptation. Not the frantic scramble to master everything, and not the paralysis that comes from feeling overwhelmed. Something more sustainable, more realistic for people who need to adapt whilst continuing to do actual work

But first, we need to look at one more uncomfortable truth about professional adaptation. Sometimes the very success that got you here becomes the biggest obstacle to getting where you need to go.

The research and data referenced in this chapter are detailed in the Notes and Sources section at the end of this book.

Chapter 3: What Got You Here May Not Get You There

Yesterday's strengths are not tomorrow's guarantees. Holding on too tightly might keep you stuck while others move on.

Recently, I had a conversation with someone who had a good career in project management for 15 years. He really was superb at what he did.

Genuinely good at his job, he understood how to coordinate complex initiatives, manage stakeholders, keep projects on track and within budget. He'd developed systems and methods that worked reliably across different types of projects and organisations.

Then his company introduced project management software that used AI to automatically handle scheduling, resource allocation, progress monitoring, and basic communication with stakeholders. Many of the skills he had worked on for years became less important overnight. Not worthless (the strategic thinking and relationship management parts were still necessary), but they were much less important to daily work.

"The frustrating thing," he told me, "is that I kept trying to prove the old way was better. I'd show them how the system missed nuances I would have caught, how automated communications lacked personal touch. I spent months fighting to demonstrate the value of approaches that had served me well for years."

He wasn't wrong about the limitations. It's true that AI tools often miss the small details and lack a personal touch. But while he was busy defending the old way of doing things, some of the other project managers on his team were quietly figuring out how to work with the new systems. They used the tools to handle the routine, repetitive tasks and put their energy into the parts that still needed a human touch, the strategy, the relationships, the judgement calls.

By the time he realised what was going on, he'd already lost months he could have spent adjusting. His skills still had value, but his need to prove he was better than the AI had stopped him from evolving with the job itself.

The Comfort of Competence And The Success Trap

Being really good at something feels great. When you've mastered a skill, when you can handle problems that leave others stuck, when people come to you for advice, it's satisfying in ways that go beyond career success. It validates the years of effort and gives you a sense of who you are and what you're here to do.

That satisfaction isn't vanity. It's just human. We're built to feel good about mastering our environment, solving problems, and making useful contributions to whatever group we're part of. The pride that comes from competence is healthy and motivating.

The trouble starts when success creates its own momentum. When something works, you do more of it. Makes sense. Your colleagues praise your approach. You get promoted because you're good at what you do. Your techniques keep delivering results. Naturally, you double down on what's working. You get better at it. You build systems around it.

All of this is brilliant when things stay relatively stable. You refine your skills, work faster, feel more confident. Those patterns of success serve you well.

Until they don't.

When the environment changes significantly, those same patterns can trap you. You're still following approaches that worked brilliantly last year but don't quite fit anymore. The more you've invested in developing specific abilities, the harder it becomes to change or let go of them. Economists call this the "sunk cost fallacy". In real working life though, it's a lot messier than a tidy logic problem.

When your skills are wrapped up with who you are, how you earn a living, and what gives you a sense of worth, letting them go isn't simple. It can feel like losing a part of yourself. And abandoning methods that have made you successful feels wrong. Not just uncomfortable. Wrong. Your brain has spent years linking these approaches to positive outcomes. Promotion, recognition, results. Changing direction feels like you're throwing away something valuable for something that might not work at all.

Even when you know, deep down, that change is the right move, the comfort of what you already do well can pull you back.

The Identity Problem

That resistance to change runs deeper than just protecting successful methods. Earlier in Chapter 1, we explored what displacement feels like on a human level. The shock, the anger, the fear of becoming irrelevant. Those feelings are real, and they matter. But underneath all that is something much deeper.

Here's what often gets missed in career advice about AI displacement. Work isn't just something we do. It's part of who we are.

That isn't vanity or pride. It's what happens when you spend years getting good at something. You build depth, you build confidence, and without realising it, that expertise becomes part of your sense of self. You don't just know how to do the work. You become someone who is known for doing it well. You don't just learn to do marketing. You become a marketer. You don't just develop project management capabilities. You become a project manager. Your identity, your confidence, even your friendships and sense of purpose often grow around that competence.

That identity serves important purposes. It gives you a sense of who you are professionally. It helps you understand your place in organisations. It gives you language for explaining your value to other people.

But when technology makes your core skills less central, it doesn't just threaten your job. It can feel like an attack on your sense of self. You're not just learning new tools. You're potentially becoming a different kind of professional entirely. That kind of disruption is predictable, but it still hurts when it arrives. You've spent years, maybe decades, getting good at what you do. That expertise doesn't just live in your head. It's woven into your reputation, how other people see you, how you see yourself.

I've seen this play out with people across all sorts of fields. The details differ. The technology, the industry, the job title. But the feeling is the same. It's the psychological whiplash of watching something you've spent years mastering suddenly count for less because software can now do it faster.

Years working on a manufacturing line learning to spot production defects through careful observation, replaced by computer vision systems that inspect thousands of items per hour with the precision human eyes cannot match. Years working in a shared service center coordinating schedules, managing documents, and building office relationships, now competing with AI assistants that automate calendars, draft emails, and organise files in seconds. A decade working supermarket checkouts, mastering transaction speed whilst handling price checks and difficult customers, replaced by self-service systems that let shoppers scan and pay without ever speaking to a person.

Training professionals working alongside AI-powered learning systems wonder if they are still doing “real” professional development work when algorithms recommend content and measure progress. QA experts learning automated testing wonder if they are still doing “real” quality assurance when software finds the flaws they used to find manually. Even a journalist friend who has spent decades building relationships with sources and writing stories now struggles to stay relevant in a media world dominated by algorithms and AI-written clickbait. He's left wondering if he's still doing “real” journalism.

The quotation marks around the word “real” in each instance are important. They reflect the psychological difficulty of maintaining professional identity whilst changing professional practice. When the things you've always done to prove your competence become less relevant, it can feel like your competence itself is being questioned.

In every case, the hardest part wasn't mastering new tools or techniques. It was coming to terms with the fact that the old mastery no longer carried the same weight it once did. That isn't resistance or pride. It's human nature. You put years into something that once mattered. Admitting it needs updating isn't a quick intellectual pivot. It's a slow, uncomfortable process most career advice skips over completely.

And that attachment isn't foolish. Your expertise was valuable. You did work hard. The system did promise stability. Those things were true. Just not true forever in a world where AI keeps advancing. That shift carries real grief, even when you're trying to stay practical.

It's worth understanding because it shapes how people respond to AI displacement. Some fight it, not because they can't learn new things but because admitting the need to learn feels like saying their old work was worthless. It wasn't. Others panic, hopping from one new skill to the next, chasing the next safe patch of ground before AI catches up there too. Neither works for long.

What helps is remembering that expertise always had a shelf life. AI has just made it much shorter.

The Investment Dilemma and Productivity Illusion

Here's where the psychological trap gets really nasty.

The more expertise you've built, the more you stand to lose when that expertise matters less. You're facing a choice that beginners don't; do you squeeze every last bit of value from what you know, or start building something new?

Early-career professionals can pivot relatively easily. They haven't invested decades yet. Late-career professionals might reasonably decide to ride out their expertise until retirement. Fair enough.

Mid-career professionals get the worst of it. You've got substantial expertise that could still provide value for years. But you've also got potentially decades of working life ahead. Failing to adapt now could be devastating later.

The natural response is trying to have it both ways. Keep your existing expertise sharp whilst building new capabilities. Sounds sensible. Usually doesn't work.

Learning new approaches whilst protecting old ones means you never fully commit to either. There is real risk in ending up mediocre at new things whilst watching your expertise in the old areas become less relevant anyway.

This dilemma gets worse because of what you might call the productivity illusion. You've spent years getting really good at particular work. You can handle complex projects faster than anyone else on your team. You spot problems that novices miss. You deliver results that less experienced colleagues can't match.

All of this can be genuinely valuable, but it can also hide a harder truth. The market for those capabilities might be shrinking. You could be the most efficient person alive at work that matters less each quarter.

That is the productivity illusion at play. Strong results with familiar methods make new learning feel wasteful. Why stumble as a beginner when you can excel with the tools you know?

Because efficiency in declining areas is worth less than basic competence in growing ones. That is tough to accept when your speed and quality are part of your identity - when excellence has defined your career for years.

Still, it has to be faced. The alternative is being excellent at work that increasingly doesn't need doing.

The Innovation Paradox and Learning Resistance

AI displacement creates a learning challenge that is different from normal professional development. This is not about adding tools within your current framework. It is about learning to work in a different paradigm.

People who have built genuine expertise often fall into an expertise trap. Deep knowledge makes you effective inside your field, but when you're focused on executing your work well day to day, you often lose awareness of broader changes developing across your industry, let alone beyond it. That narrowing of focus is not stubbornness or lack of curiosity. It is simply a by-product of what can happen when you become deeply skilled at something. The better you get at your specific work, the more your attention naturally concentrates there.

With years of practice, you develop what psychologists call mental models. These are the internal frameworks you build for understanding your work. They are the patterns you have seen succeed repeatedly, the shortcuts that tell you what good looks like, the instincts that help you spot problems before they fully emerge. When you can look at a situation and immediately know what needs doing, that is your mental model at work. It is the accumulated wisdom of thousands of hours doing your job.

These models make you valuable. They let you solve familiar problems quickly without having to think through every step from scratch. Over time, they become so efficient that you stop questioning them. You just know what works.

AI does not simply give you new tools to use inside those models. It often replaces the models themselves. When the parameters change, whether through new technology, new industry structures, or new customer expectations, the same models that made you effective can become constraints rather than assets.

Take a copywriter. Over years of practice, they built a mental model that says good copy comes from understanding audience psychology, crafting persuasive structure, and refining drafts until the tone feels right. To form that mental model, the copywriter painstakingly spent years developing those skills. Learning what resonates with readers, what falls flat, what persuades and what turns people off. Hundreds of projects. Thousands of revisions. All of that experience compressed into instincts about what makes copy work.

That model is not wrong. But when AI can produce readable copy in seconds, that hard-won framework no longer explains what the copywriter's role is. Are they editing AI output now? Providing strategic direction the algorithm cannot? Something else entirely? The old mental model does not help answer these questions. It was built for a different kind of work.

This is the core point. Your mental models define what expertise looks like. AI changes what expertise means. That is not a small shift. It is a change in the rules that shaped your expertise.

I have seen this repeatedly from professionals whose hard-won expertise is losing relevance. They understand the new tools, sometimes better than anyone, yet still treat them as add-ons to the old way of working. They miss that the field itself is being redefined.

This creates an innovation paradox. The habits that made you effective now pull against needed change. When a new approach does not match your pattern library, it feels wrong or impractical. Your instinct says, “this is not how good work is done here”. The problem is that your instinct is based on a world that is changing. The approaches that feel wrong might actually suit the new reality better.

This is also why disruption so often comes from outsiders. Without heavy investment in the current way, they are free to break patterns, challenge sacred cows, and try things experts dismiss. They see possibilities that experienced people write off as unnecessary or impractical.

Whatever your experience, you are not starting from zero. You carry assumptions about what matters, how work gets done, and what competence looks like. AI asks you to question all of it. The more experience you have, the more there is to examine. Even early in a career, those first frameworks can get in the way.

This is not a lack of ability. It is a specific learning challenge. You are being asked to learn approaches that contradict what your experience tells you is correct. Your mental models are not wrong. They may simply be answering questions that now matter less in the AI era.

Understanding why this feels hard does not make it easy, but it clarifies the task. The resistance you feel is not laziness. It is your brain protecting years of investment in methods that used to work. Recognising that pattern is the first step toward working around it.

Structural Barriers to Change

Beyond the psychological challenges, AI displacement creates practical barriers that make adaptation difficult regardless of how willing you are to change.

The expectations problem hits differently depending on where you are in your career. If you're early in your professional life, people expect you to be learning and developing. Taking entry-level positions in new areas feels normal. If you're late in your career, you might have savings that let you take time for retraining without immediate income pressure.

Mid-career professionals face the hardest constraints. You're expected to be competent and productive from day one in new roles. Taking positions where you'll initially be less capable than you're accustomed to being feels like moving backwards. The mental discomfort of feeling incompetent after years of feeling expert can be significant.

Then there's the money problem. How do you maintain your income and responsibilities whilst learning approaches that AI has made necessary? Early-career professionals can often accept lower compensation whilst they learn. Late-career professionals might have savings to draw on. Mid-career professionals often have mortgages, families, obligations that make extended learning periods impractical.

You can see that change is necessary. You can't see a practical path for making that change. That's not mental resistance. That's structural reality.

Your professional network adds another layer of difficulty. Networks are usually strengths. People in similar roles who understand your challenges. Colleagues who can offer advice and opportunities. Relationships built over years of shared experience.

But when AI disrupts your field, those same networks can become echo chambers. When everyone you know professionally is struggling with similar adaptation challenges, you don't get exposure to different approaches or perspectives. The collective wisdom of your network might reinforce outdated assumptions rather than challenging them because nobody has figured out what works yet.

Networks also carry implicit expectations about career progression and appropriate roles. What counts as moving forward versus moving sideways. Which opportunities are worth pursuing versus which ones are beneath your experience level. Which changes make sense for someone at your stage.

When AI forces you to consider paths that don't fit those expectations, it can feel like betraying your professional identity. Like disappointing people who've supported you. Like admitting you're not as competent as everyone thought.

The challenge isn't choosing between your network and your adaptation. It's maintaining valuable relationships whilst remaining open to opportunities and approaches that your network might not understand or support. That's difficult when the people whose opinions you value most are the ones least likely to understand why you're considering unconventional directions.

For those in senior or management positions, there's another trap that's particularly insidious. As you become more expert and more senior, you naturally start delegating routine tasks to others whilst focusing on strategic work. This progression makes sense and usually leads to increased responsibility and compensation.

But when automation starts handling the routine tasks that junior staff used to do, the delegation trap becomes apparent. You've been managing people who do work that's now being automated away. By the time you recognise that your role has fundamentally changed, the junior staff you were managing might no longer be needed. Your position might shift from managing people to overseeing automated systems, or it might be restructured entirely if the technology can handle both the routine work and its coordination.

This trap is particularly dangerous because it can catch senior professionals off-guard even when they championed the automation. They understood the operational benefits but didn't anticipate how eliminating middle layers would reshape their own responsibilities and value proposition.

These aren't problems you can solve through better mindset or more determination. They're structural constraints that require practical strategies. Understanding that these barriers exist helps. It clarifies why adaptation feels so difficult. It's not just you. The system makes it hard.

Moving Forward

You hopefully now have a better understanding of why AI displacement makes adaptation so difficult. The barriers are real - psychological, structural, practical.

The question is: what do you do about it?

Not in some theoretical sense. What do you actually do on Monday morning when you need to adapt but you're also managing current work, financial pressure, and all the realities that make dramatic change impossible?

Traditional career advice doesn't work here. “Upskill” and “reskill” assume you have time and clarity you probably don't have. “Build a portfolio” assumes you already know which skills will matter. “Network strategically” assumes your network isn't facing the same displacement you are.

You need something different. Something that helps you orient yourself when the usual markers disappear. Something that builds genuine capability without requiring perfect or massive time investments.

But before we get to practical solutions, there's one more piece of the puzzle to understand: the actual machinery driving these changes. It's not just AI in the abstract. There are specific technological and economic forces reshaping work right now. Understanding these forces helps you respond strategically rather than just reacting anxiously.

Let's look at what's actually happening in workplaces today.

Chapter 4: The Machinery Behind the Shift

Dark factories run through the night, ghost warehouses operate without staff, and robots join production lines. This isn't coming. It's already here.

Over the previous three chapters we've explored why traditional career security feels increasingly fragile and why old approaches no longer work reliably. Now it's time to look at what's actually driving these changes.

Understanding the mechanics matters not because you need to predict every development, but because clarity helps you stop wasting energy on vague anxiety and start focusing on practical responses that work. And those responses need to account for more than just which jobs are changing - they need to address how people learn new capabilities when traditional pathways are disappearing.

The term "Industry 4.0" has been floating around business circles for a few years now, often sounding more like corporate jargon than anything affecting ordinary working lives. But the reality behind the phrase is starting to arrive in concrete, measurable ways. And whilst some of what's happening is genuinely impressive from a technical standpoint, it's also reshaping employment in ways that deserve honest discussion.

So let's look at what's actually occurring, what the likely trajectory is, and most importantly, what this means for how you prepare yourself to work effectively in environments where AI and automation are becoming standard infrastructure rather than experimental additions.

What Industry 4.0 Actually Means

Industry 4.0 refers to the growing fusion of AI, robotics, sensors, and data analytics into how goods are made, moved, and managed. Earlier revolutions mechanised muscle. This one automates coordination and decision-making.

These technologies don't just make production faster; they make it self-managing.

The distinction matters because what starts in factories soon moves into offices, warehouses, and workplaces everywhere. The technologies driving autonomous manufacturing can manage supply chains, coordinate logistics, handle customer service, and supervise building operations. What works for making products can work for managing inventory, processing claims, or coordinating deliveries. The same underlying capabilities apply across different contexts.

The nature of human work is changing fundamentally. Some roles shift towards oversight of AI systems, monitoring output and making decisions where human judgement remains necessary. But here's the uncomfortable reality: there won't be enough of these oversight positions to absorb everyone whose work gets automated. When systems can operate with minimal human supervision, the workforce requirements shrink accordingly. Understanding this shift means positioning yourself for work that retains value, not pretending the transition will be painless for everyone.

Current Realities

That shift is no longer theoretical. It's already visible on factory floors and in logistics hubs around the world.

In late 2024, Xiaomi, a Chinese technology company, opened what it calls a "dark factory" on the outskirts of Beijing. The facility produces smartphones on production lines that run 24 hours a day without human workers present during routine operations. The lights on the factory floor stay off because the machines don't need them. Robots assemble components, AI systems coordinate logistics, sensors monitor quality, and the operation runs autonomously during standard production. One smartphone rolls off the line every second. No tea breaks, no shift changes, no human supervision required for normal production runs.

Similar facilities are emerging across China and other parts of Asia, with European manufacturers exploring parallel approaches. BMW is piloting humanoid robots from Figure AI at its Spartanburg plant in South Carolina, testing how automated systems can handle physically demanding tasks whilst human workers focus on complex assembly, quality validation, and process improvement. The company says it isn't replacing people, instead, it's repositioning them towards the kind of work that machines still can't replicate (for now).

In Western Europe, companies such as Ocado and DHL Robotics are developing high-density automated warehouse systems where robotic arms, guided by AI and real-time data, pick, pack, and dispatch orders with minimal human oversight. Amazon UK has expanded its use of autonomous mobile robots across multiple fulfilment centres, creating hybrid environments where people work alongside machines rather than being replaced by them. These examples show that automation isn't confined to Asia. It's becoming a central part of operations across Western economies too.

Tesla is also pushing hard into the robotics space. Its Optimus project aims to develop general-purpose humanoid robots capable of performing physical tasks in industrial and domestic environments. While still in development, these robots have already demonstrated the ability to sort, carry, and assemble components, signalling how physical automation will extend well beyond traditional factory settings.

The business case for automation is straightforward. Labour costs drop for routine tasks. Production can run continuously. Quality control becomes more consistent for standardised operations. From a purely economic perspective, the model works for certain types of production.

The issue for Western manufacturers isn't technical viability. What matters is how quickly competitive pressure forces adoption, and how companies integrate these systems with people rather than simply replacing them.

Let's look a little closer at Amazon. It's worth exploring in a bit more detail because what's happening there is being scrutinised and examined deeply by other multi-national conglomerates yet to pull the trigger on crossing their own AI chasm.

Amazon's deployment shows what the transitional stage looks like. By 2023, the company had deployed 750,000 robots across its global logistics network. By mid-2025, that number exceeded one million robots across operations. The facilities aren't fully dark. Instead, they represent a partnership model where robots handle the physically repetitive work whilst humans focus on judgement calls, exception handling, and continuous process improvement. A warehouse worker who previously spent their day walking miles to collect items now supervises robotic systems, troubleshoots problems the machines can't solve, and makes decisions about complex orders or unusual situations. The role has shifted from physical execution to system oversight. Whether that shift represents opportunity or displacement depends largely on which side of the transition you land on.

In October 2025, Amazon announced approximately 14,000 corporate role cuts, citing AI-enabled efficiency and resource reallocation. One million robots deployed. Fourteen thousand jobs eliminated. The pattern isn't subtle: automation at scale, operational restructuring, reduced headcount. The machinery enables the shift. The corporate restructuring completes it.

Amazon's deployment matters beyond its own workforce. As one of the first Western companies to implement automation at this scale and openly link it to headcount reduction, they're providing the business case that other logistics, retail, and distribution companies are studying closely. When boards evaluate their own automation investments, Amazon's numbers will become the proof that the model works. The pathway is visible. The economic logic is documented. Other companies will follow.

Picture a warehouse at midnight, lights dim, conveyors humming whilst no one's there. Trucks roll in and out, sensors track stock levels, and only a handful of technicians check systems remotely as required from an off-site office. These "ghost logistics centres" are being tested now in several locations. Pilot projects in Europe and the US are already testing partial versions of this model, particularly for night-time operations. Deliveries arrive, automated systems sort and store inventory, orders get fulfilled, and trucks get loaded with limited human presence on site. While today, these facilities still require human expertise for maintenance, strategic decisions, system improvements, and handling situations the automation wasn't designed to manage, that won't remain true indefinitely. Robots servicing robots, eliminating human presence entirely. It is no longer a question of possibility, but rather a question of timeline and constraint.

Beyond manufacturing and logistics, automation driven by AI is now spreading well beyond factory floors. Long-established industrial firms such as ABB, Siemens, Bosch, and FANUC are embedding AI into existing robotic and control systems, upgrading the machinery that already runs factories, warehouses, energy systems, and transport networks. This is not speculative technology but automation layered onto environments that are already operational at global scale.

Parallel to this, major platform and infrastructure companies are shaping how these systems are coordinated. Microsoft, Amazon, Google, and Oracle are deploying AI across enterprise software, cloud platforms, databases, and operational tooling that underpin vast swathes of modern work. Model developers including OpenAI, Anthropic, xAI, and DeepSeek are advancing the reasoning and coordination capabilities that allow these systems to act across tools and environments, while Nvidia provides much of the computational backbone that makes large-scale deployment feasible.

At the same time, device and household ecosystem players such as Apple and Samsung are extending automation into everyday life. Rather than humanoid robots, this takes the form of orchestration across devices, on-device intelligence, and home and workplace automation that blends quietly into daily routines. In parallel, smaller start-ups are focused on reducing cost and complexity, pushing autonomous and semi-autonomous systems out of specialist environments and into ordinary settings.

These aren't distant possibilities. As I write this book in 2025, they are active development programmes with working prototypes and expanding capabilities. The companies behind them have already invested billions of dollars into the technology and infrastructure. That level of financial commitment doesn't happen for experiments that might not proceed. The timeline for widespread deployment remains uncertain, but the direction is locked in. It's not a question of if, but when.

Economic and Social Implications

The competitive dynamics work both ways. When manufacturers in one region can produce goods at dramatically lower costs using extensive automation, companies elsewhere face uncomfortable choices. They can accept higher production costs and lose price competitiveness. They can move production to regions with cheaper labour and accept supply chain risks. Or they can invest in similar machine systems and fundamentally reshape their workforce requirements.

None of these choices are comfortable for workers or communities depending on traditional manufacturing employment models. But the competitive pressures are real. A company that maintains traditional staffing headcount whilst competitors automate and go the robotic route will likely face profit margin pressure that eventually becomes unsustainable.

The shift goes deeper than physical automation. Earlier waves replaced human muscle with machine power. This wave is replacing human coordination and decision-making with algorithmic driven systems for routine operations. AI doesn't just move boxes or assemble products. It plans production schedules, optimises supply chains, manages inventory, coordinates logistics, and handles customer interactions. The automation extends into the cognitive side of the work, not just the physical tasks.

This creates pressure across different types of employment simultaneously. Factory workers see production jobs change as automated systems handle routine assembly. Warehouse workers watch their roles evolve from pure manual labour to system supervision and exception handling. Office workers discover that coordination, scheduling, and analysis tasks get handled by machine intelligence, shifting their focus towards strategic decisions and relationship management.

The disruption doesn't stop at one sector. The same underlying technologies are now being applied across multiple industries, reshaping how work gets done in each. But it's worth noting that "disruption" doesn't automatically mean "elimination." Many jobs are transforming rather than disappearing. The challenge lies in developing the capabilities needed for the transformed versions of these roles.

Perhaps most significantly, Industry 4.0 changes who gets displaced and who remains. In previous automation waves, companies typically automated the lowest-skilled positions first whilst expanding middle management and technical oversight roles. The pyramid lost its base but grew in the middle.

Dark factories and ghost logistics centres invert that pattern. When Xiaomi's facility runs with minimal human presence, it's not just eliminating assembly line workers. It's removing shift supervisors, quality control staff, maintenance schedulers, and production coordinators. The roles that survive tend to be either very senior (strategic decision-making that algorithms can't handle) or highly specialised (complex troubleshooting that requires deep technical knowledge). The middle tier where most career progression happened simply shrinks.

This creates a difficult reality for workforce planning. Traditional career paths assumed you'd start at entry level, prove yourself, move into supervisory roles, then progress to management. Industry 4.0 facilities need far fewer people at every level, but the squeeze hits hardest in those middle positions where people used to build experience and advance their careers.

The Lost Ladder and the Learning Pathway Crisis

As explored briefly in the Productivity Paradox section (back in Chapter 2), the automation of work creates an obvious problem: jobs disappear or transform faster than people can adapt. But there's a second disruption that's quieter and potentially more damaging. The pathways people once used to learn new capabilities are disappearing at the same time.

For decades, entry-level positions functioned as invisible apprenticeships. You learned by proximity, handling straightforward tasks repeatedly until they became automatic, making mistakes when the consequences were manageable. The job paid you whilst you figured things out. You climbed a ladder with predictable rungs. That ladder is breaking.

The tasks that entry-level workers typically performed are exactly the tasks AI systems automate first. When those positions disappear, they take the learning layer with them. You can't learn to be a senior accountant without a junior accounting role to start in. You can't become a customer service manager without years handling frontline queries, learning to read customer frustration, understanding which problems need escalation and which need creative solutions. Those representative roles where you developed judgment through repetition are precisely what AI chatbots now handle.

Back in January 2025, the World Economic Forum published its Future of Jobs Report 2025, surveying over 1,000 employers representing more than 14 million workers across 55 countries. The numbers are worth delving into.

World-wide, employers expect that 59% of workers will need training by 2030. Stop and think about that. Three in every five people currently employed. Walk into any office building, any factory floor, any retail operation. Six out of every ten individuals you see will need significant reskilling in the next five years just to remain employable.

Now here's where it gets uncomfortable. Only 48% are expected to receive it.

Let that sink in. The gap between who requires reskilling and who receives it represents roughly 11% of the global workforce. We're talking about tens of millions who must adapt but won't receive institutional support to do so.

That gap isn't abstract. It's the colleague in finance who's quietly retraining at night. The neighbour in logistics trying to learn data skills online after work. The HR coordinator whose job is being redesigned by systems they had no say in choosing.

The report makes brutally clear where resources are flowing. Eighty-five percent of employers plan to prioritise upskilling their existing workforce. Seventy percent intend to hire staff who already possess new skills rather than develop current employees. Forty percent explicitly plan to reduce their workforce as certain skills become less relevant.

Companies are making rational business decisions. Training someone whose skills remain valuable to your future operations makes economic sense. Training someone whose role you're eliminating doesn't, regardless of their organisational knowledge. From a shareholder perspective, the logic is sound. Why invest resources in developing the capabilities of people you are letting go from positions that won't exist, when you could concentrate those same resources on maximising productivity from the smaller workforce you're retaining?

But here's the harsh truth the report reveals: businesses are explicitly passing the retraining burden to regional governments and individual workers. When asked about solutions to skills gaps, employers consistently point to government-funded reskilling programmes, public education improvements, and individual responsibility for capability development. The costs of adaptation are being pushed away from company balance sheets onto public budgets and personal savings. Companies gain the productivity benefits whilst the social costs get transferred elsewhere.

The data reveals another pattern worth examining: not everyone gets equal access to retraining, even among those whose employers are investing in workforce development.

The roles seeing the fastest growth require existing technical foundations. AI and Machine Learning Specialists top the list globally, followed by Big Data Specialists, FinTech Engineers, and Software Developers. These aren't entry-level positions. When companies talk about upskilling their workforce, they're typically talking about taking someone who already understands systems architecture and teaching them AI implementation, not taking someone from an administrative role and turning them into a data scientist.

Meanwhile, the fastest-declining roles tell the opposite story. Administrative assistants, data entry clerks, accounts assistants, customer service representatives, cashiers, bank tellers. Many of these workers have deep organisational knowledge and strong work ethics. What they often lack is the technical foundation that makes retraining into emerging roles realistic within the timeframes employers are working with. Moving from data entry to data analysis isn't just learning new software. It's developing statistical thinking, understanding data structures, and building analytical frameworks from scratch. That's not impossible, but it requires significant time investment that most employers aren't willing to fund when they can hire someone who already possesses those capabilities.

Age plays a role too, though it's rarely stated explicitly. Younger workers are statistically more likely to receive training investment, partly because employers can amortise that investment over more working years. A 28-year-old and a 52-year-old with identical capabilities face different probabilities of receiving training for the same role because the employer anticipates decades of return on one investment but not the other.

Geography matters as well. Workers in tech hubs and financial centres have better access to both employer-sponsored training and external reskilling programmes. Workers in regions where traditional industries are declining often face a double disadvantage: local employers are eliminating positions whilst regional training infrastructure remains limited.

If companies won't invest, perhaps governments will? Not quite.

The assumption that governments will step in requires serious scrutiny. Whether national authorities should bear responsibility for training workforces that generate private sector profit remains a fundamental question. Yet in today's economic climate, with cost-of-living pressures stretching public budgets thin, most lack the financial capacity to fund mass reskilling programmes at the scale required. We're talking about reskilling three in five workers across entire economies whilst those same public bodies struggle to maintain existing services.

Even if funding materialised, there's a more fundamental problem: where would governments find the skilled instructors capable of delivering AI literacy, advanced data analytics, and technological fluency to millions of workers simultaneously? The very skills employers are demanding are in short supply. Those qualified to teach them are already employed in private sector roles, often at salaries the public sector can't match. You can't build a training programme without the expertise to deliver it.

And then there's the responsiveness problem. Government programmes operate on political and bureaucratic cycles that move glacially compared to labour market shifts. Curriculum development realistically takes years. Educational standards need approval. Learning outcomes must be defined. Course materials require creation and validation. Then comes funding approval, which moves through budget cycles, parliamentary reviews, and competing priorities. Then rollout: finding venues, recruiting instructors, managing enrolment. By the time a government training initiative launches to address skills gaps identified during the planning phase, those skills may already be evolving or approaching obsolescence. You're being asked to aim at a target that keeps moving whilst you're still loading the rifle.

The only realistic pathway that might work would likely involve some sort of Government Public-Private Partnership arrangement, where businesses contribute expertise and governments provide funding and coordination. But even this approach depends entirely on national capability and political will, and represents an ideal outcome that only nations with exceptional institutional infrastructure, political consensus, and financial resources can realistically achieve. The countries whose governments successfully navigate this challenge will likely attract investment in AI-driven industries. Multinational corporations choosing where to build operations increasingly assess which nations can reliably produce skilled workforces their AI-enabled operations require. If your nation can't deliver that capability pipeline efficiently, the jobs will likely go elsewhere, creating competitive dynamics where successful nations gain advantage whilst others risk becoming less attractive for investment, further compounding their workforce challenges.

There's a common assumption that AI-driven work might naturally distribute globally through remote employment models. After all, if the work is digital, why would it concentrate geographically? The reality depends on which category of AI work we're discussing. Companies that build AI technology itself (Anthropic, OpenAI, xAI, Google DeepMind) remain intensely office-based, requiring secure access to compute infrastructure and rapid collaboration that's difficult to replicate remotely. But that's a tiny sector employing perhaps a few thousand people globally. The vast majority of AI displacement is happening in AI-adopter companies across customer service, administration, logistics, retail, financial services, and professional services. These organisations use AI tools to enhance operations rather than building the technology themselves. For the millions of workers in these sectors facing role transformation or elimination, the retraining challenge remains fundamentally the same: building demonstrable capabilities without institutional support, often whilst still working full-time in roles that are themselves disappearing.

The institutional pathways that once supported professional development are breaking down faster than new ones emerge. For individual workers facing this reality, waiting for employers or governments to solve the problem means falling further behind. The next section examines what's actually happening in labour markets right now, and why understanding these signals matters for anyone trying to navigate displacement.

The Labour Market Signals

Those World Economic Forum projections paint a stark picture of what's coming by 2030. But here's the uncomfortable question: are we already seeing the early stages play out?

The answer appears to be yes. Whilst projections about future displacement matter, immediate data from 2025 demonstrates that labour market disruption is already underway across multiple regions. The transformation isn't waiting for 2030. It's happening now, and the patterns are becoming visible if you know where to look.

In the United States, the Bureau of Labor Statistics reported that employers added only 22,000 jobs in August 2025, with the agency stating employment had "changed little since April". This extraordinarily weak performance (employers had been forecast to add 75,000 positions) worsened when the BLS released its annual benchmark revision on the 9th of September. The revision revealed that between April 2024 and March 2025, the economy had generated 911,000 fewer jobs than initially estimated, a downward revision of approximately 0.6% of total employment.

The United Kingdom has seen similar patterns. Proposed mass dismissal programmes rose by 5% in 2024/2025, reaching 3,715 programmes planning a total of 267,800 proposed dismissals. The manufacturing sector saw a particularly sharp increase, with notified proposed dismissals rising by 12%, whilst public administration, education, and health recorded a 19% rise. Anthony Wilcox, partner at TWM Solicitors, noted that "the increasing use of AI is making employers more comfortable with the idea that a slimmed down workforce will find a way of coping with their increased workload".

In Ireland, whilst AI-related job creation has surged (with AI job postings doubling since 2023), research indicates that 63% of employment is exposed to AI transformation. Cities like Dublin and Cork face disproportionate impact due to their concentration of ICT, pharmaceutical, and financial industries, with Dublin showing 71% of employees in relatively highly exposed roles. This represents a reversal of prior automation trends, where rural manufacturing roles faced the greatest displacement.

The Asia-Pacific region presents perhaps the most complex picture. A Boston Consulting Group survey of over 4,500 employees across nine APAC markets, conducted in July 2025, found that 78% use AI at least weekly, substantially higher than the 72% global average. Yet 53% of APAC workers fear job loss from AI, compared to 36% globally. Job displacement fears vary dramatically by market: **Thailand** (71%), **South Korea** (66%), and **Singapore** (65%) show the highest concern, whilst **Japan** registers only 40%. AI adoption is especially strong among frontline employees, with 70% in APAC using GenAI regularly compared to just 51% globally.

Across OECD countries, analysis indicates that jobs with high automation risk (defined as roles where more than 25 of 100 core skills are considered easily automatable) constitute approximately 27% of employment. However, the OECD Employment Outlook 2023 notes "there is little evidence so far that AI is leading to job losses," suggesting that whilst automation potential is substantial, actual displacement remains concentrated in specific sectors and roles.

Global layoff tracking reveals acceleration throughout 2025. By October, US-based outplacement firm Challenger, Gray & Christmas reported 153,074 job cuts in October alone (the highest October total since 2003), with year-to-date cuts exceeding 1 million. Artificial intelligence was explicitly cited in 31,039 October cuts, bringing the year-to-date total of AI-attributed layoffs to 48,414. Technology and warehousing sectors led reductions globally, with several major corporations (including Amazon, Microsoft, Salesforce, and Klarna) explicitly citing AI automation as enabling workforce reductions.

The reasons companies cite for these cuts reveal important nuances. Cost-cutting remains the primary driver, responsible for the largest share of announced layoffs. Some expert's express scepticism about AI displacement claims. Peter Cappelli, a management professor at the Wharton School who studies workforce trends, noted: "We invest significant time analysing companies genuinely attempting to implement AI, and there's scant evidence that it leads to job reductions anywhere near the scale being discussed...Introducing AI to preserve jobs is an exceedingly intricate and time-consuming process".

Cappelli's point highlights an important distinction: whilst companies cite AI in layoff announcements, proving that AI technology actually required those specific cuts is far more difficult. The gap between corporate claims and technical necessity matters.

These figures represent partial views rather than comprehensive employment data. The US federal government shutdown has prevented official September and October employment reports, creating information gaps. European Union data shows some sectoral variation, with ongoing analysis noting the challenges of assessing real-time displacement across diverse labour markets.

The immediate data doesn't prove AI is the sole cause of these employment changes, and there's likely a data lag we haven't seen yet. The full picture will probably look worse when more comprehensive figures arrive. But here's what's already clear: companies are citing AI and automation when they announce restructuring, and whilst some of that is genuine transformation, there's also opportunistic headcount reduction happening. Label it "AI-driven efficiency," and suddenly cutting staff looks strategic rather than desperate. The balance sheet improves, investors are pleased, and the narrative sounds forward-thinking rather than cost-cutting.

Whether every AI-attributed job loss genuinely required AI or whether some companies are using automation as convenient cover for workforce reductions they'd planned anyway, the net result is the same. Those WEF projections aren't describing a distant future. They're describing what's already underway. The pace varies by region and sector, the motivations are mixed, but the pattern is unmistakable.

AI job displacement isn't coming. It is already a reality.

Looking Ahead

The overall trajectory is clear, even if the exact timing remains uncertain. AI-driven autonomous manufacturing and logistics systems are set to expand across Europe and North America, driven by the same competitive pressures influencing industries worldwide. The technology has already proven itself, and for company owners and shareholders, the economic logic and dividends will be hard to ignore.

But the reach of automation now extends far beyond factories and warehouses. Generative AI tools are transforming professional and creative work, from copywriting and design to law, finance, and medicine. In offices, AI systems are handling scheduling, analysis, and reporting at speeds no human can match. In customer service, chatbots already resolve millions of interactions once managed by entire departments. The same pattern repeats across sectors: routine work, whether physical or cognitive, is being redefined or absorbed by automation.

The remaining obstacles are less about engineering than about regulation, infrastructure, politics, and mindset, not just in boardrooms but among consumers and workers too.

Will people still want to buy a particular car brand once they realise it was built entirely by machines? Will consumers care who, or what, made their products? And how will workforces respond when this efficiency starts to mean job losses? Think of everyday shopping decisions. When you walk into a supermarket, you can already choose between own-brand, premium-brand, and organic produce. You can buy Fair Trade coffee, ethically sourced cotton, or bananas that promise a fair price for farmers. What happens when "human made" and "robot made" become part of that same conversation and decision process?

When the advert says, "Buy this human-made product - save a job."

It might sound far-fetched now, but consumer identity has always adapted to the values of its time. Imagine picking up a tin of stew and seeing, under the ingredients list, a notice identifying the product as "AI and Robotics Made." Or scanning a barcode that reveals the line, "Human verified production. Thank you for keeping people in work." As I said, far-fetched (and a little tongue in cheek), but as machines take over more and more of the routine work, the mark of little to no human involvement in the process might stop being seen as a cost-saving advantage and start being seen by consumers as a reason to think twice about what they buy.

Public pushback has already reshaped other debates. In 2025, we've seen mass demonstrations around the world driven by politics, national identity, war, and migration. When industrial displacement becomes personal, when it's your town, your job, your livelihood, it's easy to imagine similar movements forming around AI automation. The technology may be inevitable, but in much of the Western world, when its real impact bites, is its acceptance likely to be automatic?

The merging of robotics with generative AI and sophisticated sensor networks will accelerate capability development. Current systems work well in controlled environments with predictable conditions. As the technology and data processing improves, they'll handle more complex, variable situations. The range of environments where minimal workforce presence becomes viable for routine operations will expand.

But here's the part most discussions avoid: this isn't a smooth transition where everyone who loses one type of work simply moves to another. It's a game of musical chairs with fewer chairs each time the music stops. When one person can oversee AI automation output that once required twenty people to fulfil, nineteen positions disappear. The work doesn't redistribute evenly; it concentrates.

BMW's trials with humanoid robots show the intent clearly. Automation takes over the physically punishing work so people can focus on judgement, improvement, and innovation. The facilities become more productive not by removing people but by repositioning contribution towards higher-value activities. That's the optimistic framing, and for some workers it will be true.

But the mathematics are unavoidable. When facilities operate with a tenth of the previous workforce, nine out of ten positions are gone. For those affected by AI displacement, the challenge isn't just developing new skills. It's accepting the reality that there won't be equivalent numbers of roles requiring those capabilities, no matter how quickly people retrain.

This is why this book emphasises adapting faster by changing how you learn. Not because faster adaptation guarantees employment, but because it maximises your chances of being among those who successfully navigate the transition. The Haversack Method can't create jobs that don't exist. What it can do is help you build adaptive capability more efficiently than traditional learning approaches, improving your odds in an increasingly competitive landscape.

Understanding these changes matters not because you need to predict every development, but because you need to position yourself for the work that remains valuable as automation expands. The professionals who navigate this transition successfully aren't those who fight the changes or pretend they're not happening. They're the ones who develop capabilities that complement rather than compete with automated systems, understanding both what the systems do well and where human judgement remains essential.

This often means developing a different relationship with technology. Instead of viewing automation as competition for your job, you learn to see it as handling the repetitive aspects while you focus on the parts that require insight and judgement. A warehouse supervisor working with robotic systems isn't competing with the robots. They're using them to handle volume while focusing on optimising workflows, managing exceptions, and improving overall performance.

The dark factories are real. Ghost logistics centres are being piloted. Facilities designed for minimal workforce presence will expand. This changes what work means and how people add value. The key is developing the flexibility and adaptive capability to evolve your contribution as the systems around you become more sophisticated.

The challenge ahead isn't surviving automation, but learning how to live and work with it. Industry 4.0 isn't a future event waiting to happen. It's already reshaping the world around us. The task now is learning to stay relevant in a system that learns faster than we do.

The following chapters provide practical tools for exactly that. Building adaptive capability that remains valuable regardless of which specific technological developments emerge next. Not by predicting the future perfectly, but by developing the flexibility to respond effectively to whatever actually arrives.

That's what the rest of this book provides.

Section Two introduces a different philosophy about learning and adaptation, one that fits the reality of AI displacement rather than pretending the old models still work. You'll learn temperance learning: finding sustainable balance, building rhythms you can maintain, and taking the long view when everything feels urgent.

Section Three gives you the Haversack Method, a practical system for building demonstrable capabilities at a pace you can sustain, using time and energy you actually have. You'll discover how to capture what matters, spot patterns, and turn scattered insights into working skills.

Section Four will show you how to make it stick when the pressure is on, maintaining these systems through setbacks, evolving your tools strategically, and integrating everything into work that's already demanding.

The machinery behind the shift isn't slowing down. But you don't have to face it empty-handed.

Let's get to work.

The employment data, research reports, and expert commentary referenced in this chapter are detailed in the Notes and Sources section at the end of this book.

Section Two: The Philosophy of Temperance

How balance beats burnout and paralysis when everything is changing.

Understanding the problem is only the first step. Section One painted a clear picture of why the ground feels unstable and why traditional approaches to career development no longer work reliably. But knowing what is wrong doesn't automatically tell you what to do instead.

This is where most people get stuck when facing AI job displacement. They can see their old approaches aren't working, but they're not sure what new strategies to adopt. The temptation is to swing between extremes: either doing nothing and hoping things will stabilise, or frantically trying to learn everything at once in case it becomes relevant.

Both extremes are understandable responses to uncertainty, and both tend to make things worse. Doing nothing leaves you unprepared when change accelerates. Doing everything burns you out before you can make meaningful progress on anything.

What you need instead is a different philosophy entirely. Not a detailed plan (those break down too quickly when circumstances change) but a way of thinking about learning and adaptation that works regardless of which specific changes come next.

I call this approach *Temperance Learning*, and it starts with an old idea that's become surprisingly relevant again. *Balance.*

Not too much, not too little, but just enough. The ancient virtue of temperance (avoiding extremes) turns out to be surprisingly practical in uncertain times.

But understanding balance is only the beginning. You also need sustainable ways to implement it, psychological tools for navigating uncertainty, and the confidence to adapt without burning out. That's what the next three chapters provide: a complete philosophy for learning and adapting when you can't predict what comes next.

When it comes to developing professionally, temperance here means learning enough to stay useful without drowning yourself in the process. It means picking up new skills whilst still backing yourself with the ones you've already got. It means adapting to change without losing track of who you are professionally.

Most importantly, it means accepting that you may never feel completely ready for whatever's coming next, but trusting that you can work out what you need to know when you need to know it. This acceptance is probably the trickiest part of temperance learning. Most of us quite like the comfort that comes from either avoiding uncertainty altogether or trying to prepare for absolutely everything that might happen. Temperance asks you to let go of both those safety blankets whilst still believing in your ability to figure things out as you go.

Chapter 5: Finding Balance

Why doing nothing or trying to do everything both fail. Temperance means learning just enough, just in time, in rhythm.

I watched someone go through what I can only call learning whiplash a couple of years back. She'd been working in human resources for about a decade when AI-powered recruitment tools started appearing in her industry. Initially, she ignored them entirely. Just another passing trend that wouldn't affect her work significantly.

Then her company implemented one of these systems, and suddenly half of her screening and initial interview work was being handled by algorithms. The wake-up call was dramatic and immediate. Within a week, she'd signed up for two online courses about AI in recruitment, registered for an industry conference, bought a couple of books about the future of work, and started following HR tech experts on LinkedIn.

For the next two months, she squeezed in reading every other evening about the growing impact of artificial intelligence in human resources. She developed a solid layman's understanding of how these systems worked and could discuss the pros and cons of different recruitment platforms knowledgeably enough for workplace conversations.

But she was exhausted, overwhelmed, and no more practically prepared for working with AI tools than when she'd started. All of that learning had been theoretical rather than applied. She knew about AI recruitment but hadn't actually learnt to use it effectively in her day-to-day work.

By month three, she'd burnt out completely and stopped all learning activities. She went back to doing her job the way she'd always done it, just with less of it since the AI was handling the routine screening. Her pendulum had swung from complete ignorance to frantic over-learning to frustrated withdrawal.

None of these positions served her well.

The Two Ditches

When people face professional disruption, they tend to end up in one of two ditches on either side of the road. Both feel safer than staying on the road itself, but both ultimately lead to problems.

The first is paralysis. People see the changes happening around them, feel overwhelmed by the scope and speed of transformation, and respond by freezing. They tell themselves they're being cautious, waiting for the dust to settle, taking time to understand the situation before making decisions.

This feels reasonable. It avoids the discomfort of making decisions with incomplete information. If you don't commit to learning anything specific, you can't be wrong about what to learn. If you don't adapt to any particular change, you can't adapt in the wrong direction.

But paralysis comes with costs. Whilst you're waiting for clarity, other people are experimenting, learning, and building capabilities that put them at an advantage. By the time things become clear enough for you to feel confident about your next move, you're likely to be significantly behind people who started adapting earlier.

The second ditch is being overwhelmed. People recognise change is happening and respond by trying to learn everything that might possibly become relevant. They sign up for courses, attend webinars, read extensively, subscribe to a podcast or two, and generally try to cover all bases.

This feels productive because you're clearly doing something. You're investing time and energy in learning. You're staying current with developments in your field. You're preparing for multiple possible futures.

But being overwhelmed has its own problems. When you try to learn everything at once, you rarely learn anything deeply enough to be practically useful. You end up with surface-level knowledge about many topics rather than working competence in any of them. The breadth of your learning prevents the depth needed for actual application.

Both are forms of avoidance. Paralysis avoids the discomfort of uncertainty by pretending decisions can be postponed indefinitely. Being overwhelmed avoids the discomfort of choice by trying to avoid having to choose priorities.

The Middle Path

The alternative to both ditches is what I call the middle path of temperance learning. This isn't about trying to find a perfect balance between doing nothing and doing everything. It's about finding a pace that lasts. Something steady enough to build progress without burning out or falling behind.

I've seen how this works in practice. A friend of mine works for a financial services firm in Dublin's IFSC. When AI tools began taking over routine market analysis, he could have ignored it and hoped it would pass, or panicked and signed up for every fintech course he could find. Instead, he took the middle path.

He set aside an hour each week to learn how the new AI systems worked. Not to compete with them, but to work alongside them. Over time, he moved from producing simple market reports, which the AI handled easily, to interpreting complex patterns and explaining their meaning to clients. He also started building stronger links with the tech team, learning how the models made their decisions and positioning himself as a bridge between automated analysis and human judgment.

Two years later, while others were either struggling to keep up or burning out from intensive retraining, he'd settled into a more strategic role that combined AI capability with human expertise. His approach wasn't flashy, but it worked.

Temperance learning means being selective about what you study without shutting out what matters. It's about giving learning enough time to make progress, but not so much that it replaces actual work.

And maybe most importantly, it's about accepting that you'll never feel completely ready for what's next, but trusting you can grow the skills you need when the moment arrives. That's hard for most of us. We're taught to believe we should have a full plan before acting. Temperance learning asks for something else: the ability to stay calm, adapt, and keep moving even when things are uncertain.

The middle path isn't a compromise between two bad choices. It's a different way of working altogether, one that treats adaptation as an ongoing process rather than a single moment of crisis. It's about finding ways to keep learning that are sustainable over years, not just months.

What Balance Actually Looks Like

Practical balance in learning isn't abstract. It shows up in the everyday choices you make about where to spend your time, what to focus on, and how to judge your own progress.

Start with time. Set aside a portion for learning, maybe around ten percent of your working hours, instead of ignoring it completely or making it your whole focus. For a standard 40-hour week, that's about four hours. Enough to build capability without tipping into burnout.

Here's what that might look like. A marketing professional could spend an hour on Monday mornings trying new AI content tools, half an hour midweek catching up on industry news, and a short session on Fridays practising data analysis. That routine builds momentum without getting in the way of normal work.

Pick learning projects that mix what helps now with what might matter later. Learn things you can use next month alongside the skills that might count next year. The 50/30/20 rule can be a good reference point: half your time improving current performance, some on adjacent skills, and the rest exploring new ground.

But these ratios aren't fixed. Your circumstances, confidence, and time all shape what balance looks like for you. Someone in a fast-moving field might spend more time pushing into new areas. Someone juggling family or heavy responsibilities might start smaller until a steady pattern takes hold. The point is to find a rhythm that feels manageable and doesn't load all your progress into one big push.

Measure progress by what changes in your work, not by hours logged or certificates collected. A project manager learning agile shouldn't just tick off training modules but instead, notice whether sprint planning and retrospectives actually improve.

Build new knowledge on what you already know. Extend, don't erase. A sales professional learning CRM automation doesn't need to drop the relationship side of their role. They can use the new tools to make those connections stronger.

And finally, hold the balance in both directions. Keep performing well in your current job while reaching into new territory. Don't get trapped in old strengths, but don't abandon what's working either. Balance is about doing good work today while quietly preparing for tomorrow.

These principles show what balance looks like. The "Practical Balance Strategies" section at the end of this chapter covers some of the habits that may help you maintain this balance week after week.

Learning Budgets

Here's the problem most people face: there's always more to learn than time available. New tools appear. Regulations change. Competitors adopt different approaches. I've seen this happen in almost every team I've worked with. The instinct is to try to keep up with all of it, but that path soon leaves you overwhelmed.

A learning budget solves this by creating deliberate constraints. Just as you set financial limits to guide spending, you set learning limits to guide where your attention goes. It sounds simple, but most people underestimate how powerful this small constraint can be.

These budgets can take different forms. Some people use time: a software developer might dedicate two hours on Tuesday evenings to new frameworks, Friday mornings to industry reading. That's it. The constraint prevents learning from consuming everything whilst ensuring consistent progress.

Others use money. Budget $500 annually for professional development. One conference, a couple of courses, some books. The financial limit forces you to choose what matters most rather than signing up for everything that looks interesting.

Still others use cognitive constraints, never actively learning more than three new things at once. A marketing manager might focus on social media advertising, basic data analysis, and AI content tools. New opportunities get declined until something reaches sufficient competence to drop from the active list.

Some combine these: three hours weekly, $200 quarterly, two major learning focuses at once. Multiple constraints working together.

The specific structure matters less than having constraints at all. Without them, most people either avoid learning entirely or scatter their efforts across too many directions. Anyone who has ever tried to learn everything at once knows how quickly it turns to noise.

Your budget should include review periods, monthly or quarterly checks on whether your investments produce value. Two months into that six-month online course, is the time and money invested delivering results? If not, then maybe it's time to redirect those resources toward something more immediately useful. Are those Tuesday evening sessions consistently building capabilities you use at work? If yes, consider increasing that time allocation. Still paying for that online platform subscription you haven't logged into since January? Cancel it and put those funds toward something you'll actually use.

The goal is not perfect optimisation. It is conscious choice that makes your professional development deliberate rather than reactive.

Here's where budgets prove most valuable: they force focus by making trade-offs visible. When you've allocated those three hours and that $200, you can't pursue every interesting opportunity. The constraints make you evaluate: which learning provides the most practical value? Which skills am I most likely to use in the next six months? Which areas build on capabilities I'm already developing?

This is uncomfortable because you're explicitly deciding not to learn certain things that might become important. But the alternative, trying to learn everything superficially, usually leaves you less prepared, not more.

In rapidly changing environments, there's always something new demanding attention. New software, industry updates, emerging trends, changing regulations. It never stops. Most people try to keep up with all of it. After all, what if you miss something crucial?

But you can't learn everything. Trying to stay current with every development means you never go deep enough on anything to make it useful. You become someone who can discuss trends at networking events but can't actually implement solutions when problems arise.

Balanced learning requires making strategic choices about what you ignore, not just hoping you'll stumble across the right things to focus on. You pick a few areas for serious time and attention whilst keeping a casual eye on everything else. You accept that you might miss some developments, trusting that depth in selected areas provides more value than shallow coverage across everything.

These budget-driven decisions prevent the scattered approach that leaves you with surface-level knowledge about many topics but working competence in none. Focus isn't just helpful. It's essential for turning learning into practical capability.

Dealing with Uncertainty

Perhaps the hardest part of keeping your learning balanced is dealing with uncertainty about what will actually prove useful. In steadier times, you could make a fair guess about which skills were worth building and expect them to stay relevant for a few years. In the AI era that's no longer true. The pace of change makes those predictions far less reliable.

Balanced learning means getting comfortable with learning things that might not pay off straight away, whilst avoiding the paralysis that comes from not knowing where to start.

This kind of uncertainty is narrower than the big career questions about industries surviving or companies succeeding. It's more immediate. Should you learn this new tool now or wait to see if it sticks? Which of the three areas on your list deserves attention first? How deep should you go before moving on?

These small choices connect to the wider issue of professional uncertainty (which we'll return to later in Chapter 7), but they also need their own approach. The goal is to keep moving without drifting into chaos.

One useful method is to treat learning like a portfolio. Instead of betting everything on one area that might turn out to matter, spread your time across a few options. Think of a financial analyst watching automation reshape their field. They might spend 40 percent of their learning time on data interpretation (a safe bet), 30 percent on AI tool integration (likely to grow), 20 percent on client advisory skills (valuable if the role shifts), and 10 percent on emerging fintech trends (low-cost awareness).

Another option is to double down on meta-skills, things that stay useful even when tools and trends move on. Learning how to get to grips with new software quickly. Knowing how to judge which information sources can be trusted. Building relationships across teams so you can learn from different perspectives. These hold their value even when the specifics of a job change.

The key is to understand and be able to separate low-stakes from high-stakes learning.

For small bets like a webinar, an article, or a quick experiment, act fast.

For larger investments such as six-month training programmes or big career pivots, take your time and look for stronger signals that the skill will stick.

Some of your bets won't pay off, and that's fine. It's the cost of staying adaptable in a moving landscape. The point isn't to predict every winner. It's to keep your overall learning portfolio healthy and balanced, knowing that a few strong returns will outweigh the rest.

The Integration Challenge

Deciding what to learn is one challenge. Putting that learning into practice is another. Many people manage the first but stumble on the second.

The trap is compartmentalising. People attend workshops, read books, or take courses, but they fail to connect that knowledge with their daily work. It sits unused while everything else carries on exactly as before.

Consider two Haulage Transport Fleet Managers attending the same workshop on AI-driven fleet management systems. The first treats it as just another training event. He takes careful notes, stores the slides, and returns to his depot planning to use the tools when the right project comes along. Three months later, he is still managing routes and fuel schedules manually because nothing felt like the ideal moment to test what he had learnt.

The second manager takes a different view. During the workshop, he identifies a few small but clear opportunities for improvement: refining fuel consumption across standard routes, spotting vehicle maintenance conflicts before they cause disruption, and generating alternative route options for changing traffic patterns. The following week, he applies one of these ideas to a short delivery run. Within a month, AI support has become part of his routine planning and he has already seen a measurable drop in fuel use and time lost to rescheduling.

When learning stays separate from everyday work, it becomes a burden instead of a benefit. Knowledge that is not applied quickly starts to drift out of reach. It either gets dropped when things get busy or turns into a kind of distraction, something that feels like progress but changes very little in practice.

Balance means weaving new knowledge into what you already do. Look for modest, real situations where you can test new ideas safely. Try a tool on an ordinary job, adjust one step in an existing process, or apply a new method to a familiar task.

This kind of integration pays off because you get real feedback quickly. You find out what works in your environment and what does not. It also keeps learning sustainable because it becomes part of improving daily performance rather than something you wait to use later.

Start small. Apply new ideas to routine work instead of saving them for major projects. Most improvements can be tested in everyday operations, where the risks are low and the results arrive quickly. This approach turns regular work into a natural testing ground while keeping progress steady and practical.

The Confidence Factor

Learning to deal with uncertainty influences more than just what you study. It affects how confident you are about your work. When your knowledge needs regular updating, it can start to seem as if you're always half a step behind, never quite caught up.

That slow leak of confidence can easily turn into a loop. Once you start doubting yourself, you might hold back from new opportunities, or go the other way and push too hard until you're worn out. Either reaction stops progress before it really starts.

A balanced approach helps you avoid both traps. You keep your strengths in play and build on them bit by bit. Nothing you already know is wasted; you're simply adding new layers and using what's there more effectively.

Keeping a steady pace also matters. Progress you can actually see builds self-belief in a way that frantic bursts never do. The small, regular steps create their own rhythm, showing that you're improving even when nothing feels dramatic.

Spreading your learning efforts helps too. If one course or experiment doesn't deliver, it doesn't shake your whole sense of competence. A financial analyst whose AI pilot project fails still has developed some good data skills that will carry on improving the more they are used.

Most importantly, balanced learning builds what could be called meta-confidence: trust in your ability to learn and adapt, rather than faith in a single skill staying relevant. That's the kind of confidence that lasts, because it's based on practice, not permanence.

Over time, you stop needing every answer in advance. You start trusting yourself to work things out as the situation changes - and that's the real foundation of professional confidence.

The Sustainability Test

One practical way to evaluate whether your approach to learning is balanced is the sustainability test. Ask yourself: could I maintain this approach for two years without burning out or falling behind in my current responsibilities?

If the answer is no, you're probably in one of the ditches. Either you're not learning enough to keep up with changes in your field, or you're learning so intensively that you can't maintain the pace without exhausting yourself.

The sustainability test is important because professional adaptation isn't a one-time event. The changes affecting most industries are ongoing processes that will continue throughout your career. Any approach that depends on unsustainable effort levels will ultimately fail when you can't maintain the required intensity.

Sustainable approaches might feel less dramatic or impressive than intensive learning binges, but they're more effective over the timeframes that actually matter for career development. The person who learns steadily for two years will generally end up with more practical capability than someone who learns intensively for six months and then burns out.

This sustainability principle applies not just to learning intensity but to the methods and tools you use to support your professional development. The systems you build to capture knowledge, the habits you establish for staying current, the networks you create for ongoing support - all of these need to work over years, not just months.

The following chapters will explore specific tools and techniques that pass the sustainability test whilst helping you navigate uncertainty effectively. These aren't dramatic solutions that promise rapid transformation, but proven approaches that work consistently over the long term, even when circumstances keep changing around you.

Practical Balance Strategies

Earlier, in the "What Balance Actually Looks Like" section, we looked at the idea of balance itself. This part is about keeping it going. The goal isn't to build a perfect system, just a few steady habits that help you learn without letting it take over your week.

The weekly learning hour. Pick one regular hour and protect it. That's all you need. Maybe it's Friday afternoon when things are quiet, or early Tuesday before the day starts rushing in. What matters is consistency, not perfection. An hour is light enough to keep going, and heavy enough to matter. If you miss a week, that's fine. Just come back to it.

Project-based learning. Use what you're already doing as the training ground. No need for side projects or long courses. If you're improving your data skills, apply them to a real report. Working on presentations? Practise in the next client meeting. When learning has a live use, it sticks faster.

Learn with others. Find a few people who are also trying to keep up. Divide the load. One follows new tools, another keeps an eye on industry shifts, and someone else shares examples worth copying. Trade notes over coffee or on a quick call once a month. It keeps everyone in the loop without burning anyone out.

Safe-to-fail experiments. Try small things where failure costs nothing. Send a test version of that new email layout to your own team before sending it to clients. Adjust how your weekly meeting runs before changing a big project review. You learn what works and what doesn't without any drama.

Learning notes. Keep short notes, nothing fancy. Just what worked, what didn't, and what you'd do differently next time. A quick line in your notebook or notes app is enough. Those notes save you repeating the same mistakes later.

The key is fit. Pick what makes sense for how you already work and drop the rest. The best systems feel natural, not forced. Good learning habits should blend into your week, not fight for space inside it.

The Long Game

One of the key insights behind temperance learning is that professional adaptation is a long game rather than a short one. The changes happening in most industries aren't one-time disruptions that you can adapt to and then move on from. They're ongoing processes that will continue for the rest of your career.

This long-term perspective fundamentally changes how you think about learning and adaptation. Consider two colleagues facing the same AI disruption in their accounting firm. One panics and spends six months intensively learning Python programming; he's convinced that coding is the only way to remain relevant. The other takes a long-game approach: she spends one hour per week learning to work with AI analysis tools, builds relationships with the IT department, and gradually develops skills in data interpretation and client advisory work.

Eighteen months later, the intensive Python learner has impressive technical skills but discovers that the firm's AI systems handle most coding tasks automatically. Meanwhile, the long-game colleague has become the bridge between automated analysis and client needs, interpreting AI outputs, handling complex client questions, and training others on the new hybrid workflow. Her gradual, sustainable approach positioned her perfectly for the changes that actually emerged.

Instead of asking, "What do I need to learn to survive this particular change?" you start asking, "How can I build sustainable capacity for continuous adaptation?" Instead of trying to predict which specific skills will be valuable in five years, you focus on developing the ability to learn whatever becomes necessary when circumstances require it.

This long-term view also helps with the emotional challenges of adaptation. When you understand that learning is an ongoing process rather than a one-time crisis, you can be more patient with yourself. You don't need to master everything immediately because you know you'll have ongoing opportunities to build your capabilities.

The methods that last rarely look dramatic. They don't create overnight breakthroughs, but they do create durable capability. The person who learns steadily for two years usually ends up stronger than the one who pushes hard for six months and burns out.

AI displacement makes this even more critical. You're not preparing for one transformation and then returning to stability. You're adapting to a world where automation keeps advancing, where yesterday's safe skills become tomorrow's automated tasks, and where the pace of change itself is accelerating. Dramatic reinvention might work once, but you can't reinvent yourself every six months for the next decade. You need approaches that work when change is permanent, not temporary.

That idea applies not only to learning intensity but to the systems that support your development. The way you collect knowledge, the habits you build for staying current, and the relationships that keep you connected all have to work over years, not months. Section Three introduces the Haversack Method, a practical system for collecting and organising what matters as you encounter it, building capability piece by piece rather than trying to absorb everything at once.

The real challenge of balanced learning is holding that long view. Professional adaptation isn't a single project to finish. It's a capacity you'll keep needing for the rest of your working life. This is temperance learning at work: finding the middle path between doing nothing and doing everything, building sustainable rhythms that you can maintain through years of change, not just months of crisis.

The long view also helps with motivation and energy. Once you see adaptation as an ongoing process rather than a crisis to fix, you can relax into the work. You don't have to master everything at once. You'll have time to adjust, build, and refine as you go.

That pacing becomes the foundation for sustainable growth. Fast bursts can help in short windows, but steady rhythms of learning will carry you further.

Finding balance isn't about perfect stability. It's about awareness, noticing when you're slipping into paralysis or overdrive and bringing yourself back to centre. With experience, you start to sense that shift earlier and correct course before you stall.

The professionals who thrive through long stretches of change aren't the ones who reinvent themselves during crises. They're the ones who keep a steady rhythm of learning, adapting, and building capacity quietly, continuously, and without drama.

That kind of rhythm needs proving. Not in theory, but in practice against real constraints and real time horizons. The question is not whether an approach sounds good in principle, but whether it can survive contact with the everyday mess of work and life. The next chapter looks at what that proof of rhythm actually feels like. It moves from mindset to method, showing how the long game becomes real through small, repeatable patterns of effort.

Chapter 6: Rhythm, Not Panic

Learning in small, steady cycles builds more resilience than binge-learning or freezing. Think waves, not avalanches.

There's a particular kind of exhaustion that comes from panic learning, and I suspect most people reading this will recognise it. It's that hollow feeling you get after spending a full weekend binge watching YouTube tutorials about something you're convinced you need to master immediately for a meeting the following week. Your brain feels stuffed with half-digested information, you can't remember most of what you watched, and you're no more capable of doing "the thing" than when you started.

I experienced this myself a few years ago when automation started affecting my own work. I convinced myself that I needed to become proficient with data analysis tools within a month. I downloaded several different analytics packages, signed up for an online course, and spent my lunchtimes and evenings working through exercises that felt increasingly disconnected from anything I might actually need to do.

After four weeks of this, I could regurgitate terminology about statistical significance and correlation coefficients, but I couldn't use any of the tools to answer simple questions about my own work. Worse, I was so tired from the intensity that I avoided anything related to data analysis in my job when possible.

That avoidance cost me more than the initial learning binge. By the time I came back to the topic, other people had started using these tools in ways that made sense for their work, whilst I was still stuck at the starting line.

The problem wasn't that I was learning the wrong things. The problem was that I was learning in the wrong rhythm.

Understanding balance, as explored in the previous chapter, provides the foundation for sustainable learning. It helps you avoid both paralysis and being overwhelmed whilst making strategic choices about where to invest your learning effort. But knowing what balanced learning looks like in principle is different from implementing it consistently in practice.

This is where rhythm becomes essential. Balance tells you how much to learn and where to focus your attention. Rhythm tells you when to learn, how to pace your efforts, and how to maintain sustainable patterns over time. Balance provides the framework; rhythm provides the execution that makes that framework work in real professional life.

The key insight I discovered through my data analysis failure (and many subsequent experiments) is that sustained learning happens through consistent small cycles rather than intensive bursts. Not because small efforts are inherently better, but because they're maintainable over the timeframes that actually matter for professional adaptation.

The Panic Learning Trap

When people realise they need to adapt to technological change, their first instinct is often to compress all the necessary learning into the shortest possible timeframe. This feels logical: the sooner you master the new skills, the sooner you'll be prepared for whatever comes next.

But panic learning creates more problems than it solves, and the issues go beyond simply feeling overwhelmed. The rhythm problems run much deeper.

When you try to absorb large amounts of information quickly, most of it never makes it from short-term memory into long-term understanding. You end up with a collection of disconnected facts and procedures rather than integrated knowledge you can apply to your own scenarios. Your brain needs time between learning sessions to process and consolidate new information, but panic learning eliminates this consolidation time.

More importantly, panic learning is fundamentally unsustainable from a rhythm perspective. You might be able to maintain intensive study for a few weeks or even months, but you can't keep that pace indefinitely. When you inevitably burn out, you often swing to the opposite extreme and avoid learning entirely.

This creates a boom-and-bust cycle that's counterproductive for long-term adaptation. You make dramatic learning efforts followed by periods of stagnation, rather than steady progress that compounds over time. The total learning over a year ends up being less than what you'd achieve through consistent, moderate effort.

The psychological appeal of panic learning is that it feels decisive and urgent. When you're worried about falling behind, throwing yourself into intensive study can feel like you're taking control of the situation. But the intensity itself often prevents the kind of thoughtful, integrated learning that helps you adapt to changing circumstances in the long term.

Panic learning also creates unrealistic expectations about how knowledge develops. It assumes that learning should feel constantly productive and immediately applicable. But genuine skill development includes periods of apparent stagnation, moments of confusion, and gradual integration that can't be rushed. When you're operating in panic mode, these natural rhythms feel like failure rather than normal parts of the learning process.

The trap isn't just about learning too intensively. It's about learning without regard to natural rhythms of attention, energy, and consolidation that make learning effective. Understanding these rhythms (and working with them rather than against them) transforms both the experience and outcomes of professional development efforts.

Rhythm Over Crisis

In the previous chapter, we saw that sustainable learning is a long game, not a crisis to be solved. The methods that last rarely look dramatic, but they create durable capability. Now we need to examine what that long game actually looks like when it becomes rhythm, when theory turns into repeatable practice.

This rhythm-focused long game differs from general strategic thinking about career development. You're not just planning for a distant future. You're establishing patterns that work, day after day, month after month, year after year. The question isn't what you want to achieve eventually, but what rhythms you can maintain consistently while still meeting your current responsibilities.

Consider the difference between two approaches to staying current with AI developments in your field. The crisis approach involves ignoring changes until they become urgent, then spending weekends frantically researching everything you can find about AI applications, attending intensive workshops, and trying to catch up all at once. This creates periods of exhausting learning activity followed by avoidance because you're burnt out.

The rhythm approach establishes a sustainable pattern: spending 30 minutes every Wednesday morning reading one article about AI developments in your industry, attending one relevant webinar per month, and experimenting with one new AI tool per quarter in low stakes work situations. Over a year, this steady rhythm often results in better understanding and more practical capability than the crisis approach, despite requiring much less total effort.

Rhythmic learning works because it replaces panic with habit, removing the need to summon motivation from nowhere each time change arrives. When something new appears on your radar, it has a place to land within your existing learning rhythm rather than demanding an emergency response.

The rhythm perspective also changes how you think about learning plateaus. Instead of treating plateaus as problems that demand harder effort, you start to see them as natural parts of learning cycles. Skills develop through periods of rapid progress followed by consolidation phases where improvement isn't immediately obvious. Sustainable rhythms account for these natural cycles rather than fighting against them.

Rhythmic learning also strengthens judgement. Because you engage with information in small, frequent doses, you get better at filtering what matters from what doesn't. You start recognising noise early, saving time and energy. This gradual sharpening of discernment often separates professionals who adapt successfully from those who struggle under the weight of too much unfiltered information.

This long-term rhythm approach requires patience because progress feels slower at first. But it is far more effective over the timeframes that actually matter for career resilience. The professional who's been learning steadily for two years through consistent small efforts often has more integrated, applicable knowledge than someone who's done three intensive learning binges followed by periods of avoidance.

Most importantly, rhythm-based long-game thinking builds learning into your identity rather than treating it as a temporary response to crisis. You become someone who stays current because learning is woven into how you work, not because pressure forces you to catch up.

What Rhythm Actually Means

Establishing sustainable long-term patterns requires understanding what rhythm actually means in the context of professional learning. This isn't about rigid scheduling or mechanical repetition. It's about finding natural cycles of effort and rest, intensity and integration, that allow you to make steady progress without burning yourself out.

Think about how musicians develop their skills. They don't try to master complex pieces by playing them at full speed from the beginning. They start slowly, work on small sections, gradually build up tempo and complexity, and practice regularly over extended periods. The rhythm of practice (short sessions, consistent frequency, gradual progression) is what allows them to develop genuine fluency rather than just memorised sequences.

Professional learning works similarly. Rather than trying to absorb everything at once, you work on small pieces, connect them to what you already know, apply them in low-risk situations, and gradually build more complex capabilities over time.

This rhythmic approach requires patience because progress feels slower initially. But it's more effective in the long run because it builds genuine understanding rather than surface-level familiarity. More importantly, it's sustainable over the timeframes that actually matter for career development.

Rhythm also means matching your learning pace to your life circumstances. If you have young children, your rhythm will be different from someone with more discretionary time. If you're dealing with high work pressure, your learning rhythm needs to accommodate that reality rather than adding unsustainable additional demands.

The key is finding patterns that feel natural rather than forced. Some people work best with daily learning habits (let's say, 15 minutes each morning working on a specific skill). Others prefer longer, less frequent sessions (a few hours every weekend dedicated to professional development). Still others work best with intensive bursts (a week of focused learning every quarter).

Different types of learning have different natural rhythms. Technical skills might require short, frequent practice sessions to maintain familiarity and build muscle memory. Conceptual understanding might develop better through longer, less frequent periods of reflection and synthesis. Strategic thinking might emerge from irregular bursts of analysis and integration.

The goal isn't finding the perfect rhythm that works for everyone, but discovering the patterns that work for your specific circumstances, learning style, and professional demands. Your rhythm should feel challenging enough to drive progress but sustainable enough to maintain indefinitely.

The Wave Pattern

Building on the concept of natural learning rhythms, a useful metaphor for sustainable learning patterns is waves on the seashore. Waves don't arrive as constant pressure; they come in cycles of intensity and rest. Each wave builds energy, crests, delivers its impact, then recedes to allow the next wave to build.

Learning works best with similar patterns. You focus intensively on something for a period, then step back to let it integrate with your existing knowledge, then focus on the next thing. This rhythm of engagement and rest allows for both progress and consolidation.

Many people try to maintain constant learning intensity, which is like trying to create waves without any troughs. It doesn't work because consolidation and integration require periods of reduced input. Your brain needs time to process and connect new information with existing knowledge.

The wave pattern also helps with motivation and energy management. When you know that periods of intensive learning will be followed by periods of integration and rest, you can sustain higher levels of effort during the intensive periods. You're not trying to maintain peak performance indefinitely.

Different types of learning have different natural wave patterns. Technical skills might require short, frequent waves (daily practice sessions with brief integration periods). Conceptual understanding might develop better through longer, less frequent waves (weekly deep learning sessions with extended reflection periods). Strategic thinking might emerge from irregular wave patterns (intensive analysis periods followed by longer integration phases).

The key is recognising these natural rhythms rather than trying to force all of your learning into the same pattern. A software developer learning a new programming language might use daily coding practice waves. A manager developing leadership skills might use monthly intensive reading waves followed by extended periods of applying concepts in real management situations.

The wave pattern also prevents the learning plateaus that discourage many people. When you understand that apparent stagnation is often the trough between waves (a necessary integration period rather than a sign of failure), you're more likely to maintain effort through periods when progress isn't immediately visible.

Most importantly, the wave pattern is infinitely sustainable. Unlike linear approaches that assume constant progress, wave patterns accept the natural ebb and flow of learning whilst ensuring overall forward movement over time.

Small Cycles, Big Results

The wave pattern suggests a practical approach to implementing sustainable learning rhythms: working in small, complete cycles that you can finish and evaluate regularly. Instead of committing to learning something over six months, you might commit to learning something over two weeks, then decide whether to continue, modify, or change direction.

These small cycles embody the wave principle in actionable form. Each cycle has a clear beginning (focus and intensity), middle (sustained effort), and end (integration and evaluation). Like waves, they're complete in themselves whilst contributing to longer-term progress.

Small cycles have several advantages over extended commitments. They're short enough that you can maintain focus and motivation throughout the entire cycle. They provide regular opportunities to assess progress and make adjustments before getting too far down unproductive paths. They prevent learning projects from becoming unwieldy commitments that compete with other responsibilities.

A typical small cycle might involve identifying one specific capability you want to develop, finding the minimum resources needed to get started, practising or experimenting for a defined period, then evaluating what you've learnt and what to do next.

Consider a junior buyer who needs to understand how AI is changing inventory management in their company. Rather than "learning inventory automation," they might commit to "spending two weeks understanding how the new demand forecasting system affects stock ordering decisions." That's specific enough to achieve in the timeframe, practical enough to apply immediately, and small enough to feel manageable.

At the end of the two weeks, you evaluate: Did this prove useful? Should I go deeper in this direction? Should I try a different approach? Should I move on to something else entirely? The short cycle gives you frequent decision points rather than locking you into extended commitments that might not prove worthwhile.

This approach also matches how most real learning happens. Major capabilities develop through multiple small cycles rather than single large efforts. Each cycle builds on previous ones whilst allowing for course corrections based on practical experience and changing circumstances.

Small cycles also reduce the psychological barriers to starting new learning. "Two weeks experimenting with inventory forecasting tools" feels much more manageable than "learning to become proficient with supply chain automation." The smaller commitment makes it easier to begin whilst still providing enough time to make meaningful progress.

Most importantly, small cycles create frequent completion experiences that build momentum and confidence. Instead of working towards distant goals that might never be reached, you complete tangible projects that demonstrate growing capability whilst providing clear stopping points when efforts aren't proving valuable.

The Integration Imperative

One of the biggest differences between sustainable learning rhythms and intensive learning efforts is the emphasis on integration timing. While Chapter 5 explored what integration looks like in principle, the rhythm approach focuses on when integration happens and how much time it requires.

Integration takes time and can't be rushed through increased effort or intensity. This timing requirement is often overlooked when people design learning plans. You need periods between learning inputs to experiment with new approaches in real work situations, notice what works and what doesn't, adjust your understanding based on feedback, and gradually incorporate new methods into your regular workflow.

This integration timing is often more valuable than the initial learning itself. When you integrate new knowledge with existing capabilities, you don't just add new skills; you multiply the effectiveness of everything you already know. But this multiplication process requires rhythm and spacing that intensive learning approaches typically eliminate.

Consider the junior buyer learning about demand forecasting systems. The initial two-week learning cycle might involve understanding how the system works and what data it uses. But the integration period that follows - experimenting with the system's recommendations, comparing them to traditional ordering decisions, adjusting their workflow to incorporate AI insights, often proves more valuable than the initial technical learning.

Many people skip adequate integration time because it feels less productive than active learning. They move from one course to the next, one book to the next, one tutorial to the next, without taking time to properly digest and apply what they've absorbed. This creates an illusion of progress whilst actually preventing real capability development.

The wave pattern naturally builds in integration time through the rhythm of intensity and rest. After a focused learning wave, you deliberately step back from new input to allow consolidation and practical application. This isn't procrastination or laziness; it's essential consolidation work that transforms information into working capability.

Different types of learning require different integration timing. Technical skills might need daily integration through regular practice. Conceptual knowledge might require weekly reflection and application. Strategic insights might need monthly synthesis with existing frameworks and approaches.

The key is recognising integration as an active process that requires dedicated time and attention, not something that happens automatically or during spare moments. When you're planning learning rhythms, integration time should be explicitly scheduled rather than hoped for.

This timing-focused approach to integration ensures that your learning wave patterns create lasting capability rather than temporary knowledge accumulation. Each wave becomes more effective because previous waves have been properly integrated before new learning begins.

Sustainable Intensity

Sustainable learning rhythms don't mean avoiding intensive effort entirely. They mean using intensity strategically rather than constantly. There are times when it makes sense to focus deeply on learning something new, but these periods need to be bounded, purposeful, and followed by periods of integration and rest.

This strategic approach differs fundamentally from the panic learning described earlier. Panic learning applies intensity reactively, driven by external pressure and anxiety about falling behind. Strategic intensity is applied proactively, planned in advance, and designed to achieve specific capability goals within realistic timeframes.

Think of it like interval training in athletics. You alternate between periods of high intensity and periods of recovery. The high-intensity periods push your capabilities forward and create rapid skill development. The recovery periods allow your mind to adapt and consolidate the gains from the intensive work, whilst preventing burnout that would undermine long-term progress.

In learning contexts, sustainable intensity might mean dedicating one day per week to focused learning or spending an hour each morning on skill development during a particular month, or taking a week-long intensive course every quarter. The key difference from panic learning is that the intensity is planned, bounded, and followed by integration time.

Our junior buyer might use sustainable intensity when preparing for a major system upgrade. Instead of panicking and trying to learn everything about the new inventory system over a weekend, they might plan a strategic intensive period: dedicating their first hour each morning for two weeks to hands-on practice with the new system, knowing this will be followed by a month of gradual integration as they apply what they've learnt to real purchasing decisions.

Strategic intensity also means matching the intensity level to the importance and urgency of what you're learning. You might learn intensively when you're preparing for a new role that starts next month, or responding to immediate changes that affect your current work. You use more moderate pacing when you're exploring potential future directions or maintaining existing capabilities.

The rhythm approach helps you avoid both extremes of constant low-level effort (which doesn't create enough momentum for breakthrough understanding) and constant high intensity (which creates burnout and prevents proper integration). Instead, you develop sensitivity to when intensive effort is warranted and when sustainable pacing better serves your long-term development.

The key is maintaining control over when and why you apply intensity, rather than letting external pressures dictate your learning rhythm. Strategic intensity feels energising because you're choosing when to push yourself hard. Panic learning feels exhausting because the intensity is imposed by circumstances rather than chosen for strategic purposes.

The Compound Effect

Perhaps the most important advantage of sustainable learning rhythms is the compound effect. When you learn consistently over extended periods, even small amounts of progress compound into significant capability development.

This compounding effect is often invisible in the short term, which is why people gravitate towards more dramatic approaches. After a week of steady learning, you might not feel dramatically more capable. After a month, the progress becomes more noticeable. After a year, the cumulative effect can be substantial.

The compound effect also applies to meta-learning - your ability to learn new things effectively. Each small cycle of learning teaches you something about how you learn best, what resources are most effective for you, how to integrate new knowledge with existing capabilities. These meta-skills compound over time, making each subsequent learning cycle more effective and efficient.

This is why people who've been using sustainable learning rhythms for years often seem to adapt to new changes effortlessly. They're not necessarily more intelligent or talented; they've just developed more effective learning systems that allow them to acquire new capabilities efficiently.

Our junior buyer, after maintaining steady learning rhythms for a year, doesn't just know more about inventory systems. They've developed judgement about which new developments are worth investigating, established relationships with colleagues who can answer technical questions, built confidence in their ability to understand complex systems, and created habits that make continuous learning feel natural rather than burdensome.

The compound effect operates at multiple levels simultaneously. Your specific knowledge grows. Your learning efficiency improves. Your confidence in handling change increases. Your reputation as someone who adapts well creates more opportunities to learn and grow. These effects reinforce each other over time.

The key insight is that compound learning works best with consistency rather than intensity. Missing occasional learning sessions doesn't significantly impact long-term compounding, but stopping and starting repeatedly does. The rhythm approach protects this consistency by making learning efforts sustainable rather than heroic.

Most importantly, compounding means that learning investments made today continue paying dividends for years. The time spent understanding new inventory forecasting systems creates foundation for understanding supply chain automation, vendor management tools, and whatever emerges next. Each learning wave builds on previous waves whilst preparing for future ones.

This compounding effect transforms learning from a cost (time and energy spent) into an investment that generates increasing returns over time. The earlier you establish sustainable learning rhythms, the longer compound effects have to work in your favour.

Dealing with Urgency

One common objection to sustainable learning rhythms is that they don't address situations where you need to learn something quickly due to external pressure. What do you do when your company announces a major technology change that will affect your role in three months? How does the rhythm approach work when urgency is imposed by circumstances beyond your control?

The answer isn't to abandon rhythmic principles entirely but to apply them more intensively whilst maintaining their core benefits. You can compress learning cycles from weeks to days, increase the frequency of learning sessions, and focus more narrowly on immediately applicable skills. But even under pressure, the basic principles of rhythm remain important.

You still need to alternate between input and integration, even if those cycles become much shorter. Instead of learning for two weeks then integrating for the next fortnight, you might learn intensively in the morning and apply what you've learnt in afternoon work sessions. The rhythm is accelerated, but it's still present.

You still need to connect new learning with existing knowledge and capabilities, but you focus on the most essential connections rather than comprehensive integration. Our junior buyer facing an urgent system changeover might focus exclusively on how the new forecasting affects their existing supplier relationships and ordering routines, leaving broader strategic implications for later exploration.

You still need to maintain some boundaries to prevent complete burnout, but those boundaries become more flexible. Instead of one hour per week, you might dedicate one hour per day to urgent learning whilst protecting evening and weekend time for rest and integration.

The key is distinguishing between genuine urgency that requires accelerated rhythm and perceived urgency that comes from anxiety about change. True urgency has external deadlines that can't be moved. Perceived urgency often reflects internal pressure to learn everything immediately, even when external timelines are more flexible than they initially appear.

Even under genuine time pressure, sustainable principles still apply. You're more likely to succeed by maintaining some rhythm structure than by abandoning all boundaries and learning chaotically. Think of it as switching from leisurely walking rhythm to running rhythm, rather than abandoning coordinated movement entirely.

Most importantly, urgent learning periods should be temporary rather than permanent. Once the immediate pressure passes, return to more sustainable rhythms rather than maintaining crisis-level intensity indefinitely. The rhythm approach provides a foundation to return to, rather than a rigid system that breaks under pressure.

Building Your Learning Rhythm

Developing a sustainable learning rhythm requires experimentation to find what works for your individual circumstances, learning style, and professional demands. There's no universal rhythm that works for everyone, but the discovery process follows predictable patterns.

Our junior buyer started by trying daily learning sessions - fifteen minutes each morning before checking emails to read about inventory management trends. This felt manageable initially, but after two weeks, the morning routine began feeling rushed when urgent supplier issues arose. The daily habit was too rigid for their unpredictable work environment.

Next, they experimented with weekly concentrated sessions, dedicating Friday afternoons to learning about demand forecasting systems. This provided better focus and didn't interfere with urgent daily responsibilities. But they discovered that by Friday afternoon, they were often mentally tired from the week's work and couldn't absorb complex technical information effectively.

The breakthrough came with a monthly intensive pattern. They began spending the first Monday morning of each month (when inventory review meetings were typically scheduled anyway) learning about new systems and approaches. This aligned with their natural work cycle and provided enough time between sessions to apply and integrate what they'd absorbed.

But even this pattern needed refinement. They discovered that Monday mornings worked well for technical learning but weren't ideal for strategic thinking. So they adapted: Monday mornings for hands-on system practice, and one Saturday morning per quarter for broader reflection about how AI was changing their industry and what skills might become important next.

The key insight from this experimentation was that effective rhythms need to match both your energy patterns and your work environment. The junior buyer learned they absorbed technical information best when alert and focused (Monday mornings) but needed quieter, less pressured time for strategic thinking (weekend mornings).

Your rhythm will also need to evolve as your circumstances change. When the junior buyer was promoted to senior buyer with additional responsibilities, they had to adjust their learning rhythm again - shorter but more frequent technical sessions, with strategic learning shifted to longer quarterly reviews.

The goal isn't finding the perfect rhythm immediately but developing sensitivity to your own learning patterns and needs. This self-awareness allows you to adjust your approach as your life circumstances, work demands, and learning goals evolve over time.

Track what works and what doesn't. Notice when you feel most alert and focused. Observe which types of learning feel natural versus forced. Use these observations to refine your approach continuously rather than forcing yourself into patterns that don't match your reality.

The Patience Paradox

One of the most counterintuitive aspects of sustainable learning rhythms is that going slower initially often allows you to go faster overall. When you take time to properly understand and integrate new knowledge, you build a stronger foundation for subsequent learning.

This patience paradox is difficult for people who are feeling pressure to adapt quickly. It requires trusting that steady progress will ultimately be more effective than dramatic but unsustainable efforts.

Remember the "Two Ditches" from Chapter 5? Paralysis (doing nothing) and being overwhelmed (doing everything). Patience isn't the same as paralysis. Paralysis waits for perfect clarity that never arrives. Patience commits to steady progress despite incomplete information. The difference matters. One avoids action hoping circumstances improve. The other takes consistent action whilst circumstances keep shifting.

Patience works, though it rarely feels that way when you're under pressure. I've watched people adapt to rapidly changing systems in different ways. Some rush through intensive courses, master the terminology, get the certifications. Others move more slowly, testing ideas in their daily work, building understanding piece by piece.

When the systems inevitably change, the patient learners often adapt more easily. Not because slow is inherently superior, but because understanding built through practical application tends to transfer better than knowledge acquired through intensive study. The rush-through-the-course approach teaches you that specific version. The gradual approach teaches you how the underlying principles work.

The patience paradox works because thorough understanding compounds more effectively than surface knowledge. When you rush through learning, you often need to relearn the same concepts multiple times as contexts change. When you learn patiently, the initial investment pays dividends across multiple applications and adaptations.

This doesn't mean learning should be unnecessarily slow or perfectionist. The goal is finding the optimal pace that balances thoroughness with practical progress. That pace usually sits between two extremes: faster than perfectionists feel comfortable with, but slower than anxiety wants you to go.

The professionals who navigate technological change most successfully are often those who started adapting earlier and more gradually, rather than those who made the most dramatic short-term changes. By the time rapid change becomes obvious to everyone, the people who've been learning patiently are already well-positioned to take advantage of new opportunities.

Moving Forward with Rhythm

Developing a sustainable learning rhythm isn't about finding the perfect schedule and sticking to it forever. It's about developing sensitivity to your own learning patterns and adjusting your approach based on what you observe about your own effectiveness.

Pay attention to when you learn most effectively. Notice which types of learning sessions leave you energised versus exhausted. Observe how long it takes for new knowledge to really integrate with your existing capabilities. Use these observations to refine your approach over time.

Our junior buyer discovered that their optimal rhythm wasn't static but evolved with their role and responsibilities. As they gained confidence with inventory systems, they could handle more complex learning challenges. As their workload increased, they needed to adjust the timing and frequency of learning sessions. The rhythm approach provided a flexible framework rather than rigid rules.

Remember that the goal isn't to optimise every aspect of your learning immediately. The goal is to establish sustainable patterns that you can maintain and improve over time. Even an imperfect rhythm is better than alternating between intensive learning binges and complete learning avoidance.

Building sustainable learning rhythms creates the foundation for navigating the deeper challenges that face professionals in uncertain times. Once you've established patterns for consistent learning and integration, you can address more complex questions about what to learn, when to pivot, and how to maintain confidence despite not knowing exactly what changes are coming next.

This rhythm-based foundation becomes particularly valuable when dealing with the fundamental uncertainty that characterises most professional environments today. You can't predict which specific skills will become crucial or which technologies will dominate your field. But you can build confidence in your ability to learn whatever becomes necessary when circumstances require it.

The steady progress that comes from sustainable learning rhythms also provides psychological stability during uncertain periods. When you know you're continuously building capabilities, you feel less vulnerable to unexpected changes. When learning becomes a natural part of your professional routine, adaptation feels manageable rather than crisis driven.

The following chapter explores how to maintain this learning momentum even when you can't predict what you're learning for. How do you stay motivated to develop capabilities when you don't know which ones will prove valuable? How do you choose learning priorities when the future remains genuinely uncertain? How do you build confidence in your adaptive capacity rather than confidence in particular knowledge remaining permanently relevant?

These questions require moving beyond rhythm and balance to address the mental challenges of functioning effectively despite ongoing uncertainty about what comes next.

Chapter 7: Living with Uncertainty

You cannot control change. You can control how you respond. Temperance learning keeps you steady in motion.

I had a conversation recently with someone who'd navigated a significant transition in banking. She'd been there for eight years, had built solid expertise in credit risk assessment, and thought she understood her industry well enough to predict where it was heading. Then new AI-driven risk analysis systems started appearing, and within eighteen months her particular type of expertise was being fundamentally transformed.

"The thing that really got to me," she said, "wasn't the technology itself. It was realising how wrong I'd been about what would happen next. I'd been so confident about the direction things were moving, and I was completely off base. Now I find myself continually second-guessing my instincts about what to learn or where to focus."

Thankfully, she has successfully adapted to the recent changes, learning to work alongside AI systems and developing hybrid approaches that combine automated analysis with human insight. Her role has evolved rather than disappeared, and she's become more valuable to her organisation through the transition. But the experience has shaken her confidence in her ability to predict what changes will come next.

This loss of confidence in predicting the future is one of the most disorienting aspects of rapid professional change. Even when you successfully navigate one major transition, it can leave you questioning whether you can trust your assessment of what's solid and what's not going forward.

The temptation is to respond by either trying to predict more carefully or giving up on prediction entirely. Neither works well. Better prediction isn't really possible when change is genuinely unpredictable. Giving up on forward thinking leads to paralysis and reactive responses that often come too late.

What works better is learning to function effectively despite uncertainty, rather than trying to eliminate uncertainty itself. This goes beyond the rhythm and balance approaches explored in previous chapters. Even when you've established sustainable learning patterns, you still face fundamental questions about direction and priority when the future remains genuinely unknowable.

Living with uncertainty requires different psychological tools other than just building learning rhythms. It means getting comfortable with provisional decisions, building confidence in your ability to adapt rather than in what you know, and trusting that you can handle what comes rather than predict what's coming.

This shift represents perhaps the most challenging aspect of navigating AI displacement: accepting that you can't control which changes arrive, whilst maintaining confidence in your ability to handle them when they do.

The Illusion of Control

Most of us prefer to believe we have more control over our professional futures than we actually do. This belief isn't entirely wrong (your choices and actions do matter significantly). But it's incomplete in ways that can become damaging when circumstances change rapidly.

When you've successfully established sustainable learning rhythms, as explored in the previous chapter, there's a natural tendency to extend that sense of control to predicting outcomes. If you can control when and how you learn, surely you can also determine what you should learn and why? This logical extension often proves problematic.

The illusion of control manifests in several ways that go beyond simple prediction failures. We create detailed career plans assuming stable industry paths. We choose learning investments based on confident assessments of which skills will remain valuable. We build professional identities around expertise that we expect to provide lasting security.

These control-seeking behaviours feel rational because they provide comfort. Having a plan feels better than acknowledging uncertainty. Investing in predictable skills feels safer than building adaptive capacity. Relying on proven expertise feels more secure than developing meta-skills for unknown challenges.

But the psychological comfort comes at a cost. When you're mentally committed to particular predictions about the future, you become less able to notice when circumstances change in ways that invalidate your assumptions. My banking colleague experienced this firsthand; her analytical skills were excellent, but they'd created overconfidence in her ability to foresee technological disruptions.

The illusion of control also leads to rigid rather than adaptive responses. People invest heavily in specific predictions about the future, then double down when early evidence suggests they might be wrong. They seek more information, better analysis, more sophisticated forecasting, rather than accepting that some aspects of professional change are genuinely unpredictable.

The alternative isn't abandoning planning or learning randomly. It's shifting focus from controlling outcomes to controlling responses. You can't determine which technologies will dominate your industry, but you can develop the capability to work effectively with whatever technologies emerge. You can't predict which companies will succeed, but you can build skills that remain valuable across different organisational contexts.

This shift from outcome control to response control requires different mental tools than traditional career planning. Instead of seeking certainty about the future, you build confidence in your ability to navigate uncertainty. Instead of preventing change through prediction, you develop capabilities that help you thrive regardless of which changes occur.

Accepting Permanent Incompleteness

One of the most mentally challenging aspects of living with uncertainty is accepting that you'll never feel fully prepared for whatever comes next. There will always be emerging technologies you don't understand, industry developments you haven't anticipated, skills you haven't yet developed.

This permanent state of gaps feels uncomfortable because it contradicts our training about how professional competence is supposed to work. Most of us learnt that competence means having thorough understanding in our area, being able to handle whatever comes up, being the person others turn to for answers.

But in rapidly changing environments, complete mastery is impossible and total preparation is impractical. The question isn't whether you'll encounter situations where you feel unprepared (you will). The question is whether you can maintain confidence and effectiveness despite those gaps.

Our banking colleague discovered this reality during her successful transition to working with AI risk assessment systems. Even after months of adaptation, she didn't fully understand how the machine learning algorithms made their decisions, couldn't predict which factors the system would weight most heavily in unusual cases, and continued learning new aspects of how to integrate AI recommendations with traditional risk evaluation methods.

Initially, this level of ongoing partial understanding felt professionally uncomfortable. She'd been used to feeling expert in credit risk assessment, having extensive expertise that colleagues relied on. Her new hybrid approach meant accepting that her understanding would always be partial and evolving rather than complete and stable.

But she's learnt to work effectively despite these gaps. She focuses on understanding enough to interpret AI outputs sensibly, maintains relationships with the technical team to clarify system behaviour when needed, and continues developing processes for combining automated analysis with human judgement. Her expertise remains partial, but it proves sufficient for making better credit decisions than either pure AI analysis or traditional methods alone.

This requires a different kind of professional self-assurance. Instead of certainty based on knowing everything relevant to your field, you need trust based on your ability to learn whatever becomes necessary. Instead of feeling secure because you have all the answers, you feel secure because you believe in your capacity to find answers when needed.

This transition from knowledge-based certainty to learning-based trust is difficult for many people, especially those who've built careers around being recognised experts in particular areas. It can feel like admitting incompetence rather than acknowledging the reality of operating in uncertain environments.

But adaptive confidence is actually more robust than static expertise because it doesn't depend on any particular information remaining relevant. When specific skills become dated, expertise-based assurance can evaporate. When circumstances change in unexpected ways, learning-based confidence adapts.

The Meta-Skills Advantage

Since you can't predict which particular competencies will matter most, it makes sense to focus significant attention on meta-skills: capabilities that help you develop other abilities regardless of which direction circumstances move.

Think of meta-skills as tools for building tools. While domain-specific expertise helps you perform particular tasks, meta-skills help you acquire new proficiencies quickly when circumstances change. It's like knowing how to fish versus simply being handed a fish - one feeds you for a meal, the other feeds you for life.

Meta-skills include learning how to learn efficiently, developing judgement about which information sources are reliable, building relationships across different areas of your field, and cultivating the knack for quickly understanding how new tools or processes work.

Our banking colleague's successful adaptation demonstrates how these foundational capabilities transfer even when specialist knowledge becomes less relevant. Her credit risk assessment expertise needed updating when AI systems began handling routine analysis, but the meta-skills she'd developed during her career proved invaluable for navigating the transition.

Her talent for quickly evaluating data source reliability helped her assess AI-generated risk reports and understand when human oversight was essential. Her experience building relationships with loan officers translated into effective collaboration with data scientists and IT specialists implementing the new systems. Her gift for explaining complex financial concepts to non-experts became crucial for interpreting AI recommendations to senior management and training colleagues on hybrid approaches.

These competencies endure even when technical know-how becomes outdated. More importantly, they compound over time. Each time you use meta-skills to develop new domain knowledge, you strengthen the meta-skills themselves.

Quick software adoption matters no matter which platforms dominate your field. Whether your industry adopts Microsoft systems, Google platforms, or specialised sector-specific software, the underlying capacity to navigate new interfaces, understand workflow logic, and identify useful features transfers across all applications.

Building cross-disciplinary relationships helps whatever the future brings. When automation changes your field, the relationships you've built with IT professionals, data analysts, or process improvement specialists become bridges to understanding new technological implementations.

Synthesising information from multiple sources stays relevant as channels evolve. Whether you're learning from industry publications, online courses, colleague insights, vendor demonstrations, or even podcasts, the skill of extracting key insights and connecting them to your particular work context applies across all information channels.

Clear communication adapts to whatever explanatory challenges emerge. Whether you're explaining traditional processes to newcomers, interpreting automated system outputs for managers, or training colleagues on hybrid human-AI workflows, this strength adjusts to your role's evolution.

Meta-skills also provide psychological benefits during uncertainty. When you trust your learning capacity, you feel less anxious about not knowing exactly what changes are coming. When you're confident building new connections, you worry less about which particular people will matter most.

Working with Partial Information

One of the practical challenges of living with uncertainty is learning to make good decisions with incomplete information. In stable environments, you can often wait until you have comprehensive data before making important choices. In uncertain environments, waiting for complete information often means waiting too long.

This creates a tension between the desire for thorough analysis and the need for timely action. The resolution isn't to abandon analysis entirely, but to become more skilled at working with partial information whilst remaining open to updating your understanding as new data becomes available.

Our banking colleague faces this challenge regularly in her current role. When the AI risk assessment system flags an unusual loan application, she rarely has complete information about why the algorithm made that determination. The applicant's financial history might be complex, the AI's weighting factors aren't fully transparent, and market conditions affecting risk calculations change daily.

Rather than delaying decisions until she understands every variable, she's developed a provisional approach. She gathers the most critical information available, makes initial assessments based on that data, and builds in review points to adjust her conclusions as additional insights emerge. She might approve a loan the AI has flagged if her analysis suggests the algorithm is overweighting temporary factors. She might reject an application the AI rates favourably if she spots risk patterns the system hasn't weighted adequately. The approach isn't about overruling the AI arbitrarily. It's about combining algorithmic analysis with human judgement, whilst acknowledging that both sources of insight remain incomplete.

Working effectively with partial information requires developing comfort with provisional decision-making. Instead of making permanent commitments based on complete analysis, you make temporary commitments based on the best information currently available, whilst building in opportunities to reassess and adjust as circumstances become clearer.

This approach feels less satisfying than making definitive decisions with all the facts in hand, but it's more effective when the landscape keeps shifting. You can start moving in a promising direction whilst remaining alert to signals that might indicate the need for course corrections.

The key is distinguishing between decisions that are easily reversible and decisions that are difficult to undo. For easily reversible decisions, you can move quickly with limited information. For decisions that are difficult to reverse, you invest more time in analysis whilst accepting that your information will never be complete.

Provisional decision-making also requires building comfort with being wrong occasionally. When you're working with incomplete data, some decisions will prove suboptimal as better information emerges. The goal isn't perfect accuracy, but reasonable quality decisions made in reasonable timeframes, with systems in place to learn from mistakes and to make adjustments in future approaches.

The Experimentation Mindset

Living effectively with uncertainty often means adopting an experimentation rather than planning mindset. Instead of trying to develop comprehensive plans based on predictions about the future, you design small tests that help you learn about emerging opportunities and threats.

This uncertainty-focused approach differs from the rhythm-based learning cycles explored in Chapter 6. Learning cycles help you build capabilities consistently over time when you know roughly what direction you're heading. Uncertainty experiments help you discover which direction might be worth heading when the road ahead itself remains unclear.

These tests have several advantages over traditional plans when you're dealing with unpredictability. They're designed to generate information rather than implement predetermined strategies. They're typically small enough that failure doesn't create significant problems. They can be modified or abandoned quickly when circumstances shift.

Most importantly, uncertainty experiments acknowledge unpredictability rather than trying to overcome it through analysis. They're based on the assumption that you'll discover important information during the test that you couldn't have known before starting it.

In professional contexts, these might involve trying new tools on small projects, exploring adjacent skill areas through short courses, building relationships with people in emerging fields, or testing alternative approaches to familiar problems.

The experimental method works best when you design multiple small trials rather than betting everything on one large investigation. This portfolio approach increases the chances that at least some efforts will prove valuable whilst limiting the damage from trials that don't work out.

The goal isn't to become expert through testing but to develop enough understanding to make informed decisions about where to invest more substantial effort when the uncertainty begins to clarify.

The experimentation mindset helps you discover which capabilities are worth developing. The next question is: which skills actually grow more valuable during disruption rather than less?

Skills that Strengthen During Change

Instead of trying to build capabilities that resist change, focus on skills that actually become more important during periods of transformation.

Skills that strengthen during change share a common thread: they become more sought-after precisely when automation increases. Human judgement matters more when systems handle routine work and all that's left are tricky decisions. Helping colleagues navigate transitions becomes critical when your organisation implements changes nobody fully understands yet. Learning quickly matters more when you can't predict what you'll need to know next quarter. Managing ambiguity becomes essential when the rulebook keeps getting rewritten.

Our banking colleague exemplifies this. Her ability to interpret AI outputs and explain them to colleagues has become increasingly useful. Her skill at bridging traditional banking practices with new technological approaches makes her indispensable during digital transformation. Her comfort with uncertainty means management turns to her when facing unfamiliar challenges.

Developing these skills often means positioning yourself at the intersection of stability and innovation. You stay connected to your field's fundamentals whilst building expertise in managing what keeps evolving. Understanding human psychology remains relevant. Understanding how people adapt to technological change becomes especially important during rapid development.

Think about which of your abilities might become more sought-after during industry changes. Communication skills strengthen when explaining things clearly matters more. Problem-solving becomes more critical when novel situations demand creative solutions. Leadership grows more essential when uncertainty creates demand for direction and stability.

These skills also become scarcer as routine work gets automated. When AI handles standard analysis, human judgement about complex situations becomes more precious. When information becomes abundant, synthesising it and understanding context grows more important.

The key is identifying which aspects of your expertise become more prized as they become less common, then deliberately developing those qualities whilst staying current with technological developments that complement human insight.

Professionals who develop strengthening skills prepare to benefit from whatever shifts emerge. They position themselves not just to survive disruption but to become more indispensable and valuable because of it.

When Humans Become Exception Handlers

Remember back in Chapter 4? We explored Industry 4.0, dark factories, Amazon's million robots, and warehouses running through the night with minimal human interactions. It gave us insights into the growing presence of AI automation within the manufacturing and logistics space.

Something I've been noticing over the past year suggests the same shift is reaching professional and office work. Job advertisements and project requirements are starting to mention specific ratios, things like "four AI agents to one human operator" or describing roles as "AI-first workflows with human oversight." What strikes me isn't just that AI is being woven into how work gets done. It's that companies are building their systems around the assumption that AI will be the primary user, with people only being brought into the workflow to handle exceptions and check quality.

This represents a fundamental change in how businesses think about human labour, and it mirrors something that happened with software development over the past decade. Companies used to design platforms primarily for people to use. Then they shifted to designing them so that other systems could connect directly, with human-facing screens and interfaces built as a layer on top. The technical term is API-first architecture, where API stands for Application Programming Interface, essentially how different software systems talk to each other. Legacy platforms in industries like banking and insurance were built around human workflows, which made adding automation messy. Modern platforms flip that. They're built for system-to-system communication first, with human interaction designed in afterwards.

AI-first platforms follow the same principle. Companies aren't just adding AI tools to existing workflows designed for people. They're building systems where AI handles the main operations, where other AI systems connect to it, and where humans manage the exceptions until AI can handle those too. It's the same progression we saw in Chapter 4 with robots and warehouses, but now it's happening to office work and professional roles.

The architectural decisions being made by the companies building these AI-first software platforms give us a major clue about what they expect will happen. Software vendors used to need significant human effort to connect each customer to their platforms. It involved pre and post sales technical implementation consultancy, custom integration code, manual configuration, solving problems when systems didn't fit. Now they're building AI-first platforms assuming automatic plug and play connections, with humans managing only the exceptions.

Think about the typical street in your local town. Underneath the road, water and gas main lines run the full length, serving every property. Those main distribution lines can be monitored and controlled remotely. But connecting each individual house to those mains? That last twenty metres from street to the front door still needs someone on-site, assessing specific property requirements, dealing with local complications, and making the connection work. That's where human judgement matters.

Software integration follows the same pattern. The main platform runs automated. Human expertise handles the final connection to each customer's unique environment. But in the age of AI-first software development, which twenty metres stay in human hands? And for how long? The boundary keeps moving and tightening. What required human oversight six months ago might be handled by an AI now. The exceptions you manage today might be automated away next month.

This may not sound immediately alarming, but it's a structural signal worth paying attention to. When businesses invest in building platforms around AI-first assumptions, they're making commitments that go well beyond what the technology can do right now. They are betting that human supervision will become increasingly unnecessary, and they're designing their systems accordingly. The professional role here isn't craftsperson anymore. It's quality controller monitoring automated processes and handling the exceptions the system can't manage yet.

For workers navigating this shift, the skills that strengthen during change become even more critical. Pattern recognition abilities matter more when your role involves spotting the subtle errors that automated processes miss. Contextual understanding becomes essential when you need to interpret whether AI outputs make sense in complex, real-world situations. Communication skills grow more important when you need to explain technology failures or translate between automated processes and human stakeholders.

This architectural shift also explains why traditional approaches to professional development prove less useful than they used to. When your role involves monitoring automated processes rather than performing routine tasks, the knowledge that proves most valuable is often contextual, situational, and difficult to write down in training manuals. It might be the shortcuts that help you quickly identify when AI outputs need checking. Or the patterns that signal when automated workflows are hitting problems. Or the institutional knowledge about why certain approaches work better in specific circumstances.

These insights rarely appear in formal training courses or documentation. They're the kind of working knowledge that builds through experience and gets captured by paying close attention to what actually works in practice versus what's supposed to work in theory.

The companies implementing AI-first architectures are creating demand for professionals who can work effectively at the intersection of human judgement and automated capability. The question isn't whether this transition will continue. The architectural decisions being made and the billions of dollars already invested suggest it will accelerate. The question is whether you're developing the adaptive capabilities that remain valuable when people shift from being primary operators to strategic supervisors of intelligent technology, knowing that even that supervision might only be temporary.

Staying Informed Without Drowning

One of the practical challenges of living with uncertainty is dealing with excessive information when you don't know exactly what will prove important. When you can't predict which developments matter most, there's a temptation to try staying current with everything that might become relevant.

This approach quickly becomes overwhelming and counterproductive. When you're trying to track everything, you often end up with superficial awareness of many developments rather than deep understanding of the ones that actually matter for your situation.

The solution isn't ignoring information entirely but developing better filters for distinguishing between signal and noise. This requires building judgement about which sources prove reliable, which types of content tend to be significant, and which developments represent genuine trends rather than temporary fluctuations.

Unlike the learning budgets discussed in Chapter 5, uncertainty-based filtering addresses the flood of unplanned information that emerges during periods of change. You're not budgeting learning time but rapidly evaluating unexpected inputs to determine what deserves attention.

Effective filtering means accepting that you'll miss some important developments. The goal isn't perfect awareness, but sufficient awareness combined with the ability to quickly get up to speed on things you've missed when they become immediately relevant.

This approach requires trusting that your learning capabilities will allow you to catch up on specific developments when necessary, rather than trying to stay current with everything just in case it becomes significant.

Practical filtering strategies include identifying two or three reliable sources for your field rather than monitoring dozens, and focusing on developments that directly affect your current responsibilities rather than hypothetical future roles. But perhaps the most effective strategy is building relationships with colleagues who can alert you to changes in adjacent areas.

Living with uncertainty becomes easier when you're part of professional connections that help you stay aware without tracking everything yourself. When you have relationships with people in adjacent fields, different industries, and various levels of your organisation, you can reach out occasionally to tap into their insights about changes that might affect your work.

Community-based awareness often proves more reliable than information-based tracking because people provide context and interpretation. A colleague who understands both your work and emerging trends can filter developments more effectively than any automated alert system.

Your connections become particularly valuable when they span different domains and perspectives. The IT professional who understands your industry, the colleague from another department facing similar automation challenges, the former classmate working in a related field. These diverse relationships provide early warning about changes that might not be obvious from within your immediate work environment.

The key is recognising that perfect information awareness is impossible during uncertain periods. Instead of trying to track everything comprehensively, focus on maintaining sufficient awareness whilst preserving mental energy for actually responding to changes. When uncertainty creates information abundance, the skill becomes not just finding relevant data but avoiding paralysis whilst building connections that help you navigate effectively.

Practical Uncertainty Management

What does living with uncertainty look like in day-to-day work?

It means building routines that help you stay oriented without requiring perfect knowledge about future directions.

This might involve regular environmental scanning, spending small amounts of time staying current with developments in your field without trying to track everything comprehensively. You could dedicate thirty minutes each week to reading industry publications, not to become an expert on every trend, but to maintain general awareness of what's changing in your professional landscape.

It might mean maintaining relationships with people who can alert you to important changes before they become obvious to everyone. These early warning systems help you spot developments whilst you still have time to respond thoughtfully rather than reactively.

Tactical approaches could include building small experiments into your regular work to test new methods before committing to them fully. When you hear about a potentially useful tool or technique, try it on low-stakes projects where failure won't create significant problems. This experimental mindset helps you adapt gradually rather than making dramatic changes under pressure.

It also means building psychological practices that help you remain calm and effective when facing ambiguous situations. This might involve mindfulness techniques that help you stay present rather than anxiously projecting worst-case scenarios, or regular reflection on your adaptation experiences to build confidence in your ability to handle whatever emerges.

Actionable uncertainty navigation includes developing comfort with "good enough" decisions rather than perfect ones. When you're operating with incomplete information, the goal becomes making reasonable choices within reasonable timeframes, then adjusting course as better data becomes available.

Document your responses to ambiguous challenges, noting what approaches worked well and what felt ineffective. This documentation helps you build a personal playbook for handling unclear situations based on your actual experience rather than theoretical advice.

The goal isn't eliminating uncertainty but developing sustainable ways of operating effectively despite it. This requires both concrete tools for navigation and mental tools for maintaining equilibrium during periods of ongoing change and unpredictability.

Moving Forward Without Maps

The metaphor that works best for me is navigation without reliable maps. In familiar territory, you can plan your route in detail because the roads, landmarks, and destinations remain stable. But today's AI-disrupted work environment increasingly resembles unmapped terrain where traditional career paths disappear overnight and new routes emerge faster than anyone can chart them.

When you're travelling through unmapped terrain, you need different navigation skills than map-following. You learn to read conditions directly rather than relying on outdated guides. You develop instincts for spotting opportunities and threats. You build capabilities in improvisation and course correction rather than rigid route-following.

Most importantly, you learn to maintain your sense of direction even when you can't see the destination clearly. You navigate by principles and general orientation rather than specific landmarks and detailed routes.

This kind of navigation requires different approaches than chart-following, but it proves more reliable when conditions change faster than guides can be updated. Professional uncertainty demands similar capabilities - maintaining general direction whilst remaining flexible about specific routes, staying alert to important changes whilst avoiding overreaction to temporary fluctuations.

The temperance learning approach provides tools for this kind of navigation. Balance helps you avoid the extremes of paralysis and panic. Rhythm helps you maintain steady progress without exhausting yourself. Living with uncertainty helps you function effectively even when you can't predict exactly where you're going.

But navigation also requires practical tools that travel with you regardless of which territory you're crossing. Just as experienced travellers carry essential equipment that proves useful across different landscapes and conditions, you need portable systems for capturing knowledge, building capabilities, and maintaining direction despite changing circumstances.

This is where the Haversack Method becomes essential. The following section introduces a practical system for creating your own professional toolkit - approaches for collecting useful information as you encounter it, organising knowledge so it remains accessible when needed, and building capabilities that transfer across different professional contexts.

These tools don't eliminate uncertainty or provide perfect maps of unmapped territory. Instead, they help you travel more confidently and effectively through whatever you encounter, building competence and collecting resources as you go.

The ground will keep shifting. That's what ground does now. But you don't have to navigate empty-handed.

Section Three: The Haversack Method

A practical system for capturing, organising, and using what you learn.

Philosophy is all very well, but at some point, you need something you can actually hold onto. The temperance learning approach provides the right mindset for navigating professional uncertainty, but mindset alone isn't enough. You need concrete tools that work in the real world, under genuine constraints, when you are dealing with genuine pressure to adapt quickly.

This is where the Haversack Method comes in. It's not a literal canvas bag slung over your shoulder, though you could certainly use one if that appeals to you. It's a simple, flexible framework for collecting, organising, and using information fragments as you encounter them.

The haversack metaphor captures something important about how learning needs to work in unstable times. A haversack is portable (it travels with you regardless of which job you're doing or which organisation you're working for). It's actionable rather than precious, designed for use rather than display. It's rough and ready rather than polished, meant to hold whatever proves helpful rather than conforming to theoretical ideals about how insights should be structured.

The Haversack Method prioritises utility over elegance. It's meant to be a working toolkit you reach for regularly, not something that sits on a shelf looking impressive whilst providing no tangible benefit. Unlike the elaborate folder structures, comprehensive bookmark collections, and detailed note-taking systems that look organised but rarely get used, this approach is designed to actually help you adapt without overwhelming you.

The following chapters show you how to build and use your own haversack. You'll learn how to collect learning fragments efficiently, arrange them just enough to be helpful, and turn scraps of information into genuine capabilities. This isn't about becoming a better note-taker or building sophisticated personal information management systems. It's about having tools that work when you need them.

Chapter 8: Enter the Haversack

Your bag of fragments. It could be a journal, folder, Excel sheet, or cloud app. The tool doesn't matter. The habit does.

By now, if you have been following along and paying attention, you will understand that in the era of AI displacement, professional uncertainty isn't temporary. The ground keeps shifting, and adaptation increasingly needs to happen alongside daily work rather than during career breaks. This reality requires different tools to facilitate continuous learning.

This is where the haversack comes in. Not as a magical solution, but as a practical system for building capabilities when the future remains unpredictable.

The haversack is simply a portable collection system. Think of it as a toolkit that travels with you regardless of employment circumstances, industry changes, or geographical moves. The name comes from the canvas bags that travellers and soldiers carried for essential supplies - lightweight, portable, focused on immediate needs rather than comprehensive storage.

Your haversack might be a notebook, a smartphone app, a simple folder, or even a collection of index cards. The specific format doesn't matter. What matters is having a system that works for you consistently.

This approach proves particularly valuable for people facing AI displacement because circumstances often change faster than formal training can accommodate. When you need to develop new capabilities quickly whilst still doing your current job, traditional learning methods often prove too slow or too rigid.

The following chapters will show you how to build and use your haversack effectively. You'll learn what to collect, how to organise it without creating admin burden, and how to convert information scraps into working skills that will help to keep you adaptable.

Why Scraps Build Skills

The Haversack Method works because it acknowledges a fundamental reality about learning during periods of rapid change. People encounter countless fragments of potentially useful information daily, but success comes from developing judgement about which pieces deserve attention.

A fragment might be anything you notice. An article headline about AI handling customer service, a colleague mentioning new software, a phrase from a training session, a technique you spot during a meeting. Most fragments pass by without significance. But occasionally something makes you pause and think "this might be useful" or "this could matter for my work."

That moment of recognition is what turns a fragment into a Scrap. It becomes something you choose to keep, not because it is immediately applicable, but because it might signal change, offer a learning opportunity, or become useful when circumstances shift.

This distinction matters because people encounter hundreds of fragments daily, yet only a few should become Scraps worth saving. A fragment becomes a Scrap the moment you decide it has potential value. That small act of selection is what keeps your haversack useful rather than overwhelming.

This selection process proves crucial when AI displacement accelerates workplace change. Traditional approaches assume comprehensive study of predetermined subjects. But during periods of uncertainty, nobody knows exactly which skills will become important. The Haversack Method works by collecting promising scraps systematically, then watching for patterns that indicate learning opportunities.

When three or more scraps cluster around the same capability area, they signal potential for developing what we call a Minimum Viable Skill (MVS). The scraps don't need to provide complete information about a topic. They need to point in the same direction, suggesting that this capability area deserves focused attention.

Consider someone working in warehouse operations who starts noticing fragments about automation. A colleague mentions new inventory tracking systems. An industry newsletter discusses robots handling routine picking tasks. A supervisor comments about staff needing to learn equipment monitoring skills. Initially, these are just fragments (background information that might or might not matter).

But if this person recognises potential relevance to their work, these fragments become scraps worth saving. When these scraps cluster together, they may suggest developing "automated warehouse collaboration" as a Minimum Viable Skill. Not comprehensive expertise in robotics technology, but functional capability that enhances current work whilst demonstrating adaptability to emerging requirements.

The MVS represents the smallest usable version of a capability that already creates value in current work. Unlike traditional skill development that requires mastering complete domains before application, a Minimum Viable Skill gets people contributing immediately whilst learning continues. This proves crucial when AI changes roles faster than comprehensive training can keep pace.

The scrap-to-skill approach works because of how we actually learn at work. Most valuable professional knowledge doesn't come from front-loaded courses or comprehensive study. It builds through accumulated insights. Small pieces that add up over time. Each useful scrap you collect and test becomes part of your working toolkit. When scraps cluster into learning opportunities, they become building blocks for MVS capabilities. These create immediate value in your current work whilst preparing you for whatever skills prove necessary next.

Here's the key insight - competence builds through selection and accumulation, not through trying to study everything comprehensively. The people who develop good judgement about which scraps to keep will be the ones who spot capability-building opportunities before they become obvious to everyone else. You're not trying to know everything. You're trying to notice what matters.

Your Haversack, Your Choice

The specific tool you choose matters far less than you think. The fancy app won't make you better at spotting useful scraps. A simple notebook won't hold you back from developing skills. What determines success is whether you'll actually use it consistently.

Your haversack needs to do three things: help you notice fragments worth keeping, let you capture scraps quickly, and make reviewing them easy. Any tool that accomplishes this will work fine. Everything else is optional.

This flexibility becomes critical when dealing with AI workplace changes. Your circumstances might shift rapidly. Different locations, different devices, different company systems. If your haversack only works in one specific setup, you're vulnerable when things change. The method needs to travel with you regardless of where you land.

Some people will prefer digital tools like their phone's notes app, Microsoft OneNote, or Google Docs. These work well if you're comfortable with technology. You'll be able to search through your scraps easily, everything gets backed up automatically, and you can save links alongside your notes. Digital systems also make pattern-spotting easier when you've collected scraps about similar topics.

Others will work better with physical tools like notebooks, index cards, or simple folders. This makes sense if you think better when writing by hand, or if you work somewhere digital devices aren't always practical. Paper systems stay simple naturally because it's actually hard work to make them complicated.

Many people will end up using both. Maybe you'll keep everything in a digital system for the long term, but capture scraps on paper during meetings or when you're out in the field. This way, you won't lose useful fragments just because the right tool wasn't handy when you needed it.

Think about someone working in customer service. Their job is changing as AI chatbots handle more of the routine questions. They're constantly encountering fragments that could become valuable scraps: how to escalate tricky cases, what to do when customers get frustrated with automated systems, ways to explain technology problems clearly. They'll need to capture these scraps whether they're at their desk, on a phone call, or walking around the office.

A phone app might work perfectly when they have quiet moments between calls. But during actual customer conversations, quickly scribbling on a notecard might be more practical. The combination will ensure they can turn promising fragments into scraps whenever the moment arises.

The tool doesn't matter nearly as much as using it regularly. A simple system that you check daily and review monthly will help you develop skills much better than a sophisticated setup that you abandon because it's too much hassle.

When AI is changing your industry quickly, this becomes even more important. You'll need to spot clustering patterns and develop Minimum Viable Skills before your job requirements change from optional to urgent. That means picking tools that help you review scraps quickly and spot connections easily, rather than tools that create perfect documentation you'll never look at again.

The goal is making it as easy as possible to use your haversack consistently whilst developing the judgement to turn random fragments into valuable scraps. Start with whatever feels natural and accessible. You can always change your approach later based on what actually works, rather than what sounds good in theory.

That's really all your haversack needs to be: something that fits how you actually work. Now comes the part that matters most.

Starting Simple and Building Habits

The real trick is getting into the habit of noticing when something might be worth keeping. Every day, you encounter loads of fragments that could become useful scraps. The challenge is training yourself to recognise them in the moment.

Say you're working in payroll and you keep hearing fragments about automation. Maybe it's an article headline about AI processing invoices, or a colleague mentioning new approval systems, or a job advert asking for "automated systems experience". Most of these fragments will just wash over you unless you start paying attention.

But once you begin looking out for potentially useful fragments, you'll start noticing them everywhere. The trick is capturing them quickly when that little voice in your head says, "this might matter."

Try starting with just one scrap a day. Not ten, not fifty. Just one. That feels easy enough that you won't skip it, but substantial enough that you're actually building the habit of noticing what matters.

When you spot a fragment worth keeping, capture it immediately. Don't wait until later when you have more time. Don't think you'll remember it properly. Capture it in the moment, even if your notes are rough. Date it, note the source if it's relevant, write down enough that you'll understand it when you review later.

The thirty-second rule helps here. If you can't capture a scrap in thirty seconds or less, your system is too complicated. Speed matters because you're building a habit that needs to work during normal working life, not just during dedicated learning sessions.

At the end of your first week, review what you've captured. Don't judge whether you chose the "right" scraps. Just look at what you noticed and saved. Are any themes emerging? Do multiple scraps point towards similar concerns or opportunities? You're not looking for perfect analysis yet. You're getting comfortable with the basic rhythm: notice, capture, review, spot patterns.

This weekly review doesn't need to be elaborate. Fifteen minutes scanning through your scraps whilst having coffee is enough. You're looking for clusters. When you spot three or more scraps pointing the same direction, that's a signal worth paying attention to.

The habit compounds quickly. Week one might feel artificial, like you're forcing yourself to notice things. Week two feels slightly more natural. By week three or four, you'll find yourself automatically registering fragments without conscious effort. That's when the method starts working for you rather than you working at the method.

Watch out for the perfectionism trap. You'll be tempted to create elaborate systems, design beautiful layouts, establish comprehensive tagging schemes. Resist that completely. Your first haversack should be almost embarrassingly simple. Date plus fragment. That's it. You can add complexity later if your collection actually needs it, but most people, once they get in the habit, will never need more than basic chronological capture with occasional review.

What matters is consistency, not perfection. One scrap captured imperfectly is worth more than ten perfect scraps you never got around to recording because your system was too complicated to use during actual working life.

The compound effect of this approach becomes visible after a few months. Small scraps will accumulate into clusters. Clusters will reveal patterns about where your industry is heading. These insights will suggest capabilities worth developing. Capabilities will become Minimum Viable Skills that create immediate value whilst preparing you for whatever comes next.

But all of that starts with noticing one fragment today and capturing it quickly enough that the habit doesn't feel like a burden.

Your first week of captures starts now.

Light Organisation That Works

Once you've been collecting scraps for a few weeks, you'll probably notice your haversack getting a bit messy. That's completely normal and nothing to worry about. You don't need elaborate filing systems or perfect categories. You just need enough organisation to spot when scraps start clustering around the same topics.

The key is finding the minimum structure that helps you recognise patterns without turning maintenance into a part-time job. Most people can handle about five or six broad groups before deciding where things belong becomes a chore. Start with obvious categories that match how you naturally think about your work.

Someone in facilities management might organise around the types of problems they handle. Building maintenance, contractor coordination, safety compliance, and new technology systems. Someone in accounts might group scraps by payment processing, vendor relations, reporting requirements, and automation changes. The categories should feel obvious, not forced.

Don't worry about getting the categories perfect from the start. You can always adjust them as your collection grows and you understand your patterns better. The goal is making it easier to spot when three or more scraps point towards the same capability area, not creating a museum-quality filing system.

The weekly tidy shouldn't take more than fifteen minutes. Scan through your recent captures, drop them into rough groups, and add brief context to anything that looks cryptic. That's it. If you find yourself spending longer than that on organisation, you're probably overdoing it.

This light organisation becomes particularly valuable when you're trying to spot clustering patterns that suggest Minimum Viable Skill development opportunities. When scraps are scattered randomly, it's hard to notice that you've collected several pieces about the same topic. When they're grouped roughly, connections become obvious.

Consider someone working in HR who's been collecting scraps about recruitment changes. Initially, they might have fragments scattered everywhere: an article about AI CV screening in their general reading list, a colleague's comment about video interview software in meeting notes, a job advert mentioning "automated recruitment tools" saved with other career research. Separately, these look like random information.

But when grouped together during a weekly tidy, the pattern becomes clear. Three scraps about recruitment automation cluster around the same capability area, suggesting it might be worth developing "AI-assisted hiring" as a Minimum Viable Skill. The light organisation made the clustering visible in a way that scattered storage wouldn't.

Look for quality over quantity during your weekly reviews. Three high-quality scraps that clearly connect are more valuable than twenty random captures. Good scraps share common characteristics: they relate to challenges you actually face, they suggest immediate applications, or they point toward capability areas that job markets are demanding. When you spot these clustering patterns, you're seeing opportunities to develop Minimum Viable Skills.

The organisation also needs to work with your daily routine rather than fighting against it. If you capture most scraps on your phone during commutes, make sure you can review and organise them easily when you get a quiet moment each week. If you collect scraps in a notebook in meetings, set aside time to review and group them once you're back at your desk.

Some people find it helpful to mark scraps that seem particularly promising as they capture them, so they are easier to spot during weekly reviews. A simple star, highlight, or even writing "good" next to useful pieces helps them stand out when you're looking for clustering patterns.

The important thing is keeping organisation light enough that it actually happens regularly. A simple system you maintain consistently will reveal clustering opportunities much better than a perfect system you abandon because it's too much work.

Remember, the organisation exists to serve clustering recognition, not to impress anyone with how tidy your notes look. When you can quickly spot that multiple scraps point towards the same skill area, you're ready to start thinking about Minimum Viable Skill development. That's what the organisation is really for.

Building Your First Haversack

Right, let's actually build the thing. You've read about tools, habits, and organisation. This section will cover some of that ground again, but in a consolidated "here's how to start today" format. That's deliberate. Some of you are ready to start building your first haversack now and will need everything in one place. Others will want to keep reading and then come back to this later.

Either approach works fine. If you'd rather keep reading before building, skip ahead to Chapter 9. This will be here when you're ready.

For everyone else, here's how to get your haversack working in the next hour.

If you don't already have something functioning as a haversack, here's how to start today rather than next week.

Choose the simplest possible format that you will actually use consistently. This might be your phone's notes app, a document on your computer, or a notebook you already carry. The goal is starting immediately, not finding the optimal solution.

If you're comfortable with technology, consider features that genuinely help without adding complexity. Voice-to-text can speed up scrap capture when typing isn't practical. Cloud sync ensures your scraps are accessible whether you're at your desk or on the move. Search capabilities help spot clustering patterns as your collection grows.

AI tools can enhance your haversack without replacing your judgement. Some people find AI helpful for cleaning up hastily written notes or suggesting links between related scraps. But do not let AI do your thinking for you. The value comes from your ability to choose which fragments deserve to become scraps, not from perfect documentation.

Commit to capturing just one potential scrap per day for the next week. Not ten, not five. Just one fragment each day that makes you think "this might be useful for my work." This low target builds sustainable habits without creating pressure that leads to abandonment.

At the end of the week, review what you've captured and try to spot any patterns. Are multiple scraps pointing towards the same area? Do any clusters suggest capability areas worth developing? This isn't about perfect analysis; it's about getting comfortable with the review process.

Watch out for a few common traps that can derail your progress early on. Don't try to capture everything that seems remotely interesting. The test for inclusion isn't importance, but likelihood that you'll actually use the information. Avoid perfectionism when you capture scraps. Better to save something quickly than lose it trying to document it perfectly.

Most importantly, don't treat your haversack as a passive collection. If you never use the scraps you collect, it becomes busywork instead of capability building.

After your first week, gradually expand your capture rate based on what feels sustainable. Some people may settle into gathering two or three scraps daily. Others will find they'll naturally collect more during certain activities and less during others. What matters is consistency, not quantity.

Begin experimenting with light organisation when your collection becomes difficult to navigate. Create three to five broad categories that match how you naturally think about your work. Don't overthink this. The categories will evolve as your haversack grows.

Start looking for integration opportunities during your second week. When you capture a potentially useful scrap, actively look for chances to test it during routine work. The goal is turning collection into capability building rather than just information accumulation.

As you build collection habits, develop instincts for recognising when fragments deserve selection as scraps. Notice what makes you pause and think 'this could matter.' Trust those recognition moments - they're often more reliable than overthinking whether something might theoretically be useful someday. Quality selection judgement improves with practice, just like any other professional skill.

Remember that your haversack will evolve significantly as you use it and as your needs change. This evolution is exactly what should happen. The best professional development tools adapt alongside growing capability rather than forcing rigid frameworks.

Most importantly, start today with whatever you have available. Don't spend days choosing the perfect system or weeks setting up elaborate organisation. The haversack that gets used immediately proves more valuable than the perfect system that never gets built.

Your first haversack will be messy, incomplete, and probably organised in ways you'll change later. That's fine. It's better to have an imperfect system that works than a perfect plan that never gets implemented.

The following chapters will show you exactly how to use your haversack to collect the right scraps, spot clustering patterns, and develop Minimum Viable Skills that keep you adaptable regardless of how your industry continues to evolve.

Chapter 9: From Scraps to Skills

A messy bag is still useful, but a little structure goes a long way. Tag, sort, or file just enough to find things again.

At this point, you understand what a haversack is and how to build one. You know the difference between fragments and scraps, and you've got the basics of collection and organisation. You might even have started gathering your first scraps.

But having a collection of useful scraps isn't the end goal. The real value comes when those scraps start working together to build actual skills you can use at work.

This is where the Haversack Method shifts from collecting information to developing capabilities. From saving potentially useful scraps to turning them into Minimum Viable Skills that make a practical difference in your daily work.

The process happens through pattern recognition. When several scraps point toward the same area, they're signalling an opportunity to develop a working skill. Not years of study, but focused capability building that creates immediate value.

For people facing AI displacement, this becomes particularly important. Traditional training often takes too long when job requirements change rapidly. The Haversack Method offers a potentially faster alternative by spotting emerging skill needs through your scraps, then developing basic competence quickly.

Spotting The Clusters

After you have been collecting scraps for a few weeks using your haversack, something predictable begins to happen. Patterns emerge. What initially looked like a loose collection of interesting observations starts to show direction. Certain scraps point towards the same areas, circling similar problems, capabilities, or questions.

This is clustering, and it is the point at which casual gathering turns into deliberate skill development.

A cluster forms when three or more scraps connect around the same underlying capability. Not simply related topics, but fragments that clearly point towards building the same type of Minimum Viable Skill. The number three matters because that is when coincidence gives way to pattern. One scrap can be dismissed as noise. Two might suggest curiosity. Three indicate direction.

Consider someone working in logistics who has been capturing scraps for a month. They might save a colleague's approach to interpreting automated route recommendations, note an article on when to override delivery algorithms, and capture a supervisor's advice on explaining system changes to drivers. On their own, these scraps resemble everyday workplace knowledge. Together, they form a cluster around "human oversight of automated logistics," an emerging Minimum Viable Skill as AI systems take on more route planning responsibility.

Clustering is not something you force. It reflects what is already pulling at your attention. The problems you are encountering on your team, the decisions you are being asked to make on a project, or the questions that keep resurfacing in your work all influence what you save. Often, you are responding to change before you are consciously aware of it. The cluster simply reveals the direction you were already moving in.

Recognising clusters requires a shift in how you conduct your weekly haversack reviews. Rather than organising scraps into tidy categories, you look for signals. What capability do these scraps suggest? What kind of judgement are they pointing towards? What skill gap is beginning to show itself?

At this point, the review process becomes Minimum Viable Skill detection.

One group of scraps about inventory systems might cluster around "AI-assisted stock control." Another set concerning conversations with long-serving staff may point towards "technology transition communication." A third, focused on checking automated reports, might indicate "AI output validation." Each cluster signals a skill taking shape before it is formally recognised or named.

Clusters often appear faster than expected during periods of workplace disruption. As AI reshapes roles across an industry, similar skill pressures emerge at the same time. That is why many people independently capture scraps about judgement, oversight, and communication. These are not trends pulled from forecasts; they are skills forming in response to real conditions.

Speed matters here. In fast-moving environments, the window between a skill beginning to matter and becoming widely visible can be short. Someone who recognises a cluster early and starts developing it gains time, confidence, and credibility over those who only react once the shift is obvious.

Clusters also reveal whether your development is primarily proactive or reactive. Scraps gathered from job ads, industry discussions, or early signals suggest proactive movement. Scraps drawn from day-to-day fires, training sessions, or immediate problems indicate reactive adjustment. Both matter, but over time, it is the proactive clusters that tend to compound into lasting advantage.

Once you learn to spot clusters reliably, your haversack becomes more than a storage system. It becomes a radar. It does not just hold information, it highlights emerging capability before it is commodified. That early recognition forms the foundation for building Minimum Viable Skills that create real professional advantage, rather than simply helping you keep pace.

From Clusters to Capabilities

Once people can reliably spot when scraps cluster around the same area, the next step will become building those clusters into working Minimum Viable Skills. This isn't about comprehensive mastery. It's about developing the smallest usable version of a capability that already creates value in current work.

The key insight is that clustered scraps often contain all the building blocks needed for an MVS. The logistics worker from the previous section doesn't need a degree in supply chain automation to develop "human oversight of automated logistics." They need to connect their scraps into a working approach they can use tomorrow.

This connection process requires shifting from collection mode to experimentation mode. Instead of asking "what else should I capture about this topic?" the question becomes "how can I test whether these scraps work together in practice?"

Consider someone working in legal support who's spotted a cluster around "AI-assisted contract review." They've captured several scraps: a colleague's method for spotting unusual clauses that automated systems miss, an article about AI errors in legal document analysis, and a technique for explaining contract risks to non-legal colleagues. Individually useful, but the real value emerges when they're combined into a systematic approach.

The MVS development starts with small experiments using real work situations. The legal support person might test their clustered approach on routine service agreements first, not on complex merger documents. Use the clause-spotting method, apply the error recognition knowledge, and practice the risk communication technique. The goal is proving the scraps work together before committing to a larger application.

These experiments often reveal gaps that weren't obvious when scraps existed separately. The clause-spotting method might work perfectly, but the error recognition knowledge might need adaptation for their specific legal software. The risk communication technique might require modification for their particular client relationships. This refinement process transforms generic scraps into personalised MVS.

Speed matters during this experimentation phase, especially when AI displacement creates urgency around skill development. Someone who can demonstrate "AI-assisted contract review" capability in March has advantages over colleagues still collecting scraps about the same topic in June. The MVS provides immediate professional value whilst building toward more sophisticated expertise.

The experimentation also helps distinguish between scraps that genuinely complement each other versus those that seemed related but don't actually work together. Not every cluster will develop into a useful MVS. Some combinations prove awkward or impractical when tested. This filtering process ensures effort goes toward developing skills that provide real workplace value.

Teaching others what you've learnt from successful experiments locks the learning in permanently. When the legal support person explains their AI oversight approach to a colleague, that person must understand not just the mechanics but why it works, when it's appropriate, and how to adapt it to different situations. This teaching requirement forces deeper comprehension than personal use alone provides.

The teaching also creates accountability for maintaining and developing the MVS further. When colleagues know someone as the person who figured out "AI-assisted contract review," that reputation motivates continued skill development whilst creating opportunities where others share related discoveries.

Perhaps most importantly, successful MVS development from clustered scraps will build confidence in the entire Haversack Method approach. You'll prove to yourself that systematic scrap collection leads to genuine capability building, not just information accumulation. This confidence encourages continued clustering recognition and experimentation with new skill areas.

The compound effect proves substantial over time. Each successful cluster-to-MVS development makes the next one easier and faster. People will develop better judgement about which scraps can work together, more efficient approaches to experimentation, and stronger instincts for teaching and sharing their discoveries.

Building Your Learning Engine

Once you've successfully turned your first cluster of scraps into a working skill, you'll probably want to keep going. The question becomes: how do you make this a regular thing without it taking over your life?

The answer is building simple habits that keep the cycle moving. Not complicated systems or elaborate processes. Just basic routines that help you spot new opportunities while you're getting on with your regular work.

This becomes particularly important when AI is changing your industry. The professionals who stay ahead are those who develop new skills before they become urgent requirements. Building a simple learning engine means you're prepared for changes rather than scrambling to catch up after they happen.

Start by keeping an eye out for patterns when you're doing things you already do. If you check job advertisements occasionally, notice which skills keep getting mentioned. If you read industry news, watch for themes that suggest your field is changing. If you chat with colleagues, listen for challenges they're starting to worry about.

You are not trying to become a trend forecaster. You're just staying alert to signals that might suggest useful scraps to collect or new clusters worth developing.

Say you've successfully built a skill around "checking AI outputs for accuracy" and it's making your work easier. During your normal weekly activities, you might notice job adverts starting to mention "AI quality control" more often. Or colleagues discussing how to explain AI mistakes to customers. Or articles about new regulations for automated systems.

These signals don't require immediate action. They just suggest areas where you might want to start collecting scraps over the coming weeks or months. Maybe there's another useful skill forming around "managing AI compliance" or "communicating about AI limitations."

The key is keeping things manageable. You're not trying to predict the future or learn everything at once. You're just staying aware of what's happening around you whilst focusing on using the skills you've already developed.

This awareness naturally feeds better scrap collection. Instead of randomly saving anything that seems interesting, you start noticing scraps that connect to emerging patterns. Your collection becomes more focused without requiring elaborate planning.

Over time, this creates a simple cycle that might look something like this. Develop skills from current clusters, use those skills at work, stay aware of new patterns, collect relevant scraps, spot new clusters, develop new skills. It's not a grand strategy. It's just a practical way of staying adaptable when AI displacement makes change happen faster than traditional training can keep up.

The cycle also gets easier with practice. Once you've successfully developed a couple of skills from clustered scraps, you get better at recognising which clusters are worth pursuing and which can be safely ignored. You develop judgement about what actually matters versus what just sounds impressive.

Most importantly, you build confidence that you can handle whatever changes come next. Instead of worrying about staying current with everything, you trust your ability to spot important shifts and develop relevant skills when needed.

This confidence changes how you think about professional uncertainty. Instead of something threatening, it becomes something manageable. You know you can adapt because you've proven you can adapt.

That's the real value of building your learning engine. Not complex systems or sophisticated development programmes. Just practical approaches that help you stay one step ahead of change without overwhelming yourself in the process.

The Haversack Archaeology Test

A useful way to evaluate whether your haversack organisation is working involves what I call the haversack archaeology test. Can you locate useful information from three months ago without significant digging? When you quickly discover relevant pieces from the recent past, your arrangement probably works adequately. When locating older items requires extensive search or reorganisation, you might need slightly more structure.

The archaeology evaluation also helps identify pieces that have outlived their usefulness. When you haven't looked for something in six months and wouldn't know where to retrieve it if needed, it's probably safe to remove from the active collection.

This check works best applied quarterly instead of continuously. You don't need to locate everything instantly, but you work better when able to discover valuable materials without turning retrieval into a research project. When organisation passes this practical test regularly, those well-organised scraps prove much more effective as foundations for building new capabilities.

What does "slightly more structure" actually mean? Nothing elaborate. Maybe adding dates to your scraps so you can find recent captures easily. Perhaps creating three or four broad categories that match how you naturally think about your work. Or simply reviewing your haversack weekly so you remember what's in there without needing to search. The goal is making retrieval easier, not building a museum-quality filing system.

But here's what's equally important: if your archaeology test passes, don't add structure just because you can. If you are finding what you need when you need it, your current system is working. Simple organisation that works beats sophisticated organisation that becomes a burden. The test exists to tell you when to evolve your system, not to make you feel inadequate about keeping things straightforward.

Chapter 10: Integration Moments

Set aside time to turn scraps into skills. Build small projects, test ideas, and consolidate fragments into something solid.

That moment when scattered pieces become working knowledge can often be surprisingly subtle. You spend weeks capturing scraps about assorted topics (shortcuts, approaches, methods for solving recurring problems), each piece seems useful on its own, but they remain disconnected materials sitting in your haversack.

Then something changes. A challenge lands on your desk that requires bringing together multiple approaches at once. Instead of starting from scratch, you open your haversack and discover scattered pieces of knowledge you've been gathering which suddenly click together as a coherent capability.

The integration moment comes when you need to develop a comprehensive approach that combines what you've collected. Instead of learning everything from scratch, you find that your gathered pieces naturally support each other. Methods enhance your ability to interpret situations. Approaches help you explain recommendations to colleagues. Insights guide your decisions about when different techniques apply best.

For the first time, those scattered materials work together as a genuine professional capability. What had been individual pieces clustered to become a learning moment and a Minimum Viable Skill - integrated expertise that creates visible value in your work.

That's what integration moments represent - the point where collected scraps stop being information and start being working skills.

For anyone navigating AI displacement, these moments can prove particularly valuable because they transform gradual learning into demonstrable capabilities when opportunities arise.

Testing Your New Capabilities

Remember our legal support worker we met in Chapter 9? She had spotted clusters of scraps around AI contract review: a colleague's method for spotting unusual clauses, an article about AI errors in document analysis, and a technique for explaining contract risks to non-legal colleagues. She could see how these pieces might work together, but seeing the connection and actually using it at work? That felt like a completely different challenge outside her comfort zone.

This gap between recognising clusters and applying them confidently is one of the most common obstacles you'll face when developing new capabilities. You've done the collection work, spotted the patterns, organised your thinking. But moving from "I think this might be useful" to "I can actually do this at work" often proves much wider than you'd expect.

Here is the thing though: developing and testing new capabilities (or Minimum Viable Skills) really shouldn't require feeling fully prepared or completely confident. You are not trying to prove you're an expert. You are trying to discover whether your clustered scraps in your haversack provide enough foundation to create genuine workplace value. When you shift from performance pressure to experimental curiosity, everything changes about how you approach capability development.

Our legal support worker did not volunteer to handle the next major merger document using her clustered AI oversight approach (that would've been madness). Instead, she tested her ideas and method on routine service agreements first. These contracts mattered for daily operations, but they weren't make-or-break situations. If her approach needed tweaking (and it probably would), the consequences stayed manageable whilst she got familiar with the newfound techniques.

You can apply this principle across diverse types of work. Take a logistics coordinator with scraps about automated routing - they might test human override judgements on routine delivery adjustments before applying them to urgent customer situations. A Payroll clerk with automation oversight clusters might experiment with new checking procedures on monthly reports before using them for a full payroll run.

The key is choosing situations where learning matters as much as outcomes. You want projects where experimenting with new approaches won't create significant problems if your initial attempts need adjustment. Keep the experiments small enough to complete quickly too; within a week or two rather than month-long trials. This gives you enough exposure to learn whether your clustered scraps work together whilst being short enough to maintain focus through the inevitable awkwardness of trying new approaches.

Most importantly, accept that some experiments won't work as expected. This isn't failure - it's valuable information about what doesn't work in your specific context. Each test teaches you something about how to refine your approach or whether to pursue different areas entirely.

One challenge you might face is waiting for perfect testing opportunities to arise naturally. In reality, the best Minimum Viable Skill development happens when you actively create opportunities rather than hoping ideal situations will emerge on their own. Integration opportunities exist in the routine work you're already doing, but they often require conscious recognition and slight modifications to become useful testing grounds.

Our legal support worker didn't wait for her supervisor to assign AI-review projects. She offered to handle the contract review backlog using her experimental approach, positioning it as an efficiency improvement rather than capability development. Smart move: this ensures you get testing opportunities regardless of external circumstances whilst connecting your development directly to workplace value (rather than abstract learning).

Look for routine tasks where you can experiment with new approaches without disrupting established workflows or creating additional admin work. Volunteer strategically for projects that align with your clustering areas whilst staying within your comfort zone for overall complexity. You want situations that challenge your developing capabilities without overwhelming your existing skills.

Testing clustered capabilities gives you several types of feedback that help you understand whether your haversack scraps are developing into genuine workplace skills. Practical feedback focuses on whether your testing actually improves work outcomes - saving time, improving quality, reducing errors, or enhancing relationships with colleagues. These concrete measures matter more than theoretical understanding or perfect execution.

Pay attention to whether familiarity grows with practice or whether approaches consistently feel unnatural. When colleagues start asking for your advice about methods you're testing, or when they comment positively on improved results, that's a strong sign your integration is succeeding beyond personal benefit. Most importantly, successful testing should make you more willing to apply new methods in appropriate situations (rather than more hesitant about their effectiveness).

Minimum Viable Skills testing often reveals gaps in understanding that weren't obvious during scrap collection and clustering. These discoveries provide valuable direction for focused learning rather than evidence that your approach isn't working. Knowledge gaps emerge when you understand concepts intellectually but lack practical familiarity with application details. Context gaps appear when techniques work well in some situations but not others; while resource gaps surface when testing reveals that effective application requires tools or support you don't currently have.

Treat gaps as information rather than evidence of failure. Each gap tells you something specific about what you need to develop further, which proves far more useful than vague uncertainty about whether your approach is working.

This experimental approach to testing clustered capabilities bridges the gap between collecting useful scraps and building real and reliable workplace skills. It transforms theoretical possibilities into practical capabilities whilst maintaining realistic expectations at a sustainable pace. Once you've proven that clusters can become working skills through testing (and you will), you're ready to tackle the more complex challenge of understanding why some knowledge converts to capability whilst other knowledge remains stubbornly theoretical.

When Knowledge Won't Convert

One of the biggest barriers to effective integration is the application gap. That's the difference between understanding how something works and being able to use it smoothly in real situations.

Our legal support worker experienced this when she tried moving beyond routine contracts to more complex agreements. She'd collected good scraps, tested her AI oversight approach successfully on simple documents, but when she tackled an international commercial contract, everything fell apart.

This gap exists because most fragments are captured without context about when, where, and how to apply them. You might collect a useful technique, but without understanding the situations where it works best and the conditions that make it effective, you're unlikely to use it successfully. The scraps look perfectly reasonable in your haversack, but practical application reveals dependencies and limitations that weren't obvious during collection.

This isn't evidence you've collected wrong scraps or misunderstood the clustering. It's normal feedback about how workplace knowledge actually functions. Most techniques have boundaries that only become visible when you try using them beyond their effective range. The banking colleague discovered her risk assessment methods worked excellently for standard applications but needed significant modification for commercial lending. She hadn't failed - she'd discovered the edges of her clustered knowledge through attempted use.

Sometimes the conversion problem stems from missing foundational knowledge you didn't realise was necessary. Your scraps might be excellent advanced techniques, but applying them requires background understanding you haven't developed yet. A facilities coordinator collected brilliant scraps about predictive maintenance systems, understood the concepts well enough to discuss them, but consistently struggled with practical application. The missing piece wasn't more maintenance scraps; it was basic understanding of how sensor data gets collected and processed.

Resource mismatches create another common barrier. Your clustered scraps might describe techniques requiring tools, software, or permissions you don't currently have. Understanding automated systems perfectly doesn't help if your organisation hasn't bought the necessary software. This doesn't make the knowledge worthless (circumstances change, budgets shift, systems get approved). Just don't expect immediate application if the infrastructure isn't there yet.

Perhaps the trickiest challenge involves techniques that work well individually but don't integrate smoothly together. You might have three excellent scraps that each address part of a problem, but combining them creates complexity that defeats their purpose. Better to discover this during testing than during important projects where smooth execution actually matters.

These conversion problems don't mean you've failed at the Haversack Method. They're normal (Expected even). The question isn't whether some scraps won't convert - they won't. The question is what you do when that happens.

The emotional aspect matters here. Unsuccessful conversion attempts can undermine your confidence if you're not prepared for them. When you've invested time collecting and organising scraps, failed conversions can feel personal. They're not. They're diagnostic information, not performance judgements.

The solution isn't abandoning scraps that don't convert immediately. Treat non-converting knowledge as conditional - potentially useful when circumstances change, when you develop supporting capabilities, or when you encounter different contexts where techniques fit more naturally. The facilities coordinator's predictive maintenance knowledge couldn't be implemented until the organisation invested in sensors, but having the understanding ready meant he could lead implementation when those investments eventually happened.

Some scraps benefit from being combined with different clusters rather than forced into their original groupings. This flexibility often reveals approaches that fit your actual working environment better than rigid adherence to original clusters.

The key insight is that knowledge conversion is ongoing rather than one-time testing. Scraps that don't work now might prove perfect later for different situations, changed circumstances, or evolved challenges. Your haversack becomes more valuable as you develop judgement about when and where to apply different pieces (rather than just accumulating techniques).

This transforms conversion challenges from frustrating failures into useful navigation information. You're building sophisticated awareness of what works where and under what conditions - far more valuable than techniques that appear universal but have hidden limitations you haven't discovered yet.

Building Integration Momentum

Our legal support worker had successfully tested her AI contract review approach and now understood why some of her collected haversack scraps wouldn't convert. Now she faced a different challenge: how do I maintain what works without it becoming another burden on top of my regular daily workload? This is where you might stumble - getting your Minimum Viable Skills working, but then letting them fade because sustaining them feels like too much extra effort.

The key is recognising that momentum builds through consistency rather than intensity. You don't need to expand every successful capability immediately. What matters is maintaining the skills that prove valuable whilst they become natural parts of your skills and workflow. The banking colleague kept her risk assessment oversight simple for months, using it only on standard applications, until it felt automatic. Only then did she consider expanding to more complex cases.

This pacing prevents the feeling of being overwhelmed that kills integration momentum. You can comfortably maintain one or two developing capabilities alongside your regular work. Trying to sustain more may create a cognitive overload that undermines both new skills and existing performance. You should always be selective about which successful experiments you keep active versus which you park for later development.

The combination of clustered scraps can often be where real enhancements are found. While individual scraps might provide modest improvements, it's the combination of complementary pieces from your haversack that can create significant capability gains. Our banking colleague found that her AI risk assessment oversight worked well on its own. However, when combined with improved client communication scraps and streamlined documentation practices it created her a comprehensive approach that improved overall confidence, impressed management, and led to expanded responsibilities.

Perhaps, the most important aspect of building momentum is recognising and acting on small wins rather than waiting for those large, dramatic breakthroughs. Each time you successfully apply a scrap, each time your developing skills save time or improve quality, each time a colleague asks about your approach, these represent progress worth acknowledging and building upon.

It's these small wins that create what you might call positive spirals. This Success builds confidence, which makes you more willing to experiment further, which creates more success, which has a knock-on effect of building more confidence. Our facilities coordinator experienced this when what he learnt from his scraps gave him the skill to spot a potential HVAC failure before it happened. That single success led to increased trust from his manager, which gave him higher levels of access to better diagnostic tools, which then enabled more sophisticated applications of his newly acquired expertise.

The compound effect of sustained integration efforts can prove substantial over time. Each capability you successfully integrate makes the next one easier because you are developing meta-skills alongside specific abilities. You get better at recognising which scraps from your haversack will work in your context, more efficient at spotting useful combinations, more skilled at judging when to apply what you've learnt.

While this compounding happens quietly, it can be substantial. You may notice that integration efficiency improves, confidence in handling change increases, and reputation as someone who adapts well to change may create opportunities for more interesting projects down the line. These effects reinforce each other and can create accelerated returns on on-going learning investments without requiring heroic effort.

Most importantly this momentum building transforms integration from conscious effort into your natural workflow. The facilities coordinator's predictive maintenance knowledge initially required deliberate attention every time he used it. After several months of consistent application, checking sensor data and spotting potential failures became automatic (integrated into how he naturally approached his work rather than something he had to remember to do).

When your Minimum Viable Skills become second nature, they stop competing with your regular work for attention and energy. You are not juggling multiple conscious techniques; you instead start working with integrated abilities that support ongoing adaptation without constant mental overhead. The time this takes varies depending on complexity and frequency of use, but consistent application matters more than speed of integration.

Building sustainable momentum means accepting that not every successful experiment needs scaling. Some capabilities prove most valuable when kept focused and simple. The goal isn't maximising what you're doing but optimising what creates genuine value in your specific work context. Quality of integration beats quantity every time.

Making Integration Stick

The ultimate goal of integration isn't just about running successful experiments. It's about the permanent incorporation of new, Minimum Viable Skills that blend into your regular workflow. This requires moving beyond conscious application to where your MVS become automatic parts of how you work – especially important when AI keeps changing what your role requires and there is no time to constantly think about new techniques.

Our legal support worker reached this point about four months after starting her AI contract review approach. She realised one afternoon that she had been using her oversight techniques all day without thinking about them. The scraps she'd carefully collected and tested had become simply how she reviewed contracts now, not something she had to remember to do. This mattered because new AI tools kept appearing in her firm, and she needed mental space to evaluate those without losing the capabilities she'd already built.

This transition happens with repeated practice across varied contexts. Eventually, your new skills will start feeling more natural as you continue to use them. Our banking colleague found this with her risk assessment methods. What started as conscious checking of AI outputs became intuitive judgement she applied without thinking, which proved crucial when her bank introduced yet another automated system.

Environmental supports can help make integration stick when you are dealing with constant AI-driven changes. This might involve modifying your workspace to remind you of new approaches, creating templates that incorporate effective techniques from your haversack, or establishing routines that include regular application of integrated methods. Our facilities coordinator set up a simple morning checklist that prompted his predictive maintenance checks until they became automatic habit - essential when his organisation kept deploying new building automation systems.

Social supports also matter quite a bit, particularly when AI displacement creates workplace anxiety. When colleagues know about the new skills you are developing and can provide feedback or reminders on your approach, you're more likely to maintain new practices during busy periods when conscious attention to integration might lapse. The legal support worker found that mentioning her approach to a colleague created informal accountability that helped sustain the practice during particularly hectic weeks when new AI tools were being rolled out.

The sign that integration has truly succeeded is when you stop thinking of your capabilities as additions to your normal approach and start thinking of them as simply how you work. At that point, your collected scraps have become genuine skills that enhance your professional capability without requiring ongoing conscious effort to maintain them - which matters tremendously when AI keeps demanding you learn more new things.

Integration moments do not always announce themselves dramatically. Sometimes they are as subtle as noticing that a previously challenging task has become routine or realising that colleagues are asking for your advice about approaches you're using naturally. These quiet confirmations that your haversack scraps have become working skills are often more meaningful than dramatic breakthrough moments, especially when they prove you can adapt to AI changes without losing what you've already built.

Our facilities coordinator experienced this when a junior colleague asked how he always seemed to catch problems before they became serious, even with all the new automated systems. He had been using his predictive maintenance approach so naturally that he had not realised others were noticing the results. That question confirmed his collected scraps had become integrated expertise rather than experimental techniques - capability that would not disappear when the next AI system arrived.

What matters most is recognising that this integration process doesn't require perfection or dramatic transformation when you are facing AI displacement. Small, consistent applications of useful scraps gradually build into reliable capabilities that support your work without adding burden. The goal is not becoming someone completely different but becoming more capable at managing the changes AI brings to your role whilst maintaining your existing value.

When your Minimum Viable Skills reach this automatic stage, they create foundation for continued adaptation as AI keeps evolving. You're not just learning specific techniques; you're developing the capacity to keep learning and integrating new approaches as circumstances keep changing. That ongoing adaptability proves more valuable than any individual skill in an environment where AI keeps shifting what work requires and threatening roles that can't adapt quickly enough.

Section Four: Putting it into Practice

Turning ideas into habits, projects, and proof you can rely on.

Philosophy and methods are useful, but they only matter if you can make them work in the messy reality of professional life. This section is about implementation.

This is where the rubber meets the road. Understanding temperance learning in theory doesn't prepare you for maintaining balanced rhythms when your industry is changing rapidly and you're not sure what skills you'll need next month. It's one thing to build a haversack and quite another to use it effectively when you're job hunting or proving your value in a changing role.

The reality is that most professional adaptation happens under pressure. You don't get to take a sabbatical to reinvent yourself. You have to adapt whilst earning, learn whilst working, and prove new capabilities whilst still demonstrating existing ones. Real deadlines, limited time, and professional uncertainty create challenges that academic approaches rarely address.

This section tackles those challenges head-on. How do you turn scattered fragments into demonstrable skills quickly enough to matter? How do you build confidence in new capabilities whilst dealing with the stress of professional disruption? How do you recover from setbacks and failed experiments without losing momentum? These aren't abstract questions. They're the practical realities that determine whether temperance learning and the haversack method remain interesting ideas or become working tools.

The following chapters work through these challenges in sequence. You'll see how scraps become demonstrable skills. You'll learn to run focused learning arcs whilst managing current work. You'll discover how to create proof that gets noticed, not lost in algorithmic screening. You'll build strategies for steadying yourself through setbacks. You'll evolve your haversack strategically as your system strains under use. You'll explore working with AI as a partner rather than competition. And you'll understand what you've actually built through sustained practice - not just skills, but a different way of navigating professional uncertainty.

Chapter 11: How Capability Forms

You will not always have the answer in the room. That is fine. Behind the scenes you are building, and one day it will show.

I can remember sitting in a meeting about six years ago, feeling completely out of my depth. The conversation had turned to data analytics, and everyone else seemed to understand concepts that were completely foreign to me. Terms like "regression analysis" and "correlation coefficients" flew around the table whilst I nodded along, hoping nobody would ask me a direct question.

The frustrating part wasn't just my ignorance. It was that I'd been meaning to learn about data analysis for months. I'd bookmarked articles, downloaded a course, even bought a book about statistics. But none of that effort translated into the ability to contribute meaningfully to the conversation happening in front of me.

Six months later, I found myself in a similar meeting with a similar topic. The difference was that this time, when someone mentioned "correlation analysis", I could ask half-decent, intelligently framed follow-up questions. When they talked about regression models, I understood enough to suggest a different approach. I wasn't the expert in the room, but I wasn't completely lost either.

The transformation hadn't happened through a dramatic learning breakthrough. It had happened through months of collecting small fragments about data analysis and gradually piecing them together into working knowledge. A formula captured from a colleague's explanation. A definition saved from an article. An example worked through during a quiet afternoon. In reality, none of these scraps seemed significant on their own, but when I put them together, they clustered into enough understanding to guide the learning I needed. I could meaningfully participate in conversations I'd previously been lost in.

That experience taught me that building professional capability often works more like sedimentary rock formation than dramatic geological events. Layers of small learning accumulate gradually until you have something solid enough to stand on.

The Awkward Middle Phase

One of the most challenging aspects of developing new capabilities is navigating what I call the awkward middle phase - the period when you know enough to recognise your ignorance but not enough to feel competent. This phase is psychologically difficult because you're simultaneously more aware of what you don't know and more capable of recognising the complexity of what you're trying to learn. Before you start learning something new, ignorance can feel blissful. Once you start learning, ignorance becomes uncomfortable.

The temptation during this phase is either to retreat back to familiar territory or to accelerate learning efforts in hopes of reaching competence faster. Both responses usually make things worse. Retreating can waste the progress you've already made. While accelerating often leads to superficial understanding that doesn't hold up under pressure.

The awkward middle phase is where the temperance learning approach proves its value. Instead of trying to rush through the discomfort, you accept it as a normal part of capability development. While you continue collecting scraps (integrating them gradually) and trusting that the accumulated understanding will eventually reach a tipping point.

The key insight here is that the awkward middle phase isn't a problem to be solved but a stage to be navigated. It's evidence that you're making progress, not a sign that your approach isn't working.

How Progress Accumulates

One of the great difficulties with gradual skill development is that progress often isn't obvious from day to day. Unlike dramatic learning breakthroughs that provide clear before-and-after moments, the scrap-to-skill approach produces subtle improvements that can be hard to notice.

This invisibility can be discouraging, especially when you're feeling pressure to demonstrate new capabilities quickly. You might wonder whether your learning efforts are having any effect at all.

But progress is happening even when you can't feel it. The vocabulary you're unconsciously absorbing, the mental models you're gradually building, the pattern recognition that's slowly developing. These changes accumulate beneath conscious awareness until they reach a threshold where they become apparent.

This accumulation isn't random. Your learning efforts compound over time. Each scrap you collect and successfully integrate makes subsequent learning in related areas faster and more effective. When you already understand basic concepts in a field, advanced topics become more accessible. When you've developed vocabulary and mental models, new information has context and structure to attach to.

The compounding effect also applies to learning skills themselves. Each time you successfully turn scraps into working capabilities, you get better at recognising valuable fragments, integrating them effectively, and applying them in real situations. Over time, this creates significant advantages. People who've been using fragmentary learning approaches for years often seem to adapt to new changes effortlessly. They're not necessarily more intelligent or talented, they've just developed more effective systems for continuous capability development.

One way to make invisible progress more visible is through deliberate documentation. Keep brief notes about what concepts confused you last month compared to this month. Notice which conversations you can follow now that would have been incomprehensible earlier. Track which tasks feel slightly easier than they did before.

This documentation isn't about comprehensive self-assessment but about creating evidence that progress is happening even when it doesn't feel dramatic. Over time, these small indicators provide reassurance that your learning efforts are effective and that accumulation is working exactly as it should.

Building Confidence Without Competence

One of the psychological challenges of skill development is maintaining confidence whilst you're still developing competence. Traditional approaches to professional development often assume that self-assurance should follow mastery (first you learn something thoroughly, then you trust yourself to use it).

But in rapidly changing environments, this sequence often doesn't work. You need confidence to experiment with new approaches before you've mastered them. You need belief in yourself to apply partial knowledge whilst you're still learning. You need the courage to admit what you don't know whilst demonstrating what you do know.

This requires developing what you might call provisional confidence - confidence in your ability to figure things out rather than in having complete knowledge. This is based on evidence that you can learn and adapt rather than evidence that you know everything relevant to a situation.

Building this requires documenting your learning successes, even small ones. When you successfully apply a scrap to solve a real problem, note it. When you understand something that confused you last week, acknowledge it. When you contribute something useful to a conversation, recognise it.

These documentation practices help you build evidence of your adaptive capacity rather than just your current skill level. Over time, this evidence supports your ability to handle whatever comes up, even when you don't start with complete preparation.

Yet even with documented progress, a persistent challenge often emerges: impostor syndrome. The feeling that your capabilities aren't legitimate because you haven't developed them through traditional, comprehensive learning processes. When your knowledge comes from accumulated scraps rather than systematic study, it can feel somehow less valid.

This feeling presents particularly strongly when you're using capabilities professionally before you feel fully competent. You might worry that colleagues will discover that your knowledge is incomplete or that you'll be exposed as someone who doesn't really know what they're doing.

But here's the reality: competence isn't binary. There's a vast range between complete ignorance and complete mastery, and most professional work happens somewhere in that middle range. You don't need perfect knowledge to contribute meaningfully to projects, conversations, and problem-solving efforts.

The antidote to impostor syndrome is focusing on contribution rather than credentials. Instead of asking "Am I qualified to do this?" ask "Can I contribute something useful to this situation?" The answer is often yes, even when your knowledge feels incomplete.

It also helps to remember that everyone's knowledge is incomplete and fragmentary to a degree. The people who seem most assured and capable are often those who've learnt to work effectively with partial knowledge rather than those who have achieved comprehensive understanding.

The Teaching Test

The "Teaching Test" is one of the most reliable ways to assess whether the scraps you have collected are developing into a genuine skill. Can you explain a concept or technique to someone else in a way that helps them understand and apply it for themselves?

The teaching reveals gaps in understanding that aren't apparent when you're just using the knowledge gained for your own purposes. When you try to help someone learn a new skill, you need to understand not just how to do it but why it works, when it's appropriate, and how to adapt it to different circumstances.

The teaching test doesn't require formal instructional opportunities. You might explain a technique to a colleague who's struggling with a similar problem, write a brief guide for your team's knowledge base, or help a friend understand something related to your field.

These informal teaching opportunities provide valuable feedback about the depth and reliability of your growing and developing capabilities. So if you can successfully help someone else learn something new, you probably understand it well enough to use it confidently in your own work.

Teaching also reinforces your own learning by forcing you to articulate concepts clearly and consider different ways of applying techniques. This articulation and consideration deepens your understanding and makes your knowledge more robust.

Testing As You Build

When you're developing new capabilities whilst working, you need to prove value incrementally rather than waiting until you feel fully competent. The most accelerated skill development happens when you create tight feedback loops between learning and application. Instead of accumulating large amounts of knowledge before attempting to use it, you constantly alternate between collecting scraps and testing them in real situations.

This approach provides immediate feedback about which learning efforts are producing useful results versus which ones remain primarily theoretical. You can adjust your learning focus based on what proves practically valuable rather than what seems important in abstract terms.

The key is looking for smaller opportunities to apply your emerging skills rather than waiting for major projects that require comprehensive knowledge. Volunteer to handle small tasks that use new capabilities. Offer to help colleagues with problems related to your developing skills. Find ways to apply new knowledge to improve existing processes.

These low-risk applications serve multiple purposes. They let you test and refine your capabilities without high-stakes pressure. They create evidence of your developing competence that you can reference in future opportunities. They help you build a reputation for being adaptable and willing to take on new challenges.

The more chances you have to test and refine developing skills in manageable situations, the faster they mature into reliable competencies. Tight feedback loops also help with motivation and momentum. When you can see immediate connections between learning efforts and improved performance, you're more likely to maintain consistent learning habits over time.

Most importantly, this constant alternation between collecting and applying helps you build confidence in your ability to use developing skills under real conditions rather than just in practice situations. Create opportunities for low-risk application rather than waiting for high-stakes situations that require proven capabilities.

Strategic Incompleteness

One mindset shift that will help with your scrap-to-skill development is embracing strategic incompleteness. Instead of trying to learn everything about a topic before using it, you might try to deliberately focus on developing just enough knowledge to be useful whilst remaining open to further learning as needed.

Adopting strategic incompleteness means accepting your knowledge will always have gaps. The trade-off is it ensures that the knowledge you do have is solid and applicable. You invest in depth where it matters most for your immediate needs whilst maintaining breadth that allows for future development down the line.

This approach requires making conscious decisions about what to learn thoroughly versus what to understand superficially. The key is to ensure that your incomplete knowledge is still relevant and useful rather than just random fragments that don't connect in meaningful ways.

Strategic incompleteness also means being honest about the limitations of your knowledge whilst still being willing to apply what you do know. This honesty builds trust with colleagues whilst positioning you as someone who's comfortable working at the edge of their competence.

Building Bridges Between Domains

The fragmented approach to skill development helps you see connections between different domains that might otherwise remain hidden. When you're collecting scraps from various sources and contexts, you start noticing patterns and principles that appear across different fields.

These cross-domain connections often prove more valuable than narrow expertise because they're inherently portable. A communication technique from customer service might solve a stakeholder problem in operations. A problem-solving approach from manufacturing might crack a service delivery challenge. When you spot the underlying pattern, the original domain becomes less important than the transferable principle. You're not just learning techniques, you're developing pattern recognition that works wherever circumstances take you.

Building these bridges requires paying attention to underlying patterns rather than just surface-level techniques. When you collect a scrap, think about how you can use it in its original context, but also how the idea behind it can be valuable in future scenarios you might find yourself in. As you collect scraps from different sources, over time, your ability to recognise patterns will improve. Eventually, you will learn to discover connections that others overlook. This in itself can be a highly useful talent in any profession. This cross-domain thinking becomes particularly crucial when AI displacement forces career pivots or industry changes.

Because you can see genuine transferable patterns, your learning isn't stuck in one place that can be threatened by the rise of artificial intelligence in your field. You are learning skills that will help you no matter what job or field you finish up in.

But pattern recognition and cross-domain thinking only matter if you can demonstrate them to potential employers or current managers. The next challenge is turning your accumulated scraps and developing skills into tangible proof that shows others what you're capable of doing.

Chapter 12: Small Arcs, Big Gains

Short bursts of learning focused on one outcome deliver more than months of vague study. Keep arcs small, frequent, and real.

Traditional learning approaches are built for stable conditions. People create comprehensive study plans, gather extensive resources, and commit to months of systematic progress through structured curricula. The plans look impressive on paper and feel reassuringly thorough when made.

In industries facing AI displacement, they also regularly fail.

Not through lack of effort or intelligence, but because rapid technological change doesn't respect your learning schedule. Work demands shift mid-study. The skill you're developing becomes less relevant whilst you're still halfway through the course. The role you're preparing for transforms before you can demonstrate the capability you've been building.

When job requirements change faster than traditional learning timelines allow, comprehensive plans become increasingly unreliable. You risk investing months in capabilities that matter less by the time you've developed them, whilst missing opportunities that required immediate, focused skill building.

There's a more effective alternative for rapidly changing environments.

Learning arcs.

These are short, focused projects aimed at developing specific capabilities within tight timeframes. Not comprehensive mastery, but targeted skill building that creates immediate value.

A learning arc might look like this: learn enough about spreadsheet automation to save an hour per week on a recurring report. Two weeks, one specific outcome, using only immediately accessible resources. No comprehensive curriculum, no grand ambitions, just enough learning to solve one particular problem.

This approach works because it matches the reality many professionals now face. Small, complete learning experiences prove more valuable than large, incomplete ones. You build actual capability quickly rather than accumulating partial knowledge that never gets applied because circumstances changed halfway through.

The arc mindset accepts that predicting which skills will matter in six months has become harder. Instead, you develop capabilities that create value now whilst building the adaptive capacity to respond effectively to whatever changes come next.

The Arc Approach

When AI displacement is actively threatening your role or industry, you don't have the luxury of gradual skill development. The Haversack Method works brilliantly for continuous learning over time, but sometimes you need to convert those collected scraps into demonstrable capabilities fast (within weeks, not months). That's where learning arcs come in.

The premise behind traditional learning methods is that you should know everything before you use it. You learn everything there is to know about a subject, then use that knowledge to accomplish your goals. In academic settings where the main goal is to understand, this step-by-step method makes sense. But when automation is eliminating positions in your field, that timeline doesn't work anymore.

The arc approach flips this sequence for urgent situations. You have already been collecting scraps in your haversack. You started spotting clusters pointing toward potential Minimum Viable Skills. Now, instead of waiting for those skills to develop gradually, you dedicate 2-4 focused weeks to turning a specific cluster into working capability you can demonstrate to current or potential employers.

Arcs acknowledge the reality that most people facing job insecurity have to juggle competing demands, current work responsibilities, job applications, and family commitments. Instead of pretending you can dedicate months to learning projects, arcs are designed to complete in a few weeks whilst you handle everything else. This constraint forces prioritisation and prevents learning from becoming another source of stress when you're already under pressure.

Perhaps most importantly for people worried about employment, arcs provide regular completion experiences. Instead of working towards distant goals that might never be reached, you finish tangible projects within weeks that demonstrate growing capability. When you're facing potential job loss, having demonstrable proof of new skills matters more than perfect theoretical knowledge.

Arcs work because they force focus through constraints, and those constraints become advantages rather than limitations. Time constraints push you to focus on essential knowledge - when you've only got a fortnight to build a demonstrable skill whilst job hunting, you can't afford to jump down interesting rabbit holes or perfect your grasp of underlying theory. You learn what's necessary to show capability and leave everything else.

Scope and resource constraints work together to keep you focused on what's achievable right now. By nailing down exactly what Minimum Viable Skill you're building before you start, you create an endpoint you can actually reach whilst managing other pressures. And by working only with resources you have to hand, you demonstrate the resourcefulness and practical problem-solving that employers value during uncertain times. You're not the person who needs perfect conditions to learn; you're the person who gets results with whatever's available.

At first, these limits may seem restrictive, but after you work with them once or twice, they become liberating. Instead of being overwhelmed by everything you could potentially study, you focus just on building one demonstrable skill that improves your employment prospects. That clarity cuts through the paralysis that comes with feeling like you need to know everything before you can show anything.

Common Arc Formats

Whilst every arc adapts to your specific circumstances, five common formats cover most situations where AI displacement creates urgency. Seeing how these formats might work through believable scenarios helps you recognise which approach fits your situation.

Problem-solving arcs focus on developing capabilities to handle specific challenges that automation struggles with.

Picture a Customer Service Manager who's been watching his company gradually expand chatbot coverage. At first it was just password resets and account balance checks. But every quarter, the bot handles more. He's not panicking yet, but he's noticing patterns. The bot completely misreads customer sarcasm or frustration. It escalates angry customers who just need someone to listen for thirty seconds. It can't spot when a "simple" question is actually masking a complex account issue. Senior leadership keeps talking about "efficiency gains" whilst his team handles the increasingly difficult cases the bot can't resolve.

If he used the Haversack Method with problem-solving arcs, those observations would be scraps collecting in his haversack. Eventually he'd spot the cluster: these bits all point towards "complex emotional and contextual problem resolution that AI genuinely can't handle." He'd design a two-week arc to build an MVS around "AI escalation triage and resolution." His outcome would be specific: a documented framework for identifying which customer issues need human judgement versus bot handling, three detailed case studies of complex problems he'd resolved that demonstrated skills bots lack, and a presentation showing leadership how his team's expertise complements rather than competes with automation. When the next quarterly review discusses further bot expansion, he'd have concrete proof of irreplaceable value.

Efficiency arcs help you demonstrate that you understand automation as a tool rather than just a threat.

Consider a Warehouse Manager in FMCG who's been running operations the same way for eight years. His system works - inventory moves efficiently, picking accuracy is solid, his team knows what they're doing. Then corporate announces they're "exploring automation opportunities" and "robotic solutions for repetitive tasks." He knows his warehouse has repetitive tasks. He starts noticing things differently now - which processes would actually benefit from automation versus which ones need human judgement, bottlenecks that technology might solve, quality control points where automation would create more problems than it fixes. He realises the people who'll survive this transition are those who can make automation work better, not those who resist it.

If he used the Haversack Method with efficiency arcs, these observations about automation opportunities and limitations would cluster around "hybrid human-robot workflow optimisation." His three-week arc would aim to build an MVS in "automated picking with human quality oversight." The outcome: a pilot system for one product line where automated systems handle routine picking whilst he and his team focus on exception handling, quality verification, and workflow troubleshooting. He'd document efficiency gains, error reduction, and the irreplaceable human elements. When corporate starts evaluating which facilities and managers understand the automated future, he'd have proof he's already building it.

Communication arcs help you adapt how you explain, persuade, and collaborate when industry practices shift.

Think about a Technical Project Manager who's been leading software development teams in the same office building for six years. He's good at his job - projects deliver on time, stakeholders stay informed, teams collaborate effectively. Then his company announces permanent remote-first policies following broader industry trends. He's run enough distributed projects to know this changes everything about how he works. Information that used to flow through hallway conversations now needs deliberate documentation. Decisions that happened in quick meetings now require async consensus (coordination across time zones without everyone online simultaneously). Technical concepts he'd explain at a whiteboard now need different approaches. He has been keeping track of what works and what doesn't in this new setting.

If he used the Haversack Method with communication arcs, these observations would cluster around "distributed technical team leadership and stakeholder communication." His two-week arc would focus on building an MVS in "async technical communication and decision-making." He'd want something demonstrable: a working system for making technical decisions across time zones with tools that are already available, documentation practices that keep everyone on the same page without too many meetings, and proof that he could finish his current project entirely through async coordination. When performance appraisals stress "thriving in the new remote-first environment," he would have real proof instead of simply assertions of adaption.

Exploration arcs help you understand emerging changes before committing to deep expertise.

Consider a Marketing Manager at an online retailer who's been building campaigns the traditional way for years - email promotions, seasonal sales, paid search, social media advertising. Then AI marketing tools start appearing everywhere. Her CEO mentions "AI-powered product recommendations" in every strategy meeting. Competitors are talking about "personalised shopping experiences at scale." She doesn't know yet whether these tools are game-changing or just hype, but she knows she can't afford to be blindsided. She starts experimenting carefully - testing an AI product recommendation tool here, exploring dynamic pricing platforms there, noting which capabilities seem genuinely useful versus which are mostly vendor marketing claims. She's learning more about AI without claiming to be an "AI expert."

If she used the Haversack Method with exploration arcs, these tests and observations would be grouped around "the strengths and weaknesses of practical AI tools for e-commerce marketing." Her two-week arc would be on building an MVS that helps with "AI-augmented personalisation and conversion optimisation."

She wouldn't try to master every AI marketing tool - she'd aim for something specific: run one complete promotional campaign using AI tools for product recommendations and personalised messaging whilst documenting what worked, what didn't, and where human judgement remained essential. When leadership asks, "how should we incorporate AI into our customer experience," she'd have informed answers based on actual trial testing rather than vendor promises or fearful resistance.

Integration arcs combine multiple capabilities you've developed separately into more sophisticated approaches.

Imagine an accountant who has been working in a shared services centre for ten years, handling bills, reconciliations, and month-end reports. She's watched automation tools gradually take over more of the routine processing work. She's learnt bits and pieces about these systems - how the invoice matching works, where the reconciliation automation breaks down, which reports can run automatically. Separately, she's developed analytical skills from years of spotting errors and explaining variances to business units.

She realises these two areas (automation systems and financial analysis) could work together powerfully if combined properly.

If she used the Haversack Method with integration arcs, her scraps about automation capabilities and her scraps about analytical interpretation would cluster towards "automated processing with human analytical oversight." Her three-week arc would aim to build an MVS in "intelligent automation monitoring and exception analysis." The outcome: a hybrid system where automated tools handle routine processing whilst she focuses on analysing patterns, investigating anomalies, and providing insights that automation flags but can't interpret. She'd prove this by going through her real monthly close process, which would show how automation can make things more efficient and how only human judgement can bring value.

When her Shared Services Centre faces further automation pressure, she'd be positioned as someone who makes automation more valuable rather than someone automation replaces.

Notice the pattern across these five formats: each person facing real displacement would collect scraps whilst working normally, spot clusters pointing towards valuable capabilities, then use focused 2-4 week arcs to turn those clusters into demonstrable Minimum Viable Skills aligned with the specific threats they're facing. The arc format varies based on what you're trying to achieve, but the underlying Haversack Method remains consistent - build something concrete that proves capability rather than just claiming you've learnt something new.

Running Your Arc

You need to organise your learning arcs well enough to give you direction and keep you on track, but not so much that the planning becomes more work than the learning itself. The goal is getting clarity about what you want to achieve and a practical approach for getting there, rather than detailed schedules or comprehensive lists of every resource you might need.

Effective arc planning starts with defining your outcome clearly. What specific skill do you wish to have in two weeks that you don't have right now? This outcome needs to be testable. You should be able to demonstrate whether you've achieved it without ambiguity.

Next, work out the minimum learning required to achieve that outcome. What knowledge or skills are absolutely necessary? What can you defer to future arcs if the core learning proves more challenging than expected? This Minimum Viable Skill focus becomes your primary target.

Then consider what resources and practice opportunities are available to you right now. What materials can you access immediately? Where can you test and apply what you're learning as you go? How can you structure your practice to provide useful feedback about whether you're making progress or heading down the wrong track?

Finally, establish simple progress markers. These informal checkpoints help you assess whether you're on track to achieve your outcome within the planned timeframe. The markers should be specific enough to provide useful feedback but flexible enough to accommodate unexpected discoveries or challenges.

The entire planning process should take no more than an hour and should give you clear direction rather than detailed schedules that become outdated within days.

Day one of your arc should feel simple, not overwhelming. Open your haversack, review the cluster you're building from, and do one small thing that moves towards your outcome. Not more research, not additional planning, not reorganising your scraps. Actual practice with the skill you're building. If your arc is about automated reporting, open the automation tool and try one basic function. If it's about presentation skills, record yourself explaining one concept. The goal is momentum through action, not perfection through preparation.

One of the hardest parts of learning arcs is keeping up the pace through the obstacles that always emerge when you learn something new. Within the compressed timeframe of a 2-4 week arc, maintaining sustainable rhythm becomes critical. Do you remember the wave pattern we discussed in Chapter 6? Learning arcs follow those same natural rhythms of intensity and rest, just compressed into shorter cycles. Instead of weekly waves, arc momentum works in daily or bi-daily waves. Periods of focused effort followed by brief integration time where your brain processes what you've absorbed.

The temptation during arcs is to maintain constant intensity because the timeframe feels urgent. But even within two weeks, you need rhythm rather than relentless effort. Burnout halfway through an arc wastes all the progress you've gained.

Early wins help establish momentum whilst building confidence for handling later challenges. Look for aspects of your learning goal that you can achieve quickly during the first few days, even if they're not the most important components. These early wins provide the mental energy needed to push through tougher phases.

Regular chances to apply what you've learnt keep the feedback loops tight. You stay motivated throughout your arc when you can relate what you're learning to practical problems you're facing right now.

External accountability can prop up your motivation when it starts to sag, especially during that awkward middle stretch where the novelty has worn off but you're not close enough to the end to feel the finish line pulling you forward. This doesn't need to be formal or complicated. Promise a colleague you'll show them what you've built by Friday. Volunteer to use your developing skill on an actual work project where other people are depending on the outcome. Mention your arc to someone and ask them to check in next week about progress. Small social commitments can be surprisingly powerful for keeping you honest with yourself.

The key is applying sustainable rhythm principles within the concentrated timeframe of an arc, rather than abandoning rhythm entirely because the project feels urgent.

Not every arc will deliver what you set out to achieve within your planned timeframe. This isn't a sign the approach is broken. It's feedback about your planning, the scope you picked, or how you executed.

Some arcs fail because the goal was too ambitious given available time or resources. When this happens, consider whether a scaled-back outcome might still be worth achieving, or whether you need to split the arc into multiple smaller projects.

Other arcs fail because the learning approach didn't work, or because resources you expected weren't available when needed. These failures provide useful information about what doesn't work in your particular situation, preventing the same mistakes in future arcs.

Still other arcs fail because priorities shifted and stopped you putting in consistent effort. These interruptions are often unavoidable parts of working life rather than planning failures.

The important part is extracting useful lessons from arc failures whilst maintaining confidence in the overall approach. Most failed arcs still produce partial progress that provides foundation for future learning, even when you don't hit the original outcome.

When an arc fails, resist the urge to extend it indefinitely hoping you'll eventually get there. It's usually better to call it done, capture whatever you did learn, and design a fresh arc that accounts for what prevented success the first time.

Once you've completed an arc, sometimes the next step is obvious. Your first arc reveals gaps or opportunities pointing directly to a second arc. Other times you'll move in completely different directions based on changing circumstances or new priorities. Both are fine.

What matters most is this: arcs are the vehicle for building Minimum Viable Skills quickly when you're under pressure. They're not the destination. The whole point is building real; demonstrable skills you can show employers or use to improve current work.

But here's the challenge. Nobody believes you've developed new skills just because you say so. Hiring managers seeing hundreds of applicants claiming they've "upskilled" need proof. Tangible demonstrations that show you can actually do the work, not just that you've studied it or completed an arc.

Building the skill through an arc matters. Proving you've built it determines whether that skill helps you stay employed or advance your career during industry disruption. That's where the next chapter becomes critical.

Chapter 13: Proof Beats Theory

Show your learning. Build a demo, run a trial, or teach someone else. It locks in skills and proves you can use them.

A logistics coordinator with thirty years of experience sits at her kitchen table, staring at another automated rejection email. Three decades of keeping supply chains running through every crisis and software change. Industry certifications earned through evening classes. A wealth of practical knowledge built scrap by scrap into genuine expertise.

She has done everything right. Built new capabilities through focused learning. She's even gone beyond just learning (she's created tangible demonstrations of what she can do). A simple automation tool that streamlined her previous employer's delivery scheduling. Documentation showing how she reduced stock discrepancies by 40%. A clear case study explaining how she integrated new inventory management software whilst training colleagues who struggled with the transition. Real proof of real capabilities, not just claims on a CV.

Her phone never rings.

What she doesn't know is that her applications likely never reach human reviewers. Applicant Tracking Systems now screen approximately 75% of job applications before any person sees them. These are not just organisational tools helping recruiters manage applications. They're gatekeepers making binary decisions about who deserves human attention.

Her carefully refined CV, the one she has spent years perfecting – with tables showing career progression and subtle visual elements that made it distinctive, uploads as gibberish. The Applicant Tracking System (ATS) software most employers use to intake resumes cannot parse complex layouts. What she sees as professional polish, the ATS algorithm sees as unreadable formatting. Her relevant skills become invisible because the system literally cannot find them in the garbled text it receives.

The job postings require a bachelor's degree. She never needed one to excel in this field for three decades, but the ATS does not evaluate equivalent experience. It simply excludes anyone without the specified credential

(regardless of demonstrated capability).
That one-year gap in her employment history, the year spent caring for an ill parent, triggers another automatic red flag. Many systems flag any gap over six months as a risk factor, treating legitimate life circumstances as professional deficiencies.

Her thirty years of continuous experience, what any human reviewer would recognise as valuable seasoning, signals something different to the algorithm. Systems trained on data favouring younger workers interpret extensive tenure as "over-qualified", or "too expensive" or simply, "not the profile we're seeking."
The system scores her as a low fit for the job requirements and pushes her application to the bottom of the digital pile. No human ever gets the chance to appreciate what she's built or what she can contribute.

This is the brutal reality facing many workers over 50 who have done everything right. You can develop genuine adaptive capacity through the methods this book teaches. You can build Minimum Viable Skills through focused learning arcs. You can create compelling proof - actual working examples, documented results, tangible demonstrations of your capabilities. And you can still be rendered invisible by automated gatekeepers designed to filter out your profile before any person evaluates your worth.

The problem is not your skills. The problem is not the proof you have created. The problem is that algorithmic barriers stand between your capabilities and the humans who might value them. Understanding these barriers and learning to work around them strategically becomes as important as building skills in the first place.

This chapter addresses both challenges: creating proof that demonstrates genuine capability (what "proof" actually means and how to build it), and ensuring that proof reaches the decision-makers who can act on it. Because proof that never gets seen might as well not exist.

The Double Barrier

Professional environments are full of people who can talk intelligently about concepts they've never applied. They've read the articles and white papers, attended the presentations and conferences, and absorbed enough buzzword vocabulary to participate in discussions. But when it comes time to use that knowledge for practical purposes, the gaps and cracks become apparent.

This disconnect between theoretical knowledge and practical capability can create real credibility problems for anyone trying to demonstrate new skills. If you can only talk about what you've learnt, potential employers and hiring managers have no reliable way to assess whether you can actually apply that knowledge effectively. Practical demonstration solves this assessment problem by providing concrete evidence of capability.

When you show someone a working example of your skills (a tool you've built, a process you've improved, a problem you've solved), they don't need to guess whether you can deliver results (they've seen the outcome). This demonstration approach has always been more persuasive than description alone.

In the AI world, what's changed is how you reach the people who can evaluate that demonstration. Before automation, a human skimmed every CV application to gauge if a candidate was a potential fit for a given role. Today, an algorithm often decides who gets seen. On its journey, your job application faces two barriers. The first barrier, is often an AI algorithm or automation. The second barrier, is the challenge of convincing humans your CV is worthy of an interview screening. Traditional career advice covers the second barrier extensively. This chapter addresses both.

The first barrier is algorithmic screening. Your CV must be read, parsed, and ranked by an Applicant Tracking System (ATS for short). Think of an ATS as a piece of software that sifts, sorts and directs all direct candidate applications before any human decision maker sees them. These ATS applications exist for legitimate reasons. They help employers manage high application volumes (a typical corporate posting can attract anywhere from 100 to 1000+ candidate applications). They also maintain compliance documentation (GDPR etc.), and enable HR and hiring stakeholders to collaborate efficiently (cutting hiring times dramatically).

So how do these Applicant Tracking Systems work? Many of them follow predictable mechanisms using AI and automation.

Typically, a parsing tool converts a candidate's CV into structured data fields. A matching algorithm then scores the CV against the job posting requirements. Another algorithm ranks the CV against other applicants in order of suitability and applies a score.

When this process is complete, the hiring team is presented with a shortlist of candidates in descending order of suitability as prescribed by the algorithm relevant to the job. The aim is to surface the best-fitting candidates at the top, so busy recruiters and hiring managers can focus their attention on those results.

During this process the algorithm runs batches of knockout questions that apply binary filters for work authorisation, degree requirements, salary expectations, availability to start or location restrictions.

The algorithm processing also rewards clean structure and matching terminology. It penalises employment gaps, unusual career paths, and creative layouts with embedded images and graphic structures.

Most CVs were not written to pass an algorithm, so the software struggles to extract their actual value.

The following are common failure patterns that demonstrate how qualified candidates can get filtered out of the hiring process through no fault of their own actual capabilities.

The format trap: catches people whose CVs look impressive to humans but break during parsing. A graphic designer with eight years of experience submitted a visually stunning infographic-style CV to highlight her portfolio. The ATS couldn't scan her CV correctly as a lot of her important information (employer names, job titles, and employment dates etc.) was embedded inside graphics and charts that the system couldn't read. Her application was automatically rejected as an unqualified, entry-level candidate despite (in reality) perfectly matching the job requirements. Industry analysis suggests over 40% of CVs contain formatting that a typical ATS cannot fully parse. Complex layouts, tables, columns, graphics, text boxes. What pleases human eyes often bewilders the algorithms.

The synonym discrepancy trap: catches candidates whose professional vocabulary differs from the job posting. A software developer applied for a front-end role. His CV listed JavaScript, React, Node.js, UI components. Precisely the right toolkit. However, the job description used slightly different terms: expertise in front-end frameworks, experience building user interfaces. The ATS rigidly stuck to the algorithm settings and gave his application a low relevance score because it wasn't configured to recognise that React is a front-end framework or that working on UI components constitutes user interface experience.

The title literalism trap: excludes career changers with transferable capabilities. After a 20-year teaching career, an educator sought a corporate training position. The position required five years of corporate training experience. She had deep expertise in pedagogy, curriculum design, and leading classrooms. The ATS auto rejected her for answering "no" to the exact experience question. It couldn't recognise that managing a classroom translates to delivering corporate workshops.

The credential trap: keeps candidates out who don't have the right qualifications, even if they have the same amount of expertise in a different field. A computer technician with 15 years of experience and various certifications applied for a technical job that needed a bachelor's degree (or equivalent experience). The ATS was set up with a binary "yes" or "no" question about whether you had a bachelor's degree. He checked no and was immediately rejected. The algorithm wasn't configured to interpret years of work as fulfilling that requirement.

The gap trap: penalises and downgrades anyone with employment breaks. A marketing manager took an 18-month break to attempt a startup venture that didn't succeed. Many ATS systems automatically filtered out his CV (Industry research suggests nearly half of companies screen out candidates with gaps over six months). His CV never reached a human reviewer who might have valued the entrepreneurial attempt as demonstrating initiative and learning.

These aren't isolated cases. Research from Harvard Business School found that 88% of employers acknowledge their Applicant Tracking System regularly filters out qualified candidates who don't match exact algorithmic criteria. The systems deliver exactly what they were designed and configured for: efficiency in narrowing applicant pools. They weren't designed to widen consideration or evaluate context and outliers.

The irony cuts particularly deep for people who've built new capabilities through focused learning. You've developed Minimum Viable Skills through deliberate arcs. You've created working examples of what you can contribute. But if automated screening eliminates your application before human review, none of that effort matters professionally. Always remember, the role of your CV is not to get you a job (that's what your interviews are for). The role of your CV is to secure you an interview with a human decision maker. Job hunting in the age of AI displacement is a job in itself. You need to build a strategy that can flex and change as you learn what works, adapt to each role's requirements, and respond when one approach hits a wall.

The second barrier is human evaluation. After your application successfully gets past the ATS barrier, you still have to convince the recruiters and hiring managers you can get the job done. Structured interviewing techniques like the STAR method (which stands for Situation, Task, Action, Result) are often used by the hiring teams in behavioural interview probing questions. They want real examples of the work you've done to showcase your suitability. They need clear achievements mapped to the role they are trying to fill.

If you can only describe what you've learnt theoretically, they will have no reliable way to assess your practical capability. But if you can point to a portfolio of work samples, walk through documented results, and tell structured stories about applying your skills to solve real problems, the conversation shifts from "can this person do the work" to "how quickly can we get them started."

Understanding both barriers is essential. You must prepare for both the ATS algorithms and the humans deliberately. But before we address tactical approaches to navigating these systems, it's worth understanding just how serious the algorithmic barrier has become. These aren't just technical frustrations. They're legal issues now being tested in court.

Algorithmic Bias in the Courts (Mobley vs Workday)

One of the most significant hiring stories of 2025 came from a US courtroom.

A man named Derek Mobley took legal action against Workday, one of the world's biggest HR software companies. His claim was simple but serious: the algorithms inside Workday's recruitment tools had quietly screened him out because of his age, race, and disability.

Mobley applied for over 100 positions through systems powered by Workday. He was rejected from every single one, often within an hour of application submission. He wasn't complaining about rudeness or poor feedback. He was questioning whether he had ever been seen at all by a human evaluator.

The lawsuit, known as Mobley v. Workday, argued that the company's AI-powered tools acted as gatekeepers, filtering and ranking candidates before human reviewers entered the picture. The legal term for this kind of harm is called disparate impact. It means that even if bias isn't deliberate, a system can still violate employment discrimination law if it disproportionately disadvantages people in protected groups.

The scale matters here. During the relevant time period, Workday's software processed over 1.1 billion job applications. If algorithmic bias exists within these systems, the number of affected applicants could reach hundreds of millions.

In May 2025, a US federal judge granted preliminary certification for Mobley's age discrimination claims to proceed as a nationwide collective action under the Age Discrimination in Employment Act. The court agreed there was a case to answer.

Workday defended itself by arguing it only provides technology. The actual hiring decisions, they said, are made by employer clients. Therefore Workday shouldn't be treated as an employer or employment agency. The court wasn't convinced by this distinction. The judge found that if a tool performs a hiring function and its outcomes show discrimination, both the user and the maker may share responsibility.

The U.S. Equal Employment Opportunity Commission has already made its position clear on this issue. Algorithmic hiring tools are not exempt from discrimination law, and vendors cannot avoid accountability simply by calling themselves third parties. The rules of fairness still apply, even when the decision-maker is a model rather than a manager.

As I write this book in 2025, the case remains ongoing. There's no final determination yet about whether Workday's systems violate employment discrimination laws. But the fact that a US federal court found the allegations sufficiently credible to allow the case to proceed as a collective action marks a turning point. AI in hiring is no longer an abstract debate about ethics. It's now a legal and operational reality.

How does bias get baked into these systems? They learn from historical hiring data. If that historical data reflects past discriminatory practices (whether conscious or unconscious), the algorithm can replicate and amplify those patterns whilst appearing objective and neutral.

The systems lack transparency. Applicants cannot see how their CVs are scored or which criteria trigger rejection. But research suggests these tools can use proxy data that correlates with protected characteristics. Schools attended, employment gaps, even phrasing style can all correlate with age, gender, or ethnicity. The systems may not intend to discriminate, but they can still produce outcomes that mirror the inequalities they were trained on.

A biased algorithm processing billions of applications can scale discrimination far beyond what individual human bias could achieve. The rapid rejection patterns, employment gap penalties, and credential requirements that auto-filter candidates may incorporate bias that would violate civil rights laws if implemented explicitly by human recruiters.

For someone who has followed the Haversack Method and built genuine capabilities, this context matters. You've run learning arcs that produced working Minimum Viable Skills. You've created proof pieces that demonstrate practical ability, not just theoretical knowledge. When these systems block your application despite demonstrable capabilities, the problem isn't your skill development. It's flawed systems that haven't been adequately tested or configured for discriminatory impact.

Bias hasn't vanished in the age of automation. It has just changed shape. Understanding these flaws doesn't eliminate them, but it does clarify what you're up against. Your MVS work is solid. Your proof pieces demonstrate real capability. Now you need specific approaches to get them past systems that weren't designed to recognise unconventional paths or recently developed skills.

Tactical Guidance for Getting Past the Algorithmic Barrier

You have built Minimum Viable Skills through focused learning arcs. You've created working examples that demonstrate real capability. Now you need those achievements to actually get on the radars of the people who can hire you. That means making your CV readable to the parsing algorithms that stand between you and interview opportunities.

Remember what we established at the start of this chapter. Your CV faces a double barrier.

First, the algorithmic screening that filters most applications before any human review. Second, the human evaluation that decides whether you get called in for interview.

This section addresses the first barrier - getting past the algorithm so humans actually see what you've built. Once again, it is important to always keep the following perspective clear in your mind. Your CV's purpose is not to get you a job (that's what interviews are for). Your CV's only purpose is to get you called for a meeting with a human decision maker.

Getting that call requires satisfying the ATS algorithm's requirements whilst maintaining content that will resonate with human readers once you clear the automated screening. Job hunting in the age of AI displacement is serious work in itself. Half-measures and outdated approaches won't cut through algorithmic filters. You need a strategy that can adapt as you learn what works.

This isn't about gaming the system or keyword stuffing dishonestly. It's about translating genuine skills and experience into formats that parsing algorithms can process accurately. Think of it as learning to speak two languages fluently - one for the algorithms, one for the human decision makers.

Start with CV structure. As mentioned at the start of this chapter, the parsing algorithms expect simple, predictable document layouts. That polished CV you've spent years refining, the one with tables showing career progression and subtle visual elements that made it distinctive, confuses the parsing software. The algorithm can't read complex formatting. So what looks like a professional presentation to humans will most likely get immediately rejected by the system.

Your CV reflects your personality, and that's normally a good thing. But when you're dealing with ATS software, stick with recognised parameters that work: a single-column layout with no tables, text boxes, graphics, or multiple columns. These formatting choices usually confuse the parsing software and cause it to misread or outright reject your information.

The software expects to read top-to-bottom in a linear flow. When it encounters a table, it often reads randomly across rows rather than following your intended sequence. That causes information to get jumbled (or lost entirely). That beautiful timeline graphic showing your career progression? The parsing algorithm literally cannot see it.

Standard section headings in your CV help the ATS categorise your information correctly. There is no need to reinvent the wheel here, so use conventional labels that are known to work: Personal Information, Summary, Skills, Experience, Projects, Education, Certifications. The algorithm will look for these specific markers to extract your data into structured fields. Creative headings like "My Journey", "What I Bring", or "What I've Mastered", might sound engaging to humans, but they leave the software uncertain where to file your information as usable data points.

File format matters more than you'd think. Save your CV as a DOCX file, or as a simple PDF exported directly from Word. Always avoid PDFs created by scanning physical documents or those generated by design software. Many systems will handle your DOCX CV file most reliably because the format preserves a text structure the algorithm expects. If you're using PDF, test it first. Copy text from it and paste into a plain text editor. If the order and content survive intact, the PDF will likely parse correctly. If it turns into gobbledygook nonsense, the algorithm will struggle with it too.

Don't include a headshot photo on your CV. Photos introduce unnecessary bias - age, gender, ethnicity, and appearance shouldn't influence whether you get an interview. Let your capabilities speak first. Practically, parsing algorithms can't read images anyway, photos break the formatting the software expects, and some systems automatically strip them during upload, leaving awkward blank spaces. Save that space for keyword-rich text the algorithm can actually process.

Keep critical information in the document body, not in headers or footers. Many parsing systems ignore or misread content placed in those areas. Your name, contact details, job titles, employment dates - all of this should live in the main text flow where the algorithm expects to find it. I've seen qualified candidates rejected because their contact information was in a header that the system couldn't parse. The algorithm thought they'd submitted a CV without even including their phone number.

Place job titles and employment dates on separate lines rather than cramming them together on one line. This helps the software distinguish between your role and the timeframe you were in that position. It is important to format dates consistently. For example, use either "January 2023" or "Jan 2023" or "01/2023". It doesn't matter, but pick one format and stick with it throughout the document. Inconsistent date formatting confuses the parsing algorithm, which might miss entire employment periods if it can't recognise the date pattern.

Your recently acquired Minimum Viable Skills need explicit representation in formats the matching algorithm recognises and scores. Create a dedicated Skills and Tools section near the top of your CV. List specific technologies, methodologies, software platforms, techniques you've actually used. Mirror the job advertisement's exact terminology here. If the posting mentions "Power BI", then write "Power BI" rather than "business intelligence tools." If it asks for "SQL", then list "SQL" even if you primarily only used it for basic queries rather than complex database administration.

This isn't dishonesty. You're not claiming expertise you lack. You're ensuring the algorithm registers that you have hands-on experience with the tools the employer actually uses. The interview process will reveal the depth of your capability (but that's a battle for another day). The matching algorithm works by identifying specific keywords. If those keywords aren't present in your CV, you don't get matched, regardless of your actual capabilities. There is no rule that says you can only have one Curriculum Vitae. It is absolutely acceptable to reword and align the language in your CV to draw synergies between your skills, experience and what the potential employer has included in the job specification you are applying for. At the end of the day, you will have to be able to stand over what you include on your application in the interview environment. Feel free to mould the language to reflect what the ATS algorithm will be sifting, accepting and rejecting candidates against.

Make sure to include a Projects section that shows that your MVS work is real legitimate experience. Every learning arc that led to a useful outcome should have a place here. Make them like job experience: give the project a clear name, indicate the tools you used, explain what you did, and, if you can, give a number for the result.

An example could be: "Building Energy Audit System (Personal Project). Created Excel dashboard tracking utility consumption across three sites using meter data and weather patterns. Identified £18,000 annual savings through optimised HVAC scheduling and equipment runtime adjustments."

Or maybe: "Customer Complaint Pattern Analyser. Reviewed 800+ complaint tickets over six months using categorisation system in Excel. Identified three recurring root causes representing 60% of volume. Delivered findings to management, resulting in process changes that cut repeat complaints by 35%."

Or perhaps: "Onboarding Efficiency Tracker (Personal Project). Built SharePoint workflow with automated task assignments and progress tracking for new hire paperwork. Reduced average onboarding completion from 14 days to 6 days, improving early retention by 15%."

Or: "Meeting Room Utilisation Study. Tracked booking patterns across 12 conference rooms for three months using Outlook calendar exports and Excel analysis. Found 40% of bookings were no-shows or ran short. Recommended scheduling policy changes that improved room availability by 25%."

These aren't hypothetical exercises. You built working solutions that solved real problems. The fact that you created them whilst learning rather than within a traditional job doesn't diminish their value. Frame them clearly so both algorithms and humans understand what you are presenting and what you accomplished. The algorithm will recognise the keywords (Excel, dashboard, SharePoint, workflow, Outlook). The humans will understand the practical value you delivered.

Keyword optimisation means aligning your wording with the employer's language were truthful. Read the job posting carefully and extract the specific nouns and phrases it emphasises. Technical skills, software platforms, methodologies, certifications, industry terminology. Note not just what's required but how it's written. If the posting says, "supply chain optimisation", then use that exact phrase rather than your preferred term "logistics coordination."

Incorporate these keywords naturally throughout your CV. In your Summary at the top. In your Skills section as direct listings. In your Project descriptions showing where you applied them. In your Experience bullets that show how you've used something before. This distribution is important. If you only include a term once in your Skills list, it might not score as highly as if you also present it in context in a Project or Experience entry. The ranking algorithm often gives more weight to terms that show up in more than one area as a sign of greater knowledge.

When your professional vocabulary differs from the posting's terminology, bridge the gap explicitly. Write "Supply chain optimisation (logistics coordination and routing)" if you've been using different terms for the same work. This signals to both the algorithm (which sees the target keyword) and to humans (who understand you're clarifying equivalence) that you have the relevant capability. You're translating, not fabricating.

Don't manufacture keywords for skills you don't actually have. Automated screening is just the first barrier. You still face human evaluation and potentially skills testing afterwards. Claiming proficiency in technologies you've never touched will get you rejected later in the process, wasting everyone's time including yours.

Many algorithmic filters apply strict rules about formal qualifications. If a posting requires a bachelor's degree and you lack one, your application often gets auto-rejected regardless of equivalent experience. You can't always overcome these filters, but you can improve your odds by front-loading alternative credentials prominently.

If you don't have the specified degree, emphasise what you do have in the Education and Certifications sections. Professional certifications, industry qualifications, completed training programmes, relevant courses. List these prominently with dates and issuing organisations. Make it easy for the algorithm (and for human reviewers who might override the filter) to see substantial learning and validation.

In your Summary, make sure to clearly connect how your experience fits the needs of the role.

For example: "Logistics coordinator with 12 years of experience managing supply chain operations in manufacturing and distribution. Certified in Lean Six Sigma and advanced Excel. Recently completed process automation training (Power Query, Power BI, workflow optimisation)."

This tells the story clearly: you have a lot of hands-on experience, formal qualifications, and you've actively gained new technical skills. It doesn't claim a degree you don't hold, but it makes the case for equivalent qualification. Sometimes this works. Sometimes it doesn't. But it's better than leaving the algorithm with nothing to match against the requirement.

Employment gaps need addressing rather than hiding. Algorithmic filters often flag unexplained time periods as negative signals. Convert gaps into neutral or positive entries by briefly explaining what you did during that time.

"January 2023 to September 2023: Family care responsibilities whilst completing online certifications in process improvement (Lean Six Sigma Green Belt) and project coordination (Google Project Management Certificate)."

"June 2024 to December 2024: Startup founder exploring facilities management consultancy. Validated market need, developed service framework, learnt building management systems and compliance software. Returned to employment to apply strategic thinking in established organisation."

These entries provide context that makes sense to both parsing systems (which see continuous activity rather than unexplained absence) and humans, (who understand legitimate reasons for gaps). You're not apologising or making excuses. You're stating facts about how you spent that time productively. The algorithm sees dates with activity labels. The human sees initiative and learning during a difficult time or a career transition.

Your Experience and Projects sections need bullets that satisfy both algorithmic screening and human evaluation. The format that works for both:

action verb, specific task or problem, tools or methods used, measurable result.

"Reduced emergency maintenance callouts by 28% by implementing preventive inspection schedule in CAFM system, tracking equipment performance patterns across five buildings."

"Streamlined employee onboarding process using SharePoint task workflows and automated reminders, cutting average completion time from 12 days to 5 days."

"Identified top three customer complaint drivers representing 60% of call volume through Excel categorisation analysis, leading to process fixes that reduced repeat issues by 40%."

"Optimised delivery route sequencing using WMS reporting data and Excel analysis, reducing average delivery time by 15% whilst maintaining service quality standards."

"Improved meeting room utilisation by 25% through Outlook calendar analysis revealing booking patterns, recommending policy adjustments that reduced scheduling conflicts."

These bullets work algorithmically because they contain concrete keywords (CAFM system, SharePoint, Excel, WMS, Outlook) that the software can match against job requirements. They parse cleanly because they follow simple structure without complex punctuation or embedded clauses. They work for human readers because they follow the STAR method's logic - Situation and Task (what problem needed solving), Action (what you did and with what tools), Result (what measurable outcome you achieved). A recruiter can quickly grasp both your capability and your impact.

Keep bullets to single lines of 15 to 25 words where possible. Longer descriptions usually mean you're explaining too much or trying to cram multiple achievements into one bullet. Split complex accomplishments into separate points. This improves both readability and parsing accuracy. The algorithm handles shorter, discrete statements better than long, complex sentences.

A two-line summary at the top of your CV serves multiple purposes. It tells the algorithm immediately that you match the role's basic profile. It tells human readers within three seconds whether they should invest time reading further. It connects your background to the specific opportunity.

Line one states who you are now, mapped explicitly to the target role. Line two provides proof points, tools, quantified outcomes.

"Warehouse operations specialist transitioning to data analyst role, combining logistics expertise with newly developed analytical skills in Python, SQL, and Power BI. Recently completed data analysis certification and built three working analytics projects processing operational data to identify efficiency improvements."

"Warehouse operations coordinator with eight years optimising logistics workflows. Hands-on with WMS software, Excel, and Power BI. Reduced fulfilment errors by 27% through process redesign and recently automated key reporting using Power Query."

"Quality assurance specialist transitioning to process improvement role, combining regulatory compliance expertise with newly developed workflow analysis and reporting automation skills. Recently completed Lean Six Sigma training and built three process improvement projects demonstrating ability to identify inefficiencies and deliver measurable results."

These summaries work because they're honest about your background whilst clearly positioning you for the role. They incorporate keywords naturally (Python, SQL, WMS, Power BI, Lean Six Sigma). They provide specific evidence of capability (certifications, projects, quantified results). And they're short enough that busy recruiters and algorithmic parsers both process them quickly.

Tailor this summary for each application. The two-line format makes customisation manageable rather than requiring complete CV rewrites. Change the skills emphasis, swap in different proof points, adjust the positioning to match each role's specific requirements. It takes five minutes per application but dramatically improves your match score.

Before submitting any application, run three quick tests. The search test: open your CV and use your word processor's Find function to search for the job posting's five most critical keywords. Does each one appear at least once? If a key requirement from the posting doesn't show up in a search of your CV, the matching algorithm likely won't find it either.

The plain-text test: copy your entire CV and paste it into a plain text editor (Notepad on Windows, TextEdit on Mac). Does the information still appear in sensible order? Are sections clearly marked? If the plain-text version becomes unreadable or jumbled text, the parsing algorithm will probably fail similarly. This test reveals formatting problems that would cause your CV to upload incorrectly.

The job-advertisement mirror: place the job posting and your CV side by side. Do your section labels use similar terminology to the posting? Do your skill names match the posting's phrasing? Does your summary address the key requirements explicitly? If there's significant language mismatch, reword to align more closely. This isn't about losing your voice - it's about speaking the employer's language so they can find you.

These checks take five minutes and dramatically improve your odds of passing automated screening. They catch formatting problems that would cause parsing failures. They identify keyword gaps that would score your application lower than it deserves. They verify that your CV actually speaks the language the employer used to describe what they need.

Each element directly addresses one of the algorithmic barriers we documented earlier. You're not being dishonest. You're ensuring the parsing and matching algorithms can actually read and accurately evaluate the genuine capabilities you've built through learning arcs. The work you've done matters. The MVS you've developed are real and valuable. This tactical approach simply ensures they reach the human decision-makers who can recognise and appreciate them.

Job searching in the age of AI displacement requires understanding that your CV faces two audiences with different requirements. The parsing and matching algorithms need structured data, matching keywords, clean formatting, and explicit credentials. The humans need context, demonstrated impact, clear achievements, and evidence you can deliver results. Your challenge is satisfying both without compromising either. Get past the algorithmic barrier so the humans can see what you've actually built.

Working with Recruitment Agencies

In the age of AI displacement, the recruitment sector (like many other industries) has taken a massive hit. Currently there is a major scramble within the Recruitment Consultancy space to adopt AI into the workflow. The aim is to let AI tools do the repetitive, time-consuming administrative functions. However, AI has also crept into the candidate selecting and shortlisting function. It is also steadily making its way into the candidate screening process in the form of chatbots and AI video interviewing.

Despite these changes, good recruitment consultants still provide a parallel job search channel that bypasses algorithmic screening entirely. When an agency submits your CV to a company HR team or hiring manager, it often goes straight to a human reviewer without passing through ATS filters first. This direct submission eliminates the parsing problems, keyword mismatches, and credential filters that trip up so many direct applications made through job boards, sites like LinkedIn, and even the companies own website.

The real value isn't just bypassing the algorithm. It's the human advocacy that comes with it. A recruitment consultant who understands both your capabilities and the employer's needs can champion your application in ways no CV alone can achieve. They position your non-linear career as an advantage rather than letting an algorithm interpret it as a disqualification. They explain why your self-taught skills matter even without formal degrees in the subject matter. They contextualise employment gaps as periods of valuable learning rather than red flags.

This advocacy happens through direct conversation with hiring managers and through the cover notes that accompany your CV. A well-written agency cover note does what your CV cannot - it tells the story behind the skills, explains why someone with a warehouse background might excel in a data analyst role (they understand supply chain patterns, bottlenecks, and operational metrics from years of hands-on experience that pure data people often miss), making the case for equivalent experience when formal qualifications are missing. These notes bypass algorithmic filtering because they're written for human decision-makers who can appreciate context and potential.

The behind-the-scenes work matters more than most candidates realise. Picture this: a hiring manager receives a shortlist of fifteen or twenty CVs for a single role. Their job now is to create two piles of CVs out of this list. A reject pile and an interview pile. If your agency recruiter has done their job correctly they've worked to position your application in that yes, invite to interview pile. Their pre-emptive conversations with the hiring manager, their strategic framing of your capabilities - this often determines which pile your CV lands in. Think of this logically, the recruitment agency isn't in business to get you a job. It's in business to generate revenue through placement fees by getting you hired. The agency recruiters commission is based on a percentage of this fee, so a good agency recruiter treats your application as if it were their own and should be shepherding and advising you through every stage of the interview process like their pay depended on it. If they don't, then get another recruiter.

Quality recruitment consultants are like good tailors or reliable mechanics - when you find one, you should stick with them. They've seen hundreds of applications succeed and fail. They'll review your CV and suggest language that better positions your capabilities for specific roles. They'll identify which of your Minimum Viable Skill projects to emphasise for particular opportunities. They'll help you frame your haversack learning arcs as evidence of adaptability rather than career uncertainty. This isn't just CV tweaking - its strategic positioning based on actual knowledge of what employer's value and what hiring managers respond to. When they give advice, take it seriously. They know what works.

Interview preparation is where good recruiters show their value for experienced workers navigating career transitions. They know the questions that trip up candidates with non-traditional backgrounds.

They'll help you frame answers that acknowledge skill gaps without undermining confidence - coaching you through how to explain why you're pivoting from logistics to analysis, or from customer service to project coordination. They've seen hundreds of interviews and will know how to best answer those probing questions that might throw you in the interview.

The practical side matters too. Good agencies handle the details that drain energy when you're already stressed - scheduling interviews, chasing feedback when employers ghost you, negotiating salary with knowledge of actual market rates. They act as buffer and champion during processes that often feel opaque and frustrating.

Not all agencies deliver this value. Some operate as pure CV forwarding services with minimal consultation or advocacy. Shop around for a professional, sympathetic, responsive recruiter who will work with you as a partner, not just process your application.

The difference shows in how they engage with you initially. Quality recruiters ask detailed questions about your capabilities, your learning journey, what you've actually built. They will want to understand your MVS work and how it applies to specific roles. They'll also ask what motivates you - career challenge, improved compensation, better work-life balance. In the era of AI displacement, be straight with them about your concerns. If AI automation contributed to you losing your job, or is currently pushing you out of your role, tell them. They need to understand what's happening (or what's already happened) so they can position you effectively with their clients who are hiring. They're selective about which opportunities they present because their reputation depends on matching candidates appropriately.

Building relationships with specialist recruiters in your industry before you need them is a smart move that may provide you with a strategic advantage. Reach out when you've completed significant learning arcs, or built notable proof pieces, not just when you're desperate for work. Share what you're learning and building. Ask for market intelligence about which skills are becoming valuable in your field. Treat it as professional networking rather than transactional job searching.

The best approach combines both strategies - optimise your CV to pass algorithmic screening for direct applications, whilst simultaneously building relationships with quality recruiters who can vouch for you through human channels. You're not choosing between algorithmic optimisation and human advocacy. You're using both to maximise your chances of getting past barriers and into interview situations where you'll have a fighting chance to land your next job opportunity.

Demonstrating Capability to Humans

You've made your CV better for algorithmic screening. You may have even engaged the services of a good recruiter to assist with introducing you to companies.

But now, you have to deal with the people who really make hiring decisions - Human Resources, in-house Talent Acquisition teams, and ultimately, the Hiring Manager. This is where demonstrating proof of ability is more important than keywords or qualifications.

Humans look for different things than automated systems do. The parsing software deemed you a potential fit because your CV had the right mix of keywords, clean formatting, and the preferred credentials. Humans on the other hand want proof that you can help them deliver solutions to their specific problems. They want to see what you've made, know how you deal with challenges and objections, and see if you will fit their existing team and be able to get things done in their environment.

Portfolio pieces give the most direct proof. These are real things that have come out of your learning arcs: tools you have made, processes you have improved, and problems you have solved.

That building energy audit dashboard you built tracking consumption patterns across multiple sites.

That one-page customer complaint summary that helped management spot three recurring service issues.

That automated onboarding workflow using SharePoint that cut completion time from two weeks to six days.

That simple meeting room utilisation analysis that reduced scheduling conflicts by 25%.

These aren't just bullet points on a CV. They are demonstrations you can walk interviewers through, showcasing exactly how you solved problems and what you got done.

The best thing about portfolio pieces is that they are very specific. Anyone can say they're good at data analysis or process improvement. But if you can actually show that you came up with a solution that solved a real problem, that's proof. Ten minutes of talking about something you've built is more useful to interviewers than thirty minutes of talking about your skills in general.

Different fields need different types of proof.

Moving into facilities management? Bring examples of maintenance tracking systems you've built - whether that's Excel dashboards analysing equipment performance or CAFM system optimisations that reduced callouts.

Positioning for HR coordination roles? Document your onboarding improvements, showing before-and-after completion times or retention improvements from better early-stage support.

Pursuing customer service management? Show the complaint analysis work you've done, the patterns you've spotted, how you've used available data to influence process improvements.

Transitioning from warehouse operations to supply chain analysis? Show the efficiency improvements you've made, the delivery route optimisations you've tested, how you've used WMS data to influence better decisions.

The content is more important than the format. A simple document walking through what you did works fine. A quick demonstration showing your solution in action works better. The goal is to show interviewers that you can do the job, not to impress them with fancy presentation.

When your career path doesn't follow the usual patterns, work samples become even more useful. The algorithm may have flagged your lack of formal qualifications as a problem. People see your MVS projects showing real capability and recognise you can do the job even without the credentials. The agency recruiter may have positioned you well with their cover letter, but now you need to back that up with real evidence.

The STAR method helps you talk about your proof pieces in a clear way. Again, STAR stands for Situation, Task, Action, Result. As mentioned earlier, it's a behavioural interviewing format many HR teams and Hiring Managers use to evaluate candidates. However, the technique can be used in reverse. When you know that interviewers are going to probe you with behavioural-type questions, you can prepare yourself to answer with behavioural-type responses. Knowing this, you can build your answers and anecdotal stories in advance so you get used to talking about your career and what you've done fluently. Remember, Hiring Managers have selected you for interview on the strength of what they've seen on your CV. So it's imperative that you are able to talk about yourself and what you've accomplished confidently.

Here's how it works with a customer service example:

Situation: “Our call centre was getting overwhelmed with repeat complaints about the same issues, but management didn't have clear visibility of the patterns.”

Task: “I needed to categorise complaints so we could identify recurring problems and fix them at the source rather than handling them one by one.”

Action: “I spent two weeks reviewing customer feedback, grouping them into themes using a simple spreadsheet system, and created a one-page summary showing the top three recurring issues with example quotes and frequency counts.”

Result: “Management used the summary to prioritise fixes. Within a month, complaints about those three issues dropped by 40%, and my categorisation approach became part of monthly reporting.”

Here's the same structure with a technical example:

Situation: “Our warehouse was experiencing 15% error rates in picking, causing customer complaints and returns.”

Task: “I needed to identify where errors occurred most frequently and implement a solution that would work with existing staff and systems.”

Action: “I analysed three months of error data using Excel and basic Python scripts, found that 70% of errors happened in the first hour of shifts, and designed a simple verification checkpoint at thirty minutes that took less than a minute to complete.”

Result: “Error rates dropped to 4% within two months, customer complaints fell by 60%, and the checkpoint process became standard procedure.”

Both stories show multiple capabilities - pattern recognition, problem-solving, practical implementation, business impact. They're far more compelling than saying “I'm good at analysis and process improvement.”

Your MVS projects from learning arcs fit the STAR structure naturally because they solved real problems with real results. That customer feedback system? Situation, Task, Action, Result. That warehouse improvement? Same structure. That's interview-ready proof regardless of whether your tools were spreadsheets or Python.

Prepare three to five STAR stories that show different aspects of your capabilities. Include at least two from recent learning arcs to show you can quickly learn and use new skills. Include examples that demonstrate what the specific role requires. Job emphasises automation? Feature your efficiency projects with whatever tools you used. Focuses on stakeholder communication? Highlight how you've explained operational issues to management or trained colleagues on new procedures.

Practise telling these stories conversationally, not reading from memory. You want to sound like someone excitedly talking about interesting work they've done, not performing rehearsed responses. The interviewer will ask follow-up questions. They'll probe details about your approach, challenge your assumptions, ask why you chose certain methods over others. This isn't hostility - it's their way of understanding how you think and whether you genuinely did the work you're describing.

Your ability to discuss details fluently shows genuine capability. If you built that customer complaint system, you should be able to explain what categories you used and why, what patterns you noticed that surprised you, how you presented findings to management. If you built that maintenance tracking dashboard, explain why you chose Excel over a purpose-built system, what data quality issues you encountered, how you validated your savings estimates. Superficial knowledge collapses under detailed questioning. Real experience generates confident, specific answers.

Digital portfolios make proof easily accessible. A simple document or LinkedIn section displaying your MVS projects helps interviewers review your work before or after conversations. Include brief descriptions of what each project does, what problem it solves, what approach you used, and what outcome you achieved. Technical projects can link to documentation or screenshots. Operational improvements can include simple before-and-after process diagrams or charts showing improvements. Keep it straightforward - you're demonstrating practical capability, not design skills.

The transition from algorithmic to human evaluation also means personality and communication style suddenly matter. The algorithm didn't care if you worked well with others, how you took feedback, or if you would fit the team culture. People put a lot of weight on these factors. When describing projects, mention how you got input from colleagues who understood the problems, how you adjusted your approach based on feedback, how you helped others understand and use what you'd built.

This isn't separate from demonstrating capability. It shows you can deliver results through and with other people, which matters enormously in most roles.

The work you've done on learning arcs has prepared you well for this stage. You made things that really worked to solve problems. You've documented how you did things and what happened. You've created proof that algorithms couldn't evaluate but humans can appreciate. Now you need to present that proof clearly, discuss it confidently, and let your genuine capability show through.

The algorithm determined whether you deserved human attention. The humans determine whether you get the job. Your proof pieces are what will tilt that decision in your favour.

Building Portfolio Whilst Learning

The proof pieces that tilt hiring decisions in your favour don't magically appear after you've finished a learning arc. They get built during the process itself, often before you feel remotely ready to show anyone your work.

This feels backwards to most people. The natural instinct says learn first, get competent, then create something worth showing. But that sequencing creates a critical problem during AI displacement when you need evidence quickly. If you wait until you feel fully competent before building demonstration pieces, you're waiting too long. The interview opportunities pass. The redundancy happens. Someone else who built their proof earlier gets the role you were preparing for.

The most effective approach flips the sequence entirely. You build demonstration pieces whilst developing the skill, not after. This produces evidence faster, but more importantly, it produces better proof. The meeting room utilisation analysis that improved scheduling by 25% wasn't built by someone who'd mastered facilities management software. It emerged during an arc from someone testing whether basic Outlook data and Excel could solve a real problem they'd noticed. The customer feedback categorisation that cut complaints by 40% came from someone two weeks into systematic analysis techniques, not someone with years of expertise.

These examples share a pattern. The proof emerged from the arc itself, not as an afterthought once the skill felt complete. When you're actively developing capability, you spot problems that technique could solve. You have noticed some gaps between current approaches and what's possible. You see opportunities that wouldn't be visible if you waited until you'd achieved some abstract threshold of readiness.

Consider a training coordinator who's noticed their organisation struggling with onboarding remote workers effectively. Traditional in-person sessions don't translate well to video calls. New hires seem disconnected, completion rates have dropped, and managers keep complaining that recent hires lack context about how things actually work. They've been collecting scraps about this problem for weeks. Articles about remote learning effectiveness. A colleague's technique for making training videos more engaging. Observations about which onboarding elements work remotely and which don't.

They spot the cluster and start a two-week arc focused on building an MVS around remote onboarding design. Now here's where timing matters. They don't spend six months studying instructional design theory, then attempt to create something. They start building in week one whilst still developing the capability. A simple prototype workflow for one department. A short video tutorial using techniques they've just discovered. A feedback survey to understand what new remote hires actually need.

By the end of week two, they have imperfect but functional results. The prototype workflow isn't polished, but three new hires used it successfully. The video tutorial has rough spots, but the managers' report back it addresses gaps the old approach missed. The survey has revealed specific needs they hadn't anticipated. This approach didn't wait for mastery. It emerged alongside skills development, capturing both what worked and what they discovered through practical applications. Believe me, that's interview-ready evidence right there. Not because it's perfect, but because it demonstrates real, genuine capability. They can walk hiring managers through a real problem they identified, explain their process, show actual implementation results, and discuss what they'd improve next time. The STAR structure fits naturally because this work solved a real problem with measurable outcomes.

Building concurrently solves another problem people face during AI displacement. When you're job hunting or worried about redundancy, motivation becomes fragile. Abstract goals like "understand remote training principles" provide no tangible progress markers. You study, read, and watch tutorials, but there's no evidence you are getting anywhere. Three weeks in, you're not sure if you've actually built any useful capability or just accumulated theoretical knowledge.

Creating proof whilst developing skills provides continuous feedback. Week one, you've got a rough prototype. Week two, you've tested it with real users. By week three, you've got documented results showing what worked. Every piece of proof shows real improvement, even when you're under a lot of stress from looking for a job or having to shift industries that could put your current career at risk.

This approach also forces practical focus. When you know you need to build something functional, you prioritise techniques that contribute directly to that goal. The training coordinator doesn't get distracted by interesting but tangential topics about cognitive psychology or educational theory. They focus on methods they can apply immediately to their prototype workflow. This constraint actually accelerates useful skill development by eliminating the paralysis that comes from trying to master everything before doing anything.

Perhaps most importantly for interview situations, building concurrently produces evidence that authentically represents your development journey. These rough edges and iterative improvements aren't flaws to hide. No, they're proof of how to work through challenges and uncertainty. When the training coordinator talks about their remote onboarding prototype in interviews, they can be honest about what they attempted first that didn't work, what they changed based on feedback, and what they would do differently next time. This openness can sometimes be more interesting than the polished presentations that hide the messy realities of learning new skills.

The facilities coordinator who builds an energy tracking dashboard whilst developing Excel skills hasn't waited until they've mastered every formula and chart type. They created a working version in week one using basic pivot tables and conditional formatting. Week two, they tested it with actual meter readings from three buildings, discovered gaps in their data collection, and then refined the approach. By week three, they've documented which patterns the dashboard revealed correctly versus which required manual investigation. That documentation becomes evidence not just of Excel capabilities, but of practical judgement about where automation helps and where human expertise remains essential in the process.

The customer service supervisor developing capabilities around complaint analysis doesn't delay until they understand every categorisation framework. They start with a simple spreadsheet tracking of current complaints, identify one obvious pattern, and implement a small process change. The before-and-after comparison, even if it only shows modest improvement, demonstrates capability that matters to potential employers facing similar challenges.

This isn't about lowering standards or accepting mediocre work. It's about recognising that evidence of rapid skill development often matters more than demonstrations of expertise. During AI displacement, organisations need people who can adapt quickly and apply new capabilities practically. Demonstrating you can go from noticing a problem to implementing a working solution in two weeks shows exactly that ability. The meeting room analysis, the customer feedback categorisation, the remote onboarding prototype all share this quality. They prove their creators can identify problems, develop relevant techniques, and deliver functional solutions quickly.

The timing advantage compounds when you're competing with others for the same roles. Two candidates both spent a month on process improvement. One studied comprehensively, completed online courses, and feels nearly ready to start building something. The other built three small improvement projects whilst developing the skill, each solving a real problem, all documented with clear before-and-after results. In the interview, the first candidate talks intelligently about improvement principles. The second candidate walks through actual implementations, discusses what worked and what didn't, and shows measurable outcomes.

The hiring decision becomes obvious.

Creating proof during arcs also reveals whether the skill you're developing actually solves problems worth solving. Sometimes clusters that look promising turn out to be less useful in practice. Finding this out in week one whilst building a prototype causes minimal wasted effort. Discovering it after months of theoretical study creates serious frustration and lost time during periods when time matters enormously.

The key is accepting that early evidence will be imperfect and incomplete. It's meant to show competence at your current level, not mastery of every aspect of a skill area. The training coordinator's remote onboarding prototype has limitations. The facilities coordinator's energy dashboard misses edge cases. The customer service supervisor's complaint analysis doesn't address every complexity. None of that prevents these pieces from demonstrating valuable capability to potential employers looking for people who can adapt and deliver results.

Your arcs naturally produce the raw material for this concurrent approach. The problems you're trying to solve, the techniques you're testing, the outcomes you're achieving all become components of your proof story. When you've built something functional during the arc, you've simultaneously created interview-ready evidence of capability. The Minimum Viable Skill you've developed and the proof you need are the same thing, created through the same process, serving both immediate practical value and longer-term career positioning.

Integration with Your Rhythm

Proof creation only becomes sustainable when it fits naturally into the haversack rhythm you've already established, not as additional work piled on top of everything else.

The weekly review session you're already doing for scrap collection serves double duty here. When you examine your haversack looking for clusters that might become MVS opportunities, you're simultaneously identifying which proof pieces you've already created during your work. That training coordinator didn't schedule separate time to "build portfolio evidence." The prototype workflow, the tutorial video, the survey results all emerged from the arc itself. The review just captures and organises what already exists.

This is why concurrent building matters so much. When you create proof during the arc rather than after, it doesn't require extra effort. You're solving real problems that need solving anyway. The facilities coordinator building that energy tracking dashboard wasn't adding portfolio work to their schedule. They were identifying cost savings opportunities whilst developing new capability with Excel and building management data. The proof is just documentation of work that would have happened regardless.

Your arc planning already includes an outcome you'll demonstrate. That outcome is your proof. When you define a two-week arc around remote onboarding design, the demonstrable outcome you set isn't separate from the proof you need for interviews. They're identical. You're not building a capability and then building proof of the capability. You're building a capability in a way that inherently produces proof.

This removes the burden most people feel when they think about creating portfolios. They imagine it as a separate project requiring dedicated time they don't have whilst job hunting or managing current work pressures. But if your haversack arc produces a working solution to a real problem, you've simultaneously created interview-ready evidence. The documentation you need for your own reference (what worked, what didn't, what you'd change) is the same documentation that proves capability to potential employers.

The rhythm becomes: collect scraps during normal work, spot clusters during weekly reviews, run focused arcs when clusters point toward valuable Minimal Viable Skills, document outcomes as you go. Proof creation isn't an additional stage. It's integrated into each part of the process.

Think about the healthcare administrator working on scheduling optimisation. Their arc involves analysing current patterns, identifying bottlenecks, implementing changes. They're not thinking "I need to build a portfolio piece." They're thinking "I need to fix this scheduling problem." But when they document the before-and-after comparison for their own learning and to show management the improvement, they've created proof. When they capture what they tried that didn't work and what adjustments they made, they've built interview material. The work serves immediate practical needs whilst simultaneously creating evidence for future opportunities.

This integration matters especially when you're under pressure from AI displacement. You don't have time or energy for separate proof-building activities. But you do have time to document the work you're already doing as you develop new capabilities. Keep simple notes during your arcs. Capture the problem you were solving, the approach you took, the results you achieved. Those notes become your proof story without requiring additional effort beyond what the arc already demands.

The haversack method's emphasis on small, focused arcs rather than comprehensive learning projects makes this integration natural. A two-week arc with a specific demonstrable outcome produces clear, bounded proof pieces. You're not trying to prove mastery of an entire domain. You're showing you can solve specific problems using developing capabilities. That's exactly what short arcs are designed to produce.

When you complete an arc, your weekly review session assesses both what you learnt and what proof you created. Often they're the same thing. The Minimum Viable Skills you built is the proof. The problem you solved demonstrates the capability. The documentation you kept for your own learning serves as interview material. Integration means recognising that these aren't separate outputs requiring separate effort.

This sustainable approach prevents the burnout that comes from treating proof creation as additional burden during already stressful periods. You're not maintaining your current work, running learning arcs, and building portfolios. You're maintaining your current work whilst running learning arcs that naturally produce proof through their normal completion. The rhythm stays manageable because you're not actually adding new categories of work, just capturing the output of work you're already doing.

The legal developments and regulatory guidance referenced in this chapter are detailed in the Notes and Sources section at the end of this book.

Chapter 14: Steadying Through Setbacks

Job loss, industry pivots, or failed attempts are not the end. With a haversack, you always have a way to rebuild.

The email arrived on a Friday afternoon. Subject line: "Important Company Update - All Staff Meeting, 5pm Today."

I'd been through enough corporate communications to know that mandatory meetings announced with less than a day's notice rarely brought good news. We'd had regular All-hands company meetings since the shift to remote working during the Covid pandemic. But this felt different. I spent the rest of the afternoon preparing myself for whatever was coming, whilst my mind ran through possibilities. Restructure. Merger. Redundancies. Each scenario felt equally likely and equally terrible.

I joined the video call watching colleagues appear in the grid of faces. Nobody was chatting in the waiting room. When our directors appeared, you could see the stress before they said a word.

The news was brief and final. The company was closing operations. All positions would be made redundant immediately. Formal notification would follow via email with information about final pay and entitlements.

The call lasted no longer than twenty minutes. All of us lost our jobs whilst sitting alone in our home offices. No box to clear out. No desk to empty. Just a sudden, disconnected silence when the meeting ended and the screen went black.

I sat staring at my laptop for a long moment, feeling that familiar weight in my chest. Relief and panic arriving together (as they always do). Relief because the uncertainty was over. We'd all seen the signs for months. Panic because I'd just watched my income disappear in that fifteen-minute video call.

But something felt different this time compared to previous career disruptions I'd experienced. Instead of spiralling into a paralysing mental fog where you can't think beyond the immediate crisis, I found myself mentally cataloguing what I'd built over the past six months. The learning arcs I had pushed through. The automation test scripts I had pulled apart and learnt from. The prompt-writing expertise I was becoming skilled in and known for. The Python and data analysis skills I was steadily growing. Two decades in my previous field hadn't prepared me for much of this, but my haversack had.

My haversack wasn't just a collection of scraps anymore. It was full of automation scripting samples, Python guides, LLM manuals, and data testing techniques. Evidence of adaptability I could demonstrate to potential employers. Tangible proof that I could learn new things, spot problems worth solving, and create value even as things were falling apart around us.

That realisation didn't eliminate the stress of suddenly needing to find work. It didn't make the financial pressure disappear or the job applications any less draining. But it provided something I'd been missing during a previous redundancy years before: a foundation of confidence built on actual evidence rather than hope. I had proof I could adapt to changing requirements. I had examples of problems I'd solved whilst developing new capabilities. I had something to show, not just something to claim.

The email arrived shortly afterwards. I read through the formal language about closure and redundancy processes. By evening, the company laptop was remotely wiped. I closed it and went to the pub for multiple beers with my wife.

When I got back to my desk the following week, I'd start reaching out to contacts and reviewing job listings. But in that moment, I just needed to process the strange mixture of ending a job working for people I really liked and respected, and the possibility that comes with sudden professional disruption.

At least this time, I wasn't starting from zero.

Inventory Before Panic

The first step after job loss shouldn't be frantically applying for everything or panic-studying whatever seems relevant. It should be taking stock of what you already have. This assessment provides a realistic foundation for recovery whilst building confidence in your existing strengths.

Your haversack becomes invaluable here. Instead of trying to remember everything you've learnt and built over recent months, you have documented evidence. The scraps you've collected, the arcs you've completed, the proof pieces you created (the ones from Chapter 12 that get past both algorithms and humans). All of this represents portable value that travels with you regardless of which specific job you've lost.

Your assessment should include both formal qualifications and informal capabilities. Yes, your degree or diploma and certifications matter. But so do the small automations you've built, the processes you've improved, the relationships you've developed, and the problems you've learnt to solve. These informal capabilities often prove more useful during transitions than formal credentials because they demonstrate what you can actually do, not just what you've studied.

Don't overlook transferable skills that might not be obvious from your job title. Communication abilities, project management experience, problem-solving approaches, learning agility. These meta-skills often translate across different contexts even when specific technical knowledge doesn't. You've probably been developing these through your arcs without explicitly naming them.

Most importantly, assess your learning systems themselves. The habits you've developed for acquiring new capabilities. The networks you've built for staying current with changes. The approaches you've tested for turning knowledge into practical skills. These represent powerful assets that will serve you regardless of which direction your career takes next. You know how to adapt. That's not nothing.

Financial pressure is real and varies enormously person to person. This book can't solve that. What it can do is help you build demonstrable capabilities whilst you're navigating whatever financial situation you're in. Your arcs continue at their normal 2-4 week pace when possible. When that's not possible, you pause and come back when circumstances allow. The system doesn't demand what you can't give.

Here's the difference this approach makes: you're better prepared for uncertainty than you would be relying on traditional methods. This preparation doesn't eliminate the challenges of transition, but it does provide tools for navigating them more effectively.

When your professional identity is built around what you can learn rather than what you currently know, losing a particular job feels less catastrophic. The job changed. You didn't stop being adaptable.

This advantage shows up in several ways. You're more comfortable with the learning required to understand new industries or roles. You're more confident about acquiring whatever capabilities might be needed for emerging opportunities. You're more creative about identifying non-obvious ways to apply existing skills in different contexts.

Perhaps most importantly, you're more realistic about what kinds of knowledge provide genuine security versus which ones create only the illusion of permanence. When your entire industry used specific software and that software gets replaced, everyone with that expertise loses value simultaneously. But the person who knows how to learn new systems quickly? They adapt whilst others panic. This realism helps you make better decisions about where to invest your limited time and energy during recovery.

While others are wondering what to learn, you're already building. While they're paralysed by too many options, you're running targeted arcs. While they're waiting to feel ready, you're creating proof pieces. The haversack method doesn't guarantee you'll find work faster, but it does mean you're not starting from zero when opportunity appears.

Maintaining Learning Momentum During Crisis

The traditional advice for job loss is straightforward: update your CV, apply widely, maybe take a short course in something relevant. That advice worked well when job markets were more stable. But AI has changed the landscape significantly.

AI has compressed timelines and changed what employers value. By the time you've completed a three-month online course, the specific tools or techniques it taught might already be less relevant. The comprehensive approach that used to work (master everything about a field, then look for roles) takes too long when industries are reshaping themselves every quarter.

This creates a trap. You know you need new skills. But conventional learning approaches demand months of study before you have anything to show. Meanwhile, you're burning through savings whilst studying theories you can't yet demonstrate. Six months later, you've learnt a lot but built nothing employers can actually see.

The haversack method offers a different approach during crisis. You're not abandoning skill development for pure job applications. You're not gambling months on comprehensive courses. You're running targeted arcs that produce demonstrable results in weeks, not months.

The shift is from exploratory to surgical. Instead of collecting scraps about topics that might become useful someday, focus on what could help right now. Skills that appear in job descriptions you're actually applying for. Capabilities that could generate freelance income whilst you're hunting for permanent positions. Industries you're seriously considering (not casually browsing).

Think about a QA specialist made redundant from a manufacturing company. Standard approach: enrol in a comprehensive software testing certification, study for months, hope it leads to interviews. By the time they're certified, they've spent hundreds or even thousands from their savings and still have no practical examples to show.

Haversack approach: notice that software QA roles keep mentioning test automation. Collect scraps about it for a week whilst job hunting. Spot the clusters. Run a three-week arc building basic test automation capability using free tools. Not trying to become an expert - that takes months. Just building enough to speak intelligently in interviews and demonstrate they can learn these systems.

The proof piece from Chapter 12 (a simple automated test suite for a practice application) becomes interview material within a month of starting. Not claiming mastery. Showing they can adapt quality thinking to software contexts. That's often enough to get past initial screening when combined with their existing QA expertise.

The arc stays manageable because it's not learning an entire new field from scratch. It's applying existing expertise (quality thinking, systematic problem-solving, attention to detail) in a new context. That's what targeted work looks like when AI has accelerated industry change. You're building on what you have, not starting from zero with something completely foreign.

Your weekly haversack review becomes essential during transition. Fifteen minutes checking which scraps connect to actual opportunities you're pursuing. Which arcs make sense given how your applications are going. What proof pieces you need based on feedback from interviews. That discipline prevents the scattered approach where you're learning five different things without completing any of them.

Typical advice says pick one thing and master it completely. But when you don't know which specific skills will get you hired, that's gambling months on a single bet. The haversack approach lets you run multiple focused arcs, building several demonstrable capabilities whilst staying responsive to what the market actually wants.

Your arcs continue at their normal 2-4 week pace when circumstances allow. When they don't (interviews demand full attention for a week, family emergency hits, temporary contract needs all your focus) you pause and come back when possible. The system accommodates real life. It doesn't demand superhuman consistency during the worst periods.

What it does demand is not abandoning systematic work entirely. The reactive approach (apply everywhere, study everything, hope something sticks) rarely works when AI has changed how quickly skills need to develop and how specifically they need to be demonstrated. You need a method that produces proof pieces fast enough to matter whilst you're still in the hunt for roles.

Even during crisis, you're still noticing things. Still collecting the occasional scrap. Still thinking about which skills matter based on actual job descriptions and interview feedback. The haversack stays alive even when arcs pause. That means when circumstances allow you to resume focused work, you're not starting from zero. You've maintained enough forward movement that building the next proof piece feels achievable rather than overwhelming.

Dealing With Rejection and Failed Experiments

That application you thought was perfect comes back with a standard rejection email.

That arc you dedicated three weeks to, hits a wall you can't get past.

That interview that seemed promising goes nowhere.

That learning project which was supposed to produce your key proof piece simply doesn't work out.

When you're already dealing with the stress of job loss or the threat of AI-related displacement, these additional setbacks can feel like evidence that nothing's working.

They are not; they're simply information.

Job application rejection rarely means what you think it means. Remember Chapter 12's algorithmic barrier? Most rejections happen before any human sees your application. The ATS filtered you out because you didn't have the exact job title it was looking for, or you had a six-month gap in your employment history, or you answered "no" to a binary yes/no question about credentials. The algorithm wasn't judging your capability. It was applying rigid filters that eliminate qualified candidates every day.

Even rejections that come after human review usually reflect specific mismatches rather than judgements about your overall value. They needed someone with three years in a particular system you've only used for six months. They wanted industry experience you're still building. They had an internal candidate all along and were going through the required hiring process. None of that says you can't do the work.

What rejection does provide is intelligence about what employers are actually looking for versus what you thought they wanted. A sales support coordinator applies for ten roles emphasising CRM data analysis. Gets no responses. Reviews the feedback (when there is any) and the job descriptions more carefully. Notices most roles emphasise stakeholder communication and cross-team coordination more than data skills.

Adjusts next five applications to highlight coordination experience, runs a two-week arc building proof around cross-functional project work. Gets three interviews.

The haversack helps here because being turned down can't erase what you've built. Your proof pieces still exist. Your completed arcs still demonstrate you can learn and deliver. Rejection just means that particular opportunity wasn't the right match for what you can currently show. There will be others.

Failed learning arcs feel different because you've invested time and energy during a period when both are precious. You dedicated three weeks to building test automation capability. Got stuck on tool configuration, couldn't produce a working example, ran out of time. That stings when you're unemployed and thought this would be your interview differentiator.

But even arcs that don't work out aren't wasted effort. You learn what doesn't work for you, which saves time on future arcs. You identify gaps in your understanding that you can address. Even unsuccessful attempts usually produce something - partial progress that gives you a foundation for trying again differently.

The QA specialist from the previous section? Their first arc on test automation failed. The Python framework they chose was too complex for their current skill level. They got lost in documentation, spent two weeks confused, produced nothing usable. Traditional approach says that's three weeks wasted. Haversack approach says that's information.

Second arc, different approach. Simpler tools. More focused outcome. Built basic automated checks for a practice application using a beginner-friendly platform. Worked. The unsuccessful first arc taught them what level of complexity they could actually handle right now. That knowledge made the second arc successful.

The important thing is not treating failed arcs as evidence you can't learn. They're evidence about which approaches work for you and which don't. Some people learn well from documentation. Others need video tutorials. Some can jump straight into complex tools. Others need to build gradually.

Arcs that don't pan out reveal your actual learning patterns versus what you hoped would work.

Keep your experimental approach whilst being more strategic about which experiments to run. During stable employment, exploratory arcs make sense. You can test interesting ideas without immediate pressure for results. During job hunting, focus arcs on capabilities directly connected to opportunities you're pursuing. You don't have margin for experiments that might not pay off.

This doesn't mean only running safe arcs. It means choosing experiments where even partial success creates useful proof pieces. The marketing coordinator learning AI prompt writing runs an arc building templated prompts for common content types. Even if the arc doesn't achieve its full outcome, they'll still have some working examples. That's strategic experimentation during crisis.

Track what you learn from both unsuccessful applications and failed arcs. Not elaborate journals (you don't have time), but simple notes in your haversack. "ATS seems to filter out career changes, need to address this in CV." "Python automation too complex right now, try Excel-based automation first." "Interviews keep asking about specific metrics, need to quantify results better."

This intelligence accumulates. After ten applications, you start seeing patterns in what works and what doesn't. After three arcs, you understand your learning style better. That knowledge makes everything more efficient. You're not randomly trying things anymore. You're running informed experiments based on actual feedback from the market.

Rejection and failure feel personal during job hunting because everything feels personal when your income has disappeared or is under threat. But treating them as data rather than judgement lets you extract value from experiences that otherwise just hurt. The haversack method doesn't prevent setbacks. It gives you a system for learning from them fast enough to adjust your approach whilst you're still in the game.

Moving Forward

One thing you'll notice as you start reaching out to your network of contacts: a lot of those people will be dealing with their own version of what you're going through. Yes, they may still be employed, but be under no doubt many are watching AI change their roles and future career landscape also. Like you, they'll be wondering what skills will matter next year. They will be having the same conversations about adaptation you have been having with yourself.

Every situation is different as is every relationship. Some contacts may be perfectly positioned to help. Others won't. Some will understand immediately what you're building. Others will need you to explain it. The key is approaching each conversation based on what you know about that specific person and their circumstances.

This shared context of AI displacement creates opportunities alongside the obvious challenges. When you reach out to people in your network, you're often talking to people who understand exactly why you're rebuilding skills whilst job hunting. They're asking themselves similar questions about adaptation. That common ground matters.

You can absolutely ask for help. A former colleague works somewhere that's hiring for a role you'd be good at? Ask for a referral introduction. Many companies still prefer internal referrals over cold applications, and many still offer referral bonuses to employees who vouch for good candidates. Getting introduced by someone internal bypasses the ATS barrier we discussed in Chapter 12. That's hugely valuable.

Showing your contact how you fit the role and how you've adapted is what matters. This is where your haversack work becomes practical. You're not asking someone to vouch for the person you were in your last job. You're showing them what you've built since then.

The proof pieces from Chapter 12 signal your direction. The customer feedback analysis reveals your ability to extract patterns from messy data. The onboarding workflow you documented shows an understanding of how to improve processes. The reporting dashboard demonstrates your ability to pull together information and make it accessible.

These aren't just portfolio pieces. They are evidence of how someone has tweaked their career direction in response to AI displacement.

When you approach someone about a specific opportunity, you're essentially saying: "Here's the role. Here's what I've been building that's relevant. Here's how I've adapted my skills to match what this kind of position needs. Would you feel comfortable introducing me?" That's different from "I lost my job, do you know anyone hiring?"

Your contact can see what you've done, understand your direction, and make an informed decision about whether vouching for you makes sense. If they work somewhere with referral bonuses, they have financial incentive. If they just want to help, they have concrete evidence you're someone who adapts rather than someone hoping for rescue.

This doesn't mean every conversation will immediately produce introductions. Some won't be in positions to help. Others work at companies that aren't hiring. A few might not feel comfortable vouching even when they could. That's normal. You're putting yourself in the shop window with people who might be able to connect you to opportunities, whilst demonstrating that you're actively building rather than passively waiting.

Your haversack gives you something current to show. You've been collecting scraps about industry changes, running targeted arcs based on actual market intelligence, creating proof pieces that didn't exist when you lost your job. That progression matters because it shows you understand how AI is reshaping your field and you're responding to it. That's valuable to professional connections who are themselves trying to figure out what adaptation looks like.

Recovery takes longer than you'd like. Initial shock and taking stock. Figuring out what opportunities exist. Building momentum as applications improve and proof pieces get stronger. Eventually things click and opportunities align. Understanding this pattern will help you maintain effort through periods where visible progress seems slow.

The haversack method provides a way to stay productive during that timeline. While others are scattered and reactive, you're running targeted arcs. While they're wondering what to learn, you're building demonstrable capabilities based on where you want to go. While they're waiting to feel ready, you're creating proof pieces that get better with each iteration. The method doesn't compress the timeline, but it ensures you're building throughout it rather than just spinning.

The most important outcome of navigating job loss whilst maintaining your haversack isn't just finding work. It's proving to yourself that the system works under pressure. You've kept building when disruption hit. You've maintained forward momentum when everything felt chaotic. You've created capabilities despite financial stress and emotional turbulence.

That proof changes something fundamental. Your professional worth is no longer tied to where you work or what your title says. It's based on what you can learn and demonstrate. When a company enters administration, they can take your job. They can't take your ability to adapt. That's the shift that steadies you through setback: understanding that no single employer can eliminate your capability to rebuild.

The remaining chapters build on this foundation. Chapter 15 addresses choosing tools now that you understand what your system actually needs. Chapter 16 explores working with AI as partner in ongoing adaptation. Chapter 17 addresses what you've actually built through using the method. The Appendix provides your structured 30-day implementation guide when you're ready to start.

You've steadied yourself through setback not by ignoring the disruption, but by proving you can still move forward inside it. Industries will keep evolving. AI will keep advancing. Roles will keep changing. Future disruption is certain. What's also certain is that you now have a method for navigating it.

And that method travels with you, regardless of what comes next.

Chapter 15: Evolving Your Haversack

Simple worked until it didn't. Time to evolve strategically. But always remember, the best haversack is the one you'll use.

You've been running your haversack for months now. Maybe longer.

It got you through crisis. You captured scraps whilst job hunting, ran focused arcs under financial pressure, built proof pieces that got you past ATS filters. The basic system worked. Phone notes, a notebook, an Excel sheet - whatever simple setup you cobbled together served its purpose when everything felt chaotic.

And now it's straining.

Not because you're doing it wrong. Rather, because you're doing it right. Success creates its own problems. The twenty scraps that were easy to review became two hundred. The single notebook that worked perfectly now has six months of material with no way to search it. The phone notes that felt natural for quick captures now require endless scrolling to find anything. What worked brilliantly at small volume hits friction at larger scale.

This is good news. It means your system proved valuable enough to keep using. Before the crisis, your haversack might have felt like an experiment. After navigating disruption with it, you know it's worth maintaining. That changes how you think about improvement.

You're not tinkering with something you might abandon. You're upgrading a tool you trust. The foundation is solid. Now you're adding capabilities based on experience rather than guesswork.

Here's what this chapter isn't. A guide to building the perfect haversack. There's no universal system that works for everyone. There's no sophisticated setup that solves all problems. What works brilliantly for someone else might be completely wrong for you.

What this chapter is. A practical guidance for recognising when your specific system needs evolution, and evolving it strategically based on actual friction rather than theoretical perfection. Your basic setup got you through crisis. Now let's make it work even better as your haversack matures.

Signs Your System Needs Evolution

The wrong time to evolve your haversack is when everything's working fine. Simple systems should stay simple as long as they're doing the job. But there are clear signals that basic setup has reached its limits and strategic improvement would help rather than complicate things further.

Review sessions that used to take fifteen minutes now stretch to forty-five because you're sifting through unsorted material. You're reorganising the same scraps multiple times trying to find the right structure. When maintenance becomes burden rather than brief routine, something needs to change.

Finding specific scraps has become painful. You remember capturing something useful about stakeholder communication three weeks ago. You know it's in your haversack somewhere. But searching through chronological captures takes so long that you give up and try to remember the content instead. If your haversack makes finding things harder than remembering things, it's not serving its purpose anymore.

You've outgrown single-tool simplicity. Phone notes worked brilliantly when you had twenty scraps. Now you have two hundred and scrolling has become obstacle rather than tool. A notebook was perfect until you needed to search for specific content across six months of material. The tool that served you well at one scale becomes hindrance at another.

Multiple capture points are causing friction. You capture on your phone during commutes, in a notebook during meetings, in laptop documents whilst working. Each makes sense in its context, but now you have three separate collections with no way to see connections across them. Missing clusters because related scraps live in different places means you can't spot the patterns.

These signals don't mean you've failed at the haversack method. They mean you've succeeded enough to reach the next level of complexity. Your basic setup got you this far. Now it's showing you what it needs to serve you better going forward.

The key is recognising these signals early, before frustration leads you to abandoning your system entirely. Adding search capability before scrolling becomes unbearable. Introducing light organisation before review sessions become impossible. Consolidating capture points before you lose track of what you've collected. Small strategic improvements made early prevent later collapse.

But absence of these signals means you don't need to evolve. If you're capturing easily, finding things quickly, and scrap review feels manageable, your current approach is working. Don't add complexity just because you can. Don't evolve because someone else's haversack looks more sophisticated. Don't optimise for theoretical elegance when practical simplicity is serving you well.

Evolution happens when problems emerge from actual use, not when you imagine problems that might emerge someday. Trust the friction points. They'll tell you when and where to evolve your haversack system.

Strategic Tool Selection (Not "Best" Tools)

"What's the best tool for a haversack?" That's the wrong question. It assumes universal answers when your needs are specific. A better question might be: "What's straining in my current setup and what would fix it?"

If you can't find your scraps when you need them, you need search capability. If they're scattered across multiple devices, you need sync. If scrap review is taking too long, better organisation would help. When scrap capture feels clunky, faster input solves the problem.

The key is matching the solution to the real problem you're experiencing, not to features that sound impressive.

Think about the QA specialist from Chapter 14. During crisis, phone notes worked fine for capturing scraps. Back at a desk job now, spending eight hours a day on a computer. Constantly pulling out the phone to capture or review feels awkward. They don't need something more sophisticated. They need a desktop-first tool that matches where they work. That's strategic selection based on changed circumstances.

Or consider someone whose notebook worked perfectly during stable employment. Now they're job hunting remotely and every interviewer wants to see proof pieces. Physical notebook doesn't translate to shareable digital format easily. They don't need elaborate knowledge management software.

They need basic digital capture that can be copied into applications and emails. Solving the real problem, not chasing features.

Your tools should solve problems you have, not problems you might theoretically encounter. Don't add sync because you could work from multiple devices someday. Add it when you're losing scraps because you've been capturing on your phone but need them on your laptop. Don't add advanced search because it exists. Add it when scrolling through captures is costing you real time.

This principle matters especially when job hunting or navigating career change. You don't have spare time or energy for learning complex new tools. You need whatever solves your immediate friction with minimum setup overhead. The fancy knowledge management system might be perfect in theory, but if it takes three days to learn and configure, it's the wrong choice right now. Better to use something simple that works today than something sophisticated that might work next week.

Tools also need to match how you actually behave and operate, not how you think you should work. Maybe you think you should be the person who meticulously tags everything with perfect taxonomy. But your typical behaviour is capturing quickly and searching later. Tools built for the aspirational you won't work for the actual you. Choose based on what you do, not what you wish you did.

Watch out for the migration trap. Switching tools because the new one looks better often creates more problems than it solves. Migration takes time. You might lose scraps in translation. You need to rebuild habits around the new tool. Only switch when your current tool creates genuine obstacles, not when you're bored or someone recommends their favourite system.

The best tool for your haversack is whatever solves your specific problems without creating new ones. That might be basic phone notes plus occasional laptop review. It might be a simple document with good search. It might be dedicated note-taking software with consolidation across devices. All of these can work brilliantly depending on your situation. None of them is universally "best."

Your tool choices will probably evolve over time as your work changes, your volume increases, or your needs shift. That's fine. But each evolution should solve a problem you're experiencing, not chase theoretical perfection. Strategic selection means letting real friction guide your choices, not imagined optimisation opportunities.

Organisation That Serves Use (Not Perfection)

You don't need elaborate organisation for your haversack. You don't need perfectly nested categories or comprehensive tags. You need just enough structure to find scraps when you need them. That's it.

The goal isn't creating beautiful archives. The goal is supporting your work. If your organisation helps you spot clusters during review and find relevant scraps during arcs, it's working. If it takes more time to maintain than it saves in retrieval, it's not.

Start with how you search for things. When you need a scrap, what's your mental query? "Where was that thing about stakeholder management?" "What did I capture about Python automation?" "Didn't I save something about remote team coordination?" Your categories should match those natural searches, not some theoretical knowledge structure.

Most people need somewhere between three and five broad categories. Technical skills. Industry trends. Process improvements. Whatever naturally emerges from the type of work you do and the scraps you tend to collect. If you're creating more than seven categories, you're probably over-organising. If you can't remember where something belongs, your system is too complex.

The test is simple: during review, can you sort new scraps without thinking hard about placement? During arcs, can you quickly locate relevant scraps without checking multiple places? If yes, your organisation is working. If you're constantly hesitating about classification or searching in the wrong places, something needs simplifying.

Tags or folders or sections - use whatever your tool provides naturally. Don't fight the interface trying to impose a perfect system. If your tool does folders well, use folders. If it does tags well, use tags. The mechanism matters less than whether it helps you find things.

Organisation should emerge from use, not be imposed before use. Start with no categories at all. Capture scraps for two weeks. Then look at what you've collected and notice natural groupings. Those groupings become your initial structure. Let it reveal itself through content rather than designing theoretical frameworks that might not match reality.

Your categories will evolve. A category that made sense six months ago might split into two as volume increases. Two categories that seemed distinct might merge when you realise they're closely related. That's fine. Organisation serves current needs, not theoretical permanence. Adjust when friction emerges, not on schedule.

Watch out for perfectionism. You'll have scraps that don't fit neatly anywhere and borderline cases that could go multiple places. You'll have messy captures that resist clean classification. All of this is normal. Pick whichever category seems closest and move on.

Remember: perfect organisation takes more time than imperfect retrieval costs you.

The real danger is spending more time organising than using. If you're constantly refining your category structure, re-sorting existing scraps, or debating where new captures belong, you've crossed from helpful structure into procrastination. This should take minutes during weekly review, not hours during special reorganisation sessions.

Remember what organisation is for: supporting review sessions where you spot clusters, and supporting arcs where you need relevant scraps quickly. If your system does those two things efficiently, it's good enough. Everything else is optimisation for its own sake.

Some scraps will never get used. Some categories will stay nearly empty. Some organisational decisions will prove wrong. None of that matters if the system helps you find the scraps you need when you need them. That's the only measure that counts.

Integration Without Bureaucracy

Your haversack shouldn't duplicate your professional systems. It should feed into them. This distinction matters because maintaining the same information in multiple places creates overhead that kills useful habits.

Think about how information flows. You capture a scrap about a useful technique. You test it during your work. It proves valuable. Now what? The scrap shouldn't live permanently in your haversack whilst also being documented in your work systems. That's duplication. The scrap served its purpose - it got you to test something. Once proven useful, it belongs in whatever system holds your working knowledge for that domain.

The haversack is a staging area, not a final destination. Scraps wait there until they're either used, proven, or discarded. Used scraps inform your work. Proven techniques get documented in professional systems. Discarded ideas get archived when they stop being relevant. The haversack stays current when scraps move through it, not by holding everything forever.

This matters especially during job hunting. You'll be collecting scraps about interview techniques, application strategies, industry trends. You run arcs building relevant skills. You create proof pieces.

Where does this material end up? Interview prep scraps inform your interviews, then get archived. Skill development scraps support your arcs, then either become proof pieces or get discarded. Industry trend scraps might feed into your CV or cover letters, serving their purpose and moving on.

Connection means your haversack links to what you're doing without creating parallel systems. When you spot a cluster pointing toward a useful capability, that cluster triggers an arc. The arc produces a proof piece. The proof piece goes in your portfolio or CV or wherever you keep demonstrable work. The original scraps that formed the cluster? They've served their purpose. Archive them or delete them. They don't need to live forever just because you captured them.

Some people struggle with this because it feels like throwing away knowledge. But you're not losing anything valuable. The knowledge became capability. The capability became proof. The proof serves your professional goals. The scraps were scaffolding. Once the structure stands, scaffolding comes down. That's efficient, not wasteful.

Watch what happens without proper connection. Your haversack fills with scraps about techniques you've already mastered and documented elsewhere. Review sessions become overwhelming because you're sorting through knowledge that should have moved into working practice months ago. You're maintaining the same information about stakeholder management in your haversack, in work documents, in training materials you created. That's bureaucracy, not organisation.

Connection also works in reverse. Useful insights from your professional systems can become scraps when they're worth capturing for future reference. You create a process improvement at work. Worth keeping a scrap about the approach in case it's useful elsewhere. You learn something valuable from a project. Capture it as a scrap even though it's documented in project files. The haversack holds personal learning, not comprehensive records of everything you've done.

The test for good connection is whether your systems feel separate or linked. If you're thinking "I should update my haversack" and "I should update my work docs" as two different tasks, they're not working together well. If updating your work naturally generates scraps worth capturing, and using scraps naturally feeds into your work, the connection is functioning.

This doesn't require complex workflows or automation. It just requires being intentional about what belongs where. Haversack holds scraps that might become useful. Work systems hold proven practices. Portfolio holds demonstrable results. Archives hold historical references. Each system has a job. Don't make them all do everything.

The haversack works well when it disappears into your natural workflow. You're not "doing haversack work" separately from "doing your job." You're working, and your haversack supports that work by capturing potentially useful scraps and helping you spot patterns. The connection is invisible because it's working.

Maintenance Becomes Habit

The best evolution happens when maintaining your haversack stops feeling deliberate. It just becomes part of how you work. This shift usually takes a few months of consistent practice, but once it happens, the system stops feeling like a separate tool and starts feeling like natural professional behaviour.

Getting there requires building sustainable routines rather than relying on motivation or discipline. The most effective approach is habit stacking, where you attach haversack maintenance to things you already do consistently.

For daily capture, link it to existing moments in your routine. After you check email each morning, spend thirty seconds capturing anything useful from yesterday. Before you leave work, note one thing worth remembering from today's conversations. During your commute, capture scraps from podcasts or articles you've been reading. The key is choosing attachment points that feel logical rather than forced. The new practice should enhance existing routines, not disrupt them.

Weekly review works the same way. If you already have coffee and read news on Saturday mornings, add haversack review to that relaxing routine. If you do meal planning on Sundays, include a quick knowledge review in that preparation time. Attach the practice to something you already do reliably, and it becomes nearly automatic.

You'll have periods when these routines lapse. Everyone does. Competing priorities emerge, circumstances change, or you just get tired and skip a few weeks. The key is getting back on track quickly rather than letting temporary lapses become permanent abandonment.

Notice when capture has been sporadic? Restart with the simplest possible approach. One scrap today beats elaborate plans to capture five scraps daily starting next week. When weekly reviews have been missed, do a brief catch-up session focusing on recent captures rather than trying to process everything you've missed. The goal is reestablishing momentum, not achieving perfect maintenance.

Most problems get solved through simplification rather than adding more structure. If capture feels burdensome, the bar is probably set too high. Lower expectations until the behaviour feels effortless, then gradually increase them as the routine becomes more automatic. If review feels pointless, you're probably not using what you've collected. Focus more on applying scraps to your work rather than just maintaining a theoretical collection.

The most successful haversack users develop compound practices where multiple behaviours support each other rather than competing for attention. Knowing you'll be reviewing scraps weekly makes you more likely to capture them thoughtfully during the week. Having useful scraps to review makes weekly sessions engaging rather than feeling like administrative work.

Capture routines that connect to review routines create compound benefits. Review routines that connect to integration create value for both activities. Identifying immediately applicable scraps during review makes it feel purposeful. When connection succeeds because of reviewed knowledge, it reinforces the value of regular reviews. These positive feedback loops make the entire system more sustainable.

The compound effect operates at multiple levels simultaneously. Daily capture builds pattern recognition that helps you notice valuable knowledge in situations where others see only routine activities. Weekly reviews build integration skills that help you apply learning more effectively. Monthly reflections build strategic thinking about your professional development priorities.

These meta-skills often prove more valuable than any specific knowledge you collect. The benefits accumulate gradually rather than appearing immediately. After a week of steady practice, you won't feel dramatically different. After a month, progress becomes more noticeable. After a year, the cumulative effect can be substantial. Small consistent practices compound into significant professional advantages over time.

This compound effect also applies to professional reputation. Colleagues notice when you consistently have useful suggestions, when you adapt to changes smoothly, when you seem to stay current without apparent effort. This reputation for competence and adaptability creates opportunities that aren't available to people who rely only on static expertise. Your haversack has evolved from basic crisis survival tool to sophisticated professional system. Now it needs to evolve one more time, from deliberate system to unconscious competence.

> When maintenance becomes routine, when integration becomes automatic, when the whole thing disappears into your natural workflow, that's when the system delivers maximum value with minimum effort.
>
> The ground will keep shifting. That's certain. What's also certain is that you now have a system that evolves with you, tools that adapt as

circumstances change, and practices that compound into lasting professional capability.

Chapter 16: Working with AI as a Partner

How AI tools can help you test, refine, and expand your haversack. Not a threat, an assistant.

This is the chapter that I almost didn't write.

Not because AI integration isn't relevant. In a book about navigating AI displacement, ignoring how AI might enhance your learning would be absurd. No, I nearly didn't write it because whatever I write about AI tools will probably be outdated before you finish reading this chapter. In the world of AI, new capabilities emerge weekly. Tools that seemed essential last month can often get replaced by something better by the end of the week. When it comes to AI, specific advice expires faster than sushi.

But here's the elephant in the room: you're reading about adapting to AI-driven workplace change whilst wondering whether you should be using AI to help you adapt. That's not just relevant. That's the entire point.

So this chapter exists, but it's deliberately ring-fenced. AI integration is optional, not required. Everything you learnt in Chapters 8 through 15 functions perfectly without AI. You can capture fragments and save them as scraps, spot clusters, run learning arcs, and build proof pieces using nothing more sophisticated than a notebook and your own thinking. No special tools required.

But if AI tools can accelerate pattern recognition, help synthesise scattered scraps, or provide low stakes testing for new capabilities, why wouldn't you use them strategically? The question isn't whether to use AI. It's how to use AI as enhancement rather than replacement for the human thinking that makes your haversack valuable.

The first time I used an AI tool to help with my haversack, I felt like I was cheating. I'd collected several fragments about project planning over the course of a month, but they were scattered notes that didn't quite connect into a coherent approach. Instead of spending hours trying to synthesise them myself, I fed them into ChatGPT and asked it to identify patterns and suggest a simple framework.

Within minutes, I had a structured approach combining my collected insights with additional context, making the whole thing more useful. The AI hadn't replaced my thinking. It had amplified it. The fragments were still mine, the context was still relevant to my specific work, but the organisation and synthesis had been accelerated dramatically.

That experience shifted how I think about AI in professional learning. Not as a replacement for human capability, but as a thinking partner that could help me process and apply information more effectively. Not a replacement for judgement, but a tool for enhancing it.

Since then, AI has become an integrated part of how I build and use my haversack. Not the most important part (the human elements of collection, reflection, and application remain central), but a valuable assistant that makes certain tasks more efficient.

What follows aren't step-by-step instructions for specific tools. Those would be obsolete before publication. Instead, you'll find principles for AI integration that should survive tool changes. How to use AI as a processing partner without outsourcing your thinking. The mistakes that undermine AI integration. The balanced partnership approach that enhances your capability rather than creating tool dependency.

Think of this chapter as future-proof guidance for a rapidly changing landscape. The specific AI tools will evolve. These principles won't.

AI as a Processing Partner

AI helps most when it processes scraps you've already collected. Not doing the thinking for you. Instead, accelerating the pattern recognition and organisation that would take longer with just manual review.

AI spots patterns across lots of text really well. When you've been collecting scraps for months and your haversack contains dozens or hundreds of items, manually reviewing everything to spot clusters could take hours. AI identifies recurring topics, related techniques, and gaps in what you've captured that might show you where to focus next.

Remember the healthcare administrator from Chapter 10 who was developing scheduling optimisation capabilities? She'd been capturing scraps for four months. A colleague's method for handling scheduling conflicts between departments. An article about patient flow optimisation. Notes from a meeting about appointment no-shows. Observations about which reminder systems worked. A case study about reducing wait times. Several bookmarked resources about staff scheduling efficiency.

Separately, these scraps looked completely unrelated. Just random captures about her changing work environment as the clinic expanded operations.

When she asked ChatGPT to review them together, the pattern became obvious. Multiple scraps were pointing toward the same capability area: "operational workflow optimisation in healthcare settings." Not basic scheduling (that's what the software handled) but the human judgement layer that sits on top of automation. Knowing when to override system recommendations for special cases. Coordinating between departments when priorities conflict. Explaining scheduling decisions to frustrated patients and staff. That cluster had been sitting in her haversack invisible until AI helped her spot it.

AI also pulls related scraps into something more coherent. Instead of scattered notes about stakeholder communication sitting in your haversack unused, you might use AI to organise them into a simple approach you can test. The AI provides initial structure. You decide whether that structure makes sense for your workplace.

What stays in your hands: choosing which scraps to examine, judging whether patterns the AI identifies matter for your work, deciding how to apply what you learn. AI processes while you guide and evaluate the output.

This works because AI handles what it does well (processing quickly, spotting connections across different scraps, suggesting organisational structures) whilst you handle what humans do well (understanding workplace context, judging quality, applying things practically). Neither replaces the other.

AI speeds up cluster recognition. Chapter 9's three-scrap rule still applies, but AI helps you spot those clusters when your haversack grows beyond easy manual scanning. It suggests ways to test new capabilities, the kind of low-stakes experimentation Chapter 10 covered. It helps organise evolved haversacks when volume outgrows simple systems, the strategic tool selection Chapter 15 discussed.

But AI can't collect the scraps that matter for your situation. Can't judge whether patterns are meaningful for your specific workplace. Can't apply knowledge to your work. That's all on you.

You stay in control. AI just processes faster.

Simple test: if your AI tool disappeared tomorrow, could you still maintain your haversack? If yes, you're using AI to boost what you do. If no, you've created dependency instead of building capability. The first one is the goal.

Five Ways This Goes Wrong

Using AI with your haversack sounds straightforward enough. It should speed up pattern recognition, help organise scraps, and test your understanding before you apply things at work. But there's a gap between "sounds straightforward" and "works well", where integration can go badly wrong.

The failures aren't random. They follow predictable patterns, and recognising those patterns helps you avoid them whilst building your own approach. When AI and the haversack method don't work well together, it's usually for one of five reasons.

What follows are five common traps worth watching for. Each shows you what goes wrong, why it happens, and how to fix it before damage gets done. These aren't theoretical problems. They're real failures that undermine the haversack method whilst making you feel productive.

One: Outsourcing Your Thinking

When you let AI do all the analytical work, you never develop your own pattern recognition and ability to connect scraps. Your haversack becomes a collection of raw material that requires AI processing to become useful. This creates reliance rather than enhancement.

Someone might capture dozens of scraps about process improvement, then ask AI to "analyse these and tell me what to learn." The AI produces a summary. They read it, feel informed, and move on. But they haven't developed the ability to spot patterns themselves. They haven't built the muscle for connecting scraps. They've outsourced the thinking that makes haversack work worthwhile.

The fix is using AI to accelerate your thinking, not replace it. Review your scraps manually first. Form initial impressions about patterns and clusters. Then use AI to test whether you've missed connections or to help organise what you've already identified. AI confirms or expands your analysis - it should never create your analysis from scratch.

Two: Accepting Everything Uncritically

AI has a dangerous quality; it can sound convincingly confident even when it's completely wrong. The technical term for this is "hallucination". It is when AI makes up facts that sound accurate but aren't. It can recommend approaches without accounting for your specific circumstances, and neglect important nuances that matter for your given situation. All whilst sounding completely authoritative.

When you accept AI outputs without filtering them through your own judgement and experience, you end up incorporating rubbish alongside genuine insights.

Someone asks AI to create a learning plan based on their collected scraps about data analysis. The AI suggests learning Python, SQL, and machine learning fundamentals. It produces a six-month curriculum that ignores the fact that this person works in accounts payable and just needs to verify automated invoice processing, not become a data scientist. The suggestion sounds authoritative. It's also completely inappropriate for their needs.

The fix is treating AI like a smart colleague who doesn't know your situation. Someone who offers useful perspectives, but whose suggestions need contextual filtering before they become useful.

Every AI suggestion should pass through three filters.

Does this make sense for my role?

Does this match my constraints?

Does this connect to work I do?

If any answer is no, then the suggestion should be requalified, modified or discarded regardless of how confident the AI seemed.

Three: Skipping the Practice

AI can explain concepts beautifully. You read the explanation, understand the logic, and feel like you've genuinely learnt something valuable. But understanding the concepts intellectually doesn't translate automatically into working capabilities. Only applied practice will build out those working skills.

Imagine someone who collects scraps about stakeholder communication. They ask AI to pull those scraps together into practical techniques, and the AI produces an excellent summary about different communication approaches. They read it, absorb the ideas, and feel reasonably prepared. Then they walk into their next stakeholder meeting and completely fumble the conversation because understanding communication theory in the abstract isn't the same as communicating effectively when you're under pressure and dealing with competing priorities.

The fix is remembering that AI can accelerate your learning, but it can't do the work for you. Whatever AI helps you understand still needs testing through real application, the kind of low-stakes experimentation Chapter 10 covered. Whatever AI helps you organise still needs validation through proof pieces that demonstrate actual capability in real situations. AI processing can make learning more efficient, but by and large, it can't replace the practice that turns intellectual understanding into something you can reliably use at work.

Four: Chasing the Latest Tools

Every week seems to bring additional news updates about new AI tools that are "better" than what is currently available. It is very easy to fall into the trap of chasing the new feature; it's a form of procrastination, not getting down to the actual work…

There is a real temptation to keep switching, constantly learning new interfaces and features, never quite developing fluency with any single approach. Your haversack work keeps restarting from zero because the tools keep changing.

Imagine someone who builds their entire haversack workflow around a specific AI tool's unique feature. It works brilliantly for six months. Then that tool changes its pricing model, removes the key features they relied on, or gets acquired and shut down entirely. Their whole system breaks. They have to rebuild from scratch using different tools because they'd optimised for tool-specific capabilities rather than transferable principles that would survive platform changes.

The fix is prioritising principles over specific tools (remember Chapter 15's migration trap warning). Basic ChatGPT used thoughtfully will generally beat fancy specialised tools used poorly. Simple AI use that can survive tool changes beats sophisticated workflows that break when platforms evolve. The goal is focusing on approaches that work across different AI tools rather than building workflows that require specific features from specific platforms.

Five: Creating AI Dependency

This one creeps up on you gradually. You start using AI for one part of your haversack work, then another, then another. Before long, your entire workflow requires AI at every step. Scrap collection gets fed through AI summarisation, pattern recognition relies on AI analysis, organisation depends on AI processing. What started as a helpful boost has become essential infrastructure. And that's when fragility enters your learning system.

Imagine someone who's built their weekly review entirely around AI. They export all their captures, feed everything to their preferred AI tool, read through the summary it produces, then file everything according to its organisational suggestions. On the surface, this feels efficient; they're getting through review sessions faster than before.

But they're not actually engaging with their scraps anymore. They're not forming their own impressions about patterns. They're not making their own decisions about what matters. The AI is doing the thinking whilst they're just executing its instructions.

Then something shifts. Maybe they're travelling somewhere without reliable internet access. Maybe the AI tool they depend on becomes temporarily unavailable due to technical issues. Maybe the pricing model changes substantially and the cost moves beyond what they can justify spending. Suddenly they can't maintain their haversack at all; not because the scraps aren't valuable, but because the human capability to process them has quietly atrophied from disuse.

The fix is building AI into your workflow as enhancement rather than foundation. Everything you do with AI should be something you could still manage manually if circumstances required it, just slower or perhaps less comprehensively. AI can make your haversack work more efficient and allow you to operate at larger scale; it shouldn't make your haversack dependent on its continued availability.

These five problems share something important: they all treat AI as replacement rather than enhancement. The approach that actually works inverts this relationship entirely. Your human judgement, your contextual understanding, your practical application stay at the centre. AI accelerates specific tasks within that human-centred process. Keep the relationship properly ordered and AI use builds genuine capability. Let it invert and you're building dependency instead.

The Future-Proof Approach

You've already built robust human processes for haversack work through Chapters 8 to 15. You can capture scraps, organise them appropriately, spot clustering patterns, run learning arcs, and build proof pieces. These capabilities are yours regardless of which tools exist or become available.

Now you can add AI strategically where it genuinely helps - accelerating pattern recognition when your haversack grows beyond comfortable manual review, organising complex clusters into initial frameworks you can then refine through experience, providing low-stakes testing for new capabilities before workplace application, filling context gaps in scraps you captured quickly.

But you maintain the ability to work without it. Your haversack doesn't require AI to function properly; AI just makes certain tasks more efficient when it's available.

Think about the QA specialist from Chapter 14 who maintained her haversack through job loss crisis. She occasionally used AI to help process the unusual volume of scraps she was capturing whilst job hunting under pressure. But her core system (identifying what to capture, recognising what mattered, applying scraps to real situations) remained entirely human. AI accelerated her processing during a particularly high-stress period; it didn't become essential infrastructure she couldn't function without.

That's the balanced partnership this chapter advocates for. Using AI as a useful assistant when it genuinely helps, but human judgement and capability as the foundation regardless of which tools happen to be available at any given time. Enhancement rather than replacement. Acceleration rather than dependency. Strategic use rather than comprehensive integration.

Four principles anchor this approach, and they should remain stable regardless of which AI tools exist or how dramatically they evolve:

You set the goals, AI processes the options. Be explicit about what you're trying to achieve before engaging AI. Instead of asking "analyse my scraps and tell me what to focus on," try something more directed: "I'm trying to develop capability in this specific area - which of these scraps seem most relevant to that goal?" If AI suggested something completely different from your current priorities, you'd follow your own judgement rather than the AI's recommendation. That's the right relationship to maintain.

AI should accelerate tasks you can already do manually. If you genuinely can't perform a task without AI assistance, you probably don't understand it well enough to perform it effectively with AI either. Before integrating AI into any haversack task, demonstrate to yourself that you can complete that task manually first. Then use AI to do it faster, perhaps more thoroughly, or at larger scale.

Filter everything through your specific context. AI doesn't know your workplace culture, your particular role constraints, your manager's current priorities, your team's ongoing challenges, or the political dynamics that make some approaches feasible whilst rendering others completely impossible. Generic advice needs careful translation through your contextual understanding before it becomes genuinely useful in your situation.

Measure actual outcomes rather than usage activity. The question that matters isn't "how much AI am I using" but rather "is my AI integration genuinely improving outcomes?" Tracking how many AI sessions you run per week or how many scraps you've processed through AI tells you nothing useful about whether this is actually helping.

What matters is whether you're spotting useful clusters faster than you were before. Whether you're building practical skills more effectively. Whether your proof pieces are getting stronger. Whether your professional adaptation is genuinely accelerating in ways you can point to.

If you're using AI sparingly but it's demonstrably helping, that's better than using it constantly whilst accomplishing very little.

The AI landscape will likely keep evolving faster than almost any other part of your professional environment; that much seems certain. New capabilities will emerge regularly. Current tools will change substantially or disappear entirely. Specific techniques that work well today will probably become obsolete at some point in time down the road.

What won't change is your ongoing need for adaptive capability that can survive tool changes and platform evolution. Your haversack method works fundamentally because it's based on human learning principles that tend to remain stable across technological disruption. AI integration should enhance that stability rather than undermining it.

Use AI strategically and keep it genuinely optional. Measure its actual impact rather than just its usage. Always maintain your human agency and judgement. Build your haversack for enhancement rather than dependency.

That approach should survive whatever comes next.

You've now worked through the entire haversack system. The philosophy of temperance learning that prevents burnout whilst maintaining forward momentum. The practical mechanics of capturing scraps, spotting clusters, and running focused arcs. The strategies for navigating setbacks, evolving your tools as needs change, and working alongside AI without creating dependency.

Chapter 17 addresses what you've actually built through using this method; the transformation that happens when these practices stop being deliberate tasks and become simply how you operate as a professional. The shift from emergency response to sustainable operating system.

When you're ready to start implementing what you've learnt, the Appendix provides your structured 30-day guide. It walks you through building your haversack from scratch, day by day, following two professionals as they navigate their first month of systematic adaptation. Not theoretical frameworks, but practical daily actions that fit within real constraints. Everything you need to begin today.

Chapter 17: What You've Built

The haversack method isn't just for crisis. It can become your professional operating system.

The 30-day challenge in the Appendix is an implementation guide that will give you everything you need to start building your haversack today. But completing that challenge raises a question that most productivity books conveniently ignore. What happens when it's not a structured 30-day project but simply how you work?

This is where many other methods fail. They provide brilliant frameworks for implementation but nothing for integration. You finish the challenge, feel accomplished, then gradually drift back to old patterns because nobody explained what "making this permanent" actually looks like.

The haversack method strives to be different because it's designed from the start for integration rather than just implementation. After months of maintaining your haversack, capturing scraps can stop feeling like a task and become as automatic as checking your phone. After completing several arcs, you might stop thinking "I need to run a learning arc" and start naturally spotting opportunities to build capabilities.

This matters particularly in the era of AI displacement that prompted this book. When automation is eliminating roles faster than traditional career advice can adapt, when your expertise might become less relevant within months rather than years, when the ground keeps shifting beneath your professional feet, you need systems that work continuously, not just during scheduled learning periods.

This chapter addresses what you're building through using the method. It's the psychological transformation that happens when these practices shift from deliberate effort to natural, muscle memory professional behaviour in a world where continuous adaptation isn't optional.

It's about understanding the shift from emergency tool to operating system. It's about recognising what professional fears the method addresses. Identity fear when expertise becomes less relevant, security fear when you can't predict which skills stay valuable, competence fear when you doubt your ability to adapt fast enough. These aren't abstract anxieties; they're rational responses to genuine AI-driven workplace disruption.

Most importantly, it's about developing a portable professional identity. Traditional identity ties to specific roles or companies. The haversack method will help you build something more durable; identity based on capabilities and approaches rather than job titles. Your scraps travel with you. Your completed arcs demonstrate adaptive capability regardless of current employment. No employer can take your adaptation system. When AI removes or disrupts your role, it can't eliminate your ability to adapt.

The ground won't stop shifting. Continuous change is the permanent reality of professional life now. The question isn't whether you can survive one disruption; it's whether you've built sustainable systems for navigating continuous disruption without burning out.

You have those systems. This chapter explores what they look like when they're not crisis responses but simply how you work.

Beyond Emergency Response

The haversack method isn't meant to be a crisis response you use once then abandon. The goal is evolution from deliberate practice to unconscious competence. Understanding that evolution matters because it changes how you think about the work you've done through this book.

If you maintain your haversack over months, capturing scraps can stop feeling like a task. It might become as automatic as checking your phone. You notice a useful technique in a conversation and add it to your collection without conscious decision. After completing several arcs, you might stop thinking "I need to run a learning arc" and instead, start naturally spotting opportunities to build capabilities.

Remember the facilities coordinator from Chapter 10 who used scraps to spot a potential HVAC failure? Or the QA specialist from Chapter 14 who maintained her haversack through redundancy whilst job hunting? Neither of them treats their haversack as a separate activity anymore. It's woven into how they work. They review their scraps whilst planning their week. They spot clustering patterns whilst preparing for challenging projects. The boundaries between learning and working dissolve because learning becomes integral to how they approach professional challenges.

This transformation doesn't happen overnight, and it never feels complete in the sense of requiring no further development. But there comes a time when being able to adapt feels as natural as any other job skill; something you do without thinking about it.

The haversack approach can become a part of who you are as a professional instead of just a tool you use sometimes. You can learn to deal with uncertainty in a calm and deliberate way instead of getting overly anxious. A person who sees professional growth as a path that never ends, not just a sequence of separate accomplishments.

This matters particularly when facing AI displacement. You don't just get over the disruption and go back to normal. We're in for continuous evolution where roles keep changing, industry keeps shifting, and the capabilities that mattered last year might become less relevant this year and next. Emergency responses work for emergencies. Ongoing challenges require ongoing systems.

What Travels with You

Traditional professional identity ties to specific roles and companies. Your identity becomes your job title, your employer, your place in the organisational hierarchy. That can provide comfort and clarity throughout a career; it gives you a clear sense of who you are professionally and where you fit. But it also creates vulnerability. When AI displacement removes roles or company restructuring changes the work that remains, that entire sense of professional self can collapse along with it.

The haversack method helps you build something different; a sense of professional self-based on what you can demonstrate rather than what your business card says. Its identity built on capabilities you've developed, problems you can solve, and value you create. This travels with you regardless of which company employs you or whether your current role exists next year.

Your scraps represent knowledge that isn't tied to one company's systems; they're patterns you've noticed, techniques you've captured, insights that transfer across different contexts. When you leave a job, your scraps leave with you. Your completed arcs prove you can identify what needs learning and build working competence within weeks. That adaptive capability works across different contexts, different industries, different circumstances.

Your proof pieces demonstrate what you can do through tangible examples that get past ATS algorithms and into conversations with decision-makers. They're evidence rather than assertions, and they speak for themselves.

When AI removes or disrupts your role, it takes your job title and organisational standing. It doesn't take your ability to capture what matters, run learning arcs, or build demonstrable capabilities. Those remain yours.

You can't predict which roles survive or which companies thrive, but you can build capabilities that work regardless. That's what the haversack method creates; not security through expertise that might become obsolete, but security through demonstrated adaptability that keeps building on itself.

What defines you professionally shifts from being about what you currently do to being about what you can learn and demonstrate when circumstances demand it. That works in any role, any industry, any employment situation because it's not tied to one job title or one company or one moment in time.

When the ground shifts, your capabilities shift with you. That's what you've been building.

The Next Horizon

As this book ends, your journey with these approaches is just starting. The concepts and techniques you've read about provide starting points rather than final destinations. How you adapt and apply them will depend on your specific circumstances, your preferences, and the challenges you're facing in your professional life.

The haversack you build will look different from everyone else's because it reflects your unique combination of interests, opportunities, and needs. The learning arcs you pursue will address problems and goals that matter to your particular situation. The confidence you build will be based on your own experiences of successful adaptation rather than abstract assurance.

You have the philosophy of temperance that helps you find balance between paralysis and being overwhelmed. You have your haversack for collecting and using what matters as you encounter it. You have techniques for turning learning into capability and capability into confidence. Most importantly, you have practical approaches that work not just in theory but in the reality of professional life where deadlines matter, relationships count, and results are expected.

The world will keep shifting; that's not a temporary condition that will eventually stabilise. It's the permanent reality of professional life now. But that's not a catastrophe to be feared. It's simply the condition under which you're learning to navigate.

The path ahead remains uncertain, but you're no longer walking it empty-handed. When the next disruption hits (and it will), you won't be starting from zero. You'll have a system for capturing what matters, building capabilities that create value, and demonstrating competence in ways that get noticed.

The Appendix gives you the 30-day implementation guide when you're ready to start. Not someday when things settle down. Today, if you choose. The ground keeps moving whether you're ready or not. The difference now is that you are.

Look, if the insights and approaches within these pages have given you pause for thought in how you're going to approach your future upskilling, do something for me. Tell someone else who's struggling with the same thing. Your colleague who's worried about their role changing. Your friend who's panicking about AI displacement. The person in your network who needs practical guidance instead of platitudes. Millions of professionals are facing AI disruption without systems for adapting. If you think what you've read here might help them, then please, pass it on.

The ground keeps moving. That's what ground does now. But armed with the Haversack Method, you've learned to walk on moving ground without losing your balance, your direction, or your sense of purpose.

The End.

APPENDIX: Your 30-Day Challenge Implementation Guide

Introduction

This implementation guide is designed to be used, not just read. If you are reading this book cover-to-cover, you may want to finish Chapter 17 first, then return here when you're ready to start your 30 days.

Throughout this book, you've explored the Haversack Method as a practical response to AI-driven workplace displacement. You've read about temperance learning philosophy, the mechanics of capturing scraps and running arcs, strategies for navigating setbacks, and ways to work alongside AI tools. But reading about a method and actually implementing it are very different challenges. This guide bridges that gap by showing what systematic adaptation looks like when practised consistently over 30 days.

It follows two people you've already met through the book as they work through their first month of building a haversack whilst navigating AI changes in their roles. One is adapting within an existing position. The other is building capabilities whilst job hunting between roles.

These aren't documentation of real people who've completed a formal 30-day challenge. They're simulations based on the principles and practices covered throughout the book, showing how the method might work under real constraints: limited time, competing priorities, uncertainty about whether small daily actions will make meaningful difference. The scenarios are realistic because they're built from the same workplace pressures and AI displacement anxieties that prompted this book.

What follows is a detailed walkthrough of how the method could work in practice over thirty days. You'll see how they might capture scraps, spot patterns, run focused arcs, and create proof pieces. Your 30 days will look different from these examples. Different scraps, different clusters, different arcs, different proof pieces. That's how it should work. The method adapts to your situation rather than forcing your situation to adapt to the method.

The Challenge Structure

The 30-day challenge combines all elements of temperance learning into one experience: building a working haversack, establishing sustainable capture and review habits, completing a focused learning arc, and creating proof that demonstrates developing capabilities.

The challenge moves through four weekly phases:

Week 1: Foundation Building

Set up your haversack and establish basic capture habits

Week 2: Habit Development

Build review routines and identify learning arc opportunities

Week 3: Focused Learning

Execute a short learning arc with specific outcomes

Week 4: Integration and Proof

Apply what you've learned and document results

Each week builds on the previous whilst remaining manageable within busy schedules. The cumulative effect should feel substantial without requiring unsustainable effort.

Pre-Challenge Preparation

This section shows how preparation might work by following two people you've already met through the book. We'll see what their 30-day challenge could look like if they decided to test the method systematically.

Again, remember the facilities coordinator from Chapter 10 who built momentum through small wins?

He's watching AI automate parts of his job. Building management systems now handle routine maintenance scheduling that used to need his experience. His role isn't disappearing, but it's changing fast enough to make him uneasy.

Before starting, he'd spend an hour getting ready - just practical decisions about tools and focus. His haversack would be a section in the notebook he already carries for site inspections. He's constantly moving between buildings, checking equipment, meeting contractors. Digital doesn't work well in basement plant rooms or on rooftops. Physical makes sense.

His learning focus would be simple: get to know the AI building systems well enough to work alongside them. The software is good at routine jobs, but it falls short once things get complicated. It can't see that maintenance clashes with a planned refurbishment. It doesn't know how to manage a tricky contractor relationship. It won't weigh short-term savings against long-term reliability. That's where his judgement matters.

For him, success would mean reviewing the system's recommendations, spotting the gaps, and stepping in when human judgement is needed. He'd keep a record of the issues he caught that the software missed. Over time, the worry about being replaced would shift into confidence, because he'd see exactly where his knowledge makes the difference.

To make it practical, he'd ring-fence ten to fifteen minutes a day for jotting scraps and quick reviews.

Saturday mornings get 30 minutes for deeper work. He'd ask a colleague to check in occasionally.

Remember the QA specialist from Chapter 14 who kept her haversack running through redundancy? What if she turned her job-hunting period into a structured 30-day challenge?

Three months after redundancy, she's balancing applications with building new capabilities. The uncertainty is real, but so is her determination. Her situation captures the other archetype: proving competence whilst between roles rather than adapting within an existing one.

Her haversack lives in a laptop document because job hunting happens at home. Her target is immediate: automation testing skills with proof pieces for interviews - actual code samples, test scenarios, documentation rather than CV assertions.

Success means completing learning arcs that produce work she can show people, having concrete examples for interview discussions, feeling confident about learning whatever tools a new employer uses. What starts as job-loss fragility ends as steady professional identity.

Her time looks different from the facilities coordinator's approach. Longer focused sessions when job hunting allows (maybe an hour or two between applications). But keeping rhythm even on interview-heavy days, even if that's just 15 minutes reviewing scraps. Staying consistent matters more than achieving perfection.

Whether you're still in your role or between roles, the preparation principles remain the same. Choose tools you already use. Pick capabilities that actually help your situation. Set success measures you can observe easily. Protect realistic amounts of time. Find someone for occasional feedback.

An hour of preparation creates the conditions for progress. What matters most is not elaborate planning, but actually starting.

Week 1: Foundation Building

The first week isn't about building comprehensive systems or developing new capabilities. It's about establishing one habit: noticing fragments in your daily work and saving the valuable ones as scraps before they disappear.

Day 1: Haversack Setup

The facilities coordinator would start by creating his haversack. He'd already decided during preparation to use his site inspection notebook, but now he'd need to actually set it up. Monday morning, before heading out to the first building, he'd flip to a fresh section near the back, write "Haversack" at the top of the page, and date it.

That's it. Nothing elaborate. Just a designated space for scraps, clearly marked so he'd know where to capture things throughout the day. He'd keep the notebook in his jacket pocket where he could reach it quickly.

The QA specialist would take a different approach. She'd open her laptop, create a new document called "Haversack - Automation Testing," and save it to her desktop where she'd see it every time she opened her computer. She'd type today's date at the top and add a simple header: "Scraps."

Setup complete in under two minutes. The point isn't creating something sophisticated. The point is having a specific place ready when fragments worth capturing appear.

Days 2-4: Initial Captures

The facilities coordinator's first capture would come unexpectedly. Walking across the car park toward the main building on Tuesday morning, he'd overhear two contractors discussing a scheduling conflict the automated system created. Something about overlapping maintenance windows the algorithm hadn't caught. He'd pull out his notebook, flip to his haversack section, and write it down. Twenty seconds. Nothing profound, just something potentially useful that would vanish by lunchtime if he didn't note it.

His early scraps would come from unexpected places. A supplier mentions offshoring concerns during a phone call - captured. An industry newsletter headline about predictive maintenance crosses his screen whilst eating lunch - captured. His manager uses a phrase about "algorithm-assisted oversight" in a budget meeting - captured.

None of these would feel particularly significant in the moment. That's not the point. The point is developing the recognition muscle: this might matter, save it now, assess value later.

The QA specialist's first captures would look different. Preparing for an interview, she'd notice the job description mentions "comfort with AI-assisted testing tools." She'd open her haversack document and type that phrase. Then she'd look at three more job postings. Each mentions AI or automation differently. She'd capture those variations. Four scraps in fifteen minutes, all pointing toward language she'd need for interviews.

Different contexts, same principle: notice fragments, save valuable ones as scraps, don't overthink it.

Days 5-6: Finding Natural Moments

By Thursday, the facilities coordinator would be paying attention to when capturing felt effortless versus when it felt forced. After site inspections works well - he'd already have his notebook out. Brief lulls during contractor meetings give him time to jot down useful techniques someone mentioned. The drive home sometimes surfaces thoughts about problems he encountered.

He'd notice he captures more scraps when his notebook is immediately accessible. The jacket pocket placement is working. He'd give himself thirty seconds after meetings or calls before moving to the next task - just enough time to capture anything worth saving.

The QA specialist would find her natural moments differently. Reading technical articles triggers multiple captures as she notices patterns in how automation testing gets discussed. Mock interview prep with a friend surfaces gaps in her knowledge - she'd capture each gap as a scrap, potential learning targets. Even rejection emails sometimes contain useful information about what companies actually seek.

Day 7: Light Organisation

Saturday morning, coffee in hand, the facilities coordinator would spend fifteen minutes reviewing his week's captures. Eleven scraps scattered through his haversack section. Some seem related. Others feel like random observations.

Patterns would emerge immediately. Four scraps relate to AI system limitations - things the algorithms struggle with. Three address contractor relationship management. Two cover strategic planning issues. Two are random observations that don't fit anywhere yet.

He wouldn't create elaborate categorisation systems. Just write "AI Limits," "Contractors," and "Strategy" at the top of three fresh pages, then copy relevant scraps under each heading. The two random scraps stay where they are. Maybe they'd find a home later. Maybe they wouldn't matter.

The QA specialist's review would reveal different patterns. Seven of her thirteen scraps relate to language used in job descriptions and interviews. Four cover specific technical capabilities companies seek. Two discuss workplace changes driven by AI tools.

She'd create two simple categories: "Interview Language" and "Technical Capabilities." Clean divisions that make sense for her immediate needs. The two scraps about workplace changes get their own small section labelled "Context" - useful background even if not directly applicable to job applications yet.

Both would end their first week recognising something important: patterns are already emerging. The scraps aren't random. They're clustering around specific themes. Those clusters will matter in Week 2.

Week 2: Habit Development and Arc Planning

The second week builds on the foundation by establishing review routines whilst identifying specific learning opportunities that could form the basis for learning arcs in Week 3.

Days 8-10: Review Habit Building

Monday morning of Week 2, the facilities coordinator would continue daily captures whilst adding something new: a brief weekly review. He'd already done light organisation on Saturday, but now he'd start examining his scraps more deliberately, looking for connections and gaps.

During his Tuesday lunch break, he'd flip through his haversack and notice something interesting. The four scraps under "AI Limits" weren't just random observations. They pointed toward a pattern: the building management system struggled consistently with situations involving multiple overlapping factors. Single-variable decisions worked fine. Complex scenarios with competing priorities broke down.

That insight wouldn't have been visible from individual scraps. It emerged from reviewing them together.

The QA specialist would approach reviews differently. Wednesday afternoon between applications, she'd open her haversack document and read through everything she'd captured. Her "Interview Language" section had grown to nine scraps, and reading them together revealed something useful: companies weren't actually asking for AI expertise. They were asking for comfort working alongside AI tools. Different requirement. Different preparation needed.

She'd add a note to that section: "They want collaboration skills, not technical mastery." That distinction would shape how she talked about her capabilities in interviews.

Days 11-13: Arc Opportunity Identification

By midweek, both would start thinking about potential learning arcs for Week 3. Not committing yet, just generating options based on what their scraps were revealing.

The facilities coordinator's "AI Limits" cluster suggested an obvious arc opportunity: spend time actually using the building management system's recommendation engine, deliberately testing it with complex scenarios to understand exactly where human oversight matters most. Not reading documentation or taking courses. Hands-on experimentation with the actual system he'd be working alongside.

He'd jot down three potential arc topics in his haversack: "Test AI system with complex maintenance scenarios," "Document contractor relationship patterns the system misses," "Map strategic planning decisions requiring human judgement." All possibilities. He wouldn't choose yet.

The QA specialist's review would surface different opportunities. Her "Technical Capabilities" scraps showed three skills appearing repeatedly in job descriptions: test automation frameworks, API testing, and performance testing. She had some experience with the first, none with the others.

She'd write down potential arcs: "Build basic API testing examples," "Learn performance testing fundamentals," "Create test automation portfolio pieces." Real options based on what employers actually sought, not what sounded impressive.

Day 14: Arc Selection and Planning

The facilities coordinator would choose "Test AI system with complex maintenance scenarios." Specific, achievable in a week, directly relevant to his role. His simple plan: spend 30-45 minutes daily next week deliberately feeding complex scenarios into the building management system, documenting where recommendations break down, identifying patterns in what the algorithm misses.

Success would mean having concrete examples of scenarios requiring human intervention and understanding why the system struggles with them. Not mastery of the software. Just enough knowledge to work alongside it effectively.

The QA specialist would choose "Build basic API testing examples." More focused than learning everything about performance testing, more immediately demonstrable than abstract framework knowledge. Her plan: spend an hour daily building simple API tests using tools mentioned in job descriptions, creating three working examples she could show in interviews.

Success would mean having actual code samples demonstrating API testing capability. Proof pieces, not claims.

Both would keep their plans minimal but clear. One page of notes covering the goal, approach, daily time commitment, and success criteria. Nothing elaborate. Just enough structure to prevent Week 3 from drifting into vague intentions.

The second week would end with both having established review rhythms, identified clustering patterns in their scraps, and committed to specific learning arcs for the following week. The foundation from Week 1 was evolving into focused capability building.

Week 3: Focused Learning Arc

The third week is where temperance learning demonstrates its practical value through a focused learning arc that turns interest into capability. This week should feel more intensive than the previous weeks whilst remaining manageable within your regular schedule.

Remember temperance learning from Section Two (the approach that balances doing nothing with attempting everything). Week 3 applies that philosophy through short, focused arcs targeting specific capabilities rather than comprehensive mastery, using timeframes that fit actual schedules and producing outcomes you can demonstrate when finished.

The scraps both captured in Week 1 revealed patterns. Week 2's reviews identified specific capabilities worth building. Now Week 3 executes learning arcs based on those discoveries - not because someone told them what to learn, but because their own observations showed what mattered for their situations.

This is how the haversack method works in practice:

Notice, Cluster, Focus, Build.

Days 15-17: Arc Initiation

Monday morning, the facilities coordinator would begin testing the building management system with complex scenarios. He'd start simply: feed the system a maintenance request that conflicted with a scheduled refurbishment. The algorithm recommended proceeding with maintenance during the refurbishment window - clearly wrong. He'd document that in his haversack: "System doesn't check refurbishment calendar before scheduling."

Tuesday, he'd try a different scenario: overlapping contractor requirements where timing mattered. The system scheduled both contractors for the same access point simultaneously. Another miss. He'd capture the pattern: "Algorithm treats each task independently, doesn't model resource conflicts."

Wednesday brought a more subtle test: maintenance timing where deferral would save significant cost but the system's efficiency metrics penalised delays. The algorithm recommended immediate action despite the financial waste. He'd note: "Optimises for speed metrics, ignores cost-benefit trade-offs."

Three days in, patterns were emerging. The system excelled at straightforward scheduling but failed when competing priorities required judgement about relative importance.

The QA specialist would spend Monday setting up her development environment for API testing. She'd chosen a popular tool mentioned in job descriptions and spent an hour working through basic examples. Nothing impressive yet, just getting comfortable with syntax and structure.

Tuesday, she'd build her first actual test: a simple API call validating response structure. Twenty lines of code that worked. She'd save it as "Example_1_Basic_Validation.py" in a portfolio folder. Small, but demonstrable.

Wednesday, she'd create a second example: testing error handling when APIs receive invalid data. Slightly more sophisticated. Another working piece of code saved. Her portfolio was growing.

Days 18-20: Application and Refinement

Thursday, the facilities coordinator would test more complex scenarios, deliberately looking for edge cases where human oversight mattered. A maintenance request during holiday periods when contractor availability was limited. Equipment failure requiring emergency response versus routine maintenance the system treated identically. Strategic decisions about replacement timing based on budget cycles the algorithm couldn't see.

Each test would reveal something about where his judgement added value. He'd capture the patterns, noting which types of complexity the system handled and which required human intervention.

Friday, he'd review his week's documentation and notice something useful: three categories of situations consistently needed human oversight. Scenarios involving organisational context the system lacked, decisions requiring trade-offs between competing priorities, situations where timing depended on factors outside the maintenance schedule itself.

The QA specialist would spend Thursday and Friday building her third example: testing authentication flows. More complex than the first two, requiring multiple API calls in sequence. She'd struggle with it Thursday, getting frustrated when tests failed. Friday afternoon, she'd figure out the sequencing issue and get it working. That struggle and solution would both go into her documentation - showing problem-solving, not just perfect execution.

Day 21: Arc Completion

Saturday, both would complete their learning arcs by creating simple demonstrations of what they'd built. The facilities coordinator would write a one-page summary in his haversack: "Where AI Building Management Needs Human Oversight." Three categories of scenarios, specific examples of each, patterns he'd identified about algorithm limitations. Nothing fancy. Just clear documentation of what he'd learnt through hands-on testing. He could show this to his manager if needed, explaining exactly where his judgement complemented the automated system.

The QA specialist would organise her three code examples into a simple GitHub repository. Each example would have clear comments explaining what it tested and why. She'd write a brief README describing the portfolio pieces. Total time invested across the week: about seven hours. Output: demonstrable capability she could discuss in interviews and link from her CV.

Both would document lessons learnt during their arcs. The facilities manager noted that hands-on experimentation taught him more in a week than months of wondering about the system's limitations. The QA specialist realised that building simple working examples proved more valuable than trying to master every aspect of API testing comprehensively.

Week 3 would end with both having completed focused learning arcs that produced tangible outcomes. Not expertise. Not mastery. Just working capability built efficiently through deliberate practice on specific, achievable targets.

The foundation from Week 1, the planning from Week 2, and the execution in Week 3 had created something demonstrable. Week 4 would focus on integrating these capabilities and creating proof pieces that could be shown to others.

Week 4: Integration and Proof Building

The final week focuses on consolidating learning whilst creating evidence that demonstrates the value of the 30-day challenge. This isn't about perfecting what you've built. It's about integrating new capabilities into regular work and creating proof pieces that show others what you can do.

Days 22-24: Application Integration

Monday morning, the facilities coordinator would start applying his Week 3 learning in actual work situations. When the building management system flagged routine maintenance during a planned refurbishment, he'd recognise the pattern immediately - the algorithm missing organisational context. He'd override the recommendation, reschedule appropriately, and document the intervention in his haversack.

Tuesday brought a contractor scheduling conflict the system hadn't caught. He'd spot it during his morning review of automated recommendations, adjust the schedule, and note another example of where his judgement added value the algorithm couldn't provide.

Wednesday, he'd review three weeks of system recommendations with his new understanding. Patterns stood out clearly now. Some recommendations needed no human input. Others required consistent oversight. He was developing instincts about which automated decisions to trust and which to scrutinise carefully.

The QA specialist would spend Monday updating her CV and LinkedIn profile with her new API testing capability. Not vague claims about being adaptable, but a link to her GitHub repository showing working code examples. Three proof pieces demonstrating actual capability.

Tuesday, she'd have an interview. When asked about API testing experience, she wouldn't say "I'm learning about it" or "I'm comfortable with new technologies. She'd pull up her repository, walk through one of her examples, explain the testing scenario and why it mattered. Demonstrable capability, not assertions.

Wednesday, she'd apply for two positions that specifically mentioned API testing. Her application would reference the repository directly. Proof that she could already do what they needed, not promises that she could learn it if hired.

Days 25-27: Proof Creation

Thursday, the facilities coordinator would create his proof piece: a one-page guide for colleagues titled "Working Effectively with AI Building Management." Three sections covering when to trust automated recommendations, situations requiring human oversight, and patterns indicating algorithm limitations. Written for other facilities staff, not technical experts.

He'd base it entirely on his three weeks of systematic testing and documentation. Real examples from their actual building management system. Practical guidance anyone on his team could use immediately.

Friday, he'd share the draft with the colleague who'd been checking in on his progress. The feedback was immediate: "This is exactly what we need. Can you present this at the next team meeting?"

The QA specialist would spend Thursday and Friday refining her proof pieces. She'd add more detailed comments to her code examples, making them clearer for reviewers who might not be familiar with the specific testing framework. She'd improve her README file, explaining not just what each example did but why those particular scenarios mattered for API testing.

Saturday, she'd record a brief video walkthrough of one example, explaining her thought process whilst building it. Two minutes showing how she approached the problem, what she tested, and why. Another proof piece for her portfolio.

Days 28-30: Challenge Assessment

Sunday morning, both would spend time reviewing their entire 30-day experience.

The facilities coordinator would flip through his haversack from Day 1 to Day 28. Sixty-three scraps captured. Patterns identified. One focused learning arc completed. A practical guide created that his team would actually use. More importantly, a systematic approach to working alongside AI that reduced his anxiety whilst increasing his confidence.

He'd write a brief assessment: "What worked - daily capturing became automatic after Week 1. Weekly reviews revealed patterns I wouldn't have spotted otherwise. Week 3's focused arc was more valuable than six months of worrying about automation. What needs adjustment - could capture more scraps during contractor meetings, need better system for reviewing complex scenarios."

Most important realisation: he wasn't learning how to compete with AI. He was learning how to work alongside it effectively, adding value where the algorithms fell short. That shift in perspective changed everything.

The QA specialist would review her laptop haversack document. Seventy-one scraps. Two clear categories that shaped her job search strategy. One learning arc that produced three demonstrable proof pieces. An interview where she'd shown capability rather than claimed it. Two job applications strengthened by actual work rather than CV assertions.

She'd note what worked: "Capturing job description language helped me understand what companies actually wanted. Building simple examples proved more valuable than trying to master everything. Creating proof pieces shifted interviews from 'Can you do this?' to 'Here's how I do this.'"

Key insight: she'd stopped feeling like someone scrambling to stay relevant and started feeling like someone who could systematically build whatever capabilities circumstances required. That confidence came from evidence, not hope.

Monday morning - Day 30 - both would decide what came next. The 30-day challenge was complete, but the method continued. Habits established. Systems proven. Confidence earned through practical experience rather than abstract assurance.

The facilities manager would start a new scrap section: "Advanced AI Oversight." Already thinking about his next learning arc.

The QA specialist would begin Week 5 of job hunting with her haversack still open, still capturing, still building. The challenge ended. The adaptation continued.

Daily Minimums and Weekly Goals

The 30-day challenge works because it establishes sustainable baselines rather than demanding heroic effort. Understanding your minimums prevents missed days from derailing the entire challenge.

Daily Minimums (Every Day):

Capture at least one scrap. Target: 30 seconds. This might be a single observation during a meeting, one headline from an article, one phrase a colleague mentions. The goal is maintaining the recognition habit, not building comprehensive knowledge.

The facilities manager kept this standard even on his busiest days - site emergencies, back-to-back contractor meetings, equipment failures demanding immediate attention. One scrap captured. Habit maintained.

The QA specialist-maintained captures even on interview days when her schedule felt chaotic. Between preparing, travelling, and recovering from interviews, she'd capture at least one observation about what companies were actually seeking or how conversations revealed capability gaps.

Weekly Minimums:

One 15-minute review session. Not elaborate analysis. Just reading through the week's scraps, adding context where needed, noting any patterns emerging. This is the session that reveals clustering and identifies arc opportunities.

Saturday morning worked for the facilities manager. Sunday afternoon suited the QA specialist's unpredictable job-hunting schedule. The specific day matters less than protecting the time consistently.

These minimums are deliberately conservative. Most days you'll exceed them. Week 3's arc work requires more time. Week 4's proof creation demands focused effort. But having low baseline expectations means you can maintain momentum even when circumstances constrain your available time.

The goal isn't perfect execution. The goal is building habits that survive real-world pressures.

Common Challenge Obstacles

Understanding typical obstacles helps you prepare responses rather than abandoning the challenge when difficulties arise.

Time Pressure emerges as the most frequent obstacle. Remember that daily minimums take 30 seconds to two minutes. Weekly reviews need 15 minutes. Week 3's arc requires 30-45 minutes daily for seven days. If time becomes genuinely scarce, reduce scope rather than stopping entirely. One scrap captured daily maintains momentum better than elaborate plans that get abandoned.

The facilities coordinator faced this during Week 2 when two major equipment failures consumed his schedule. He maintained daily captures but postponed his weekly review by two days. The challenge continued.

Motivation Lapses happen to everyone. Focus on maintaining minimums rather than optimal performance during low-motivation periods. The QA specialist experienced this after a particularly discouraging interview in Week 3. She captured one scrap that evening and nothing more. Next day, rhythm resumed.

Perfectionism kills more challenges than time pressure. Your haversack will be messy. Your learning arc won't be comprehensive. Your proof pieces won't be polished. Functional implementations beat perfect plans that never get executed. The facilities manager's one-page guide wasn't elegant, but his team used it immediately.

Competing priorities are permanent features of professional life, not temporary obstacles. Use existing transition times for challenge activities rather than creating new time slots. The QA specialist captured scraps whilst waiting for interviews to start, during lunch breaks between applications, in the evening whilst reviewing her day. Integration with existing routines proves more sustainable than building entirely new schedules.

When obstacles arise, adjust rather than abandon. The challenge adapts to your circumstances. Your circumstances don't need to adapt to the challenge.

Post-Challenge Planning

Day 30 marks completion of the structured challenge, not the end of using the method. The question is how to continue the practices you've established without the rigid 30-day framework.

Continuation Planning should be based on evidence from your challenge experience. What provided genuine value? The facilities coordinator found weekly reviews most useful - patterns emerged that daily work obscured. He'd continue those. Daily capturing had become automatic, requiring no conscious effort to maintain.

The QA specialist discovered that focused learning arcs with clear proof-piece outcomes worked better than vague skill development goals. She'd plan her next arc based on job market signals from recent applications and interviews.

Habit Refinement adapts what you tested during the challenge. Maybe daily capturing works better in the morning than evening for your schedule. Perhaps weekly reviews need 20 minutes rather than 15. The challenge provided data. Use it to adjust your approach for sustainability.

Next Arc Planning happens naturally if you've maintained your haversack. Your scraps reveal what matters next. The facilities manager's new "Advanced AI Oversight" section was already showing clustering patterns around strategic planning decisions. His next arc was emerging organically.

The 30-day structure proved the method works under your specific circumstances. Now you're building the adaptive capabilities that will serve you regardless of how your industry or role evolves.

Closing

The 30-day challenge you've just read about isn't theoretical. It shows what systematic adaptation looks like when stripped of elaborate planning and heroic effort. Two people, different circumstances, same framework. Both built demonstrable capabilities whilst managing real constraints.

Your 30 days will look different from theirs. Different scraps. Different clusters. Different learning arcs. Different proof pieces. That's how it should work. The method adapts to your situation rather than forcing your situation to adapt to the method.

What remains consistent is the progression: notice fragments, save valuable scraps, spot clustering patterns, run focused arcs, create demonstrable proof. This isn't complicated. It's systematic.

The facilities coordinator and QA specialist both discovered something important through their 30 days. They weren't learning how to predict which specific skills would matter next year. They were proving they could systematically build whatever capabilities circumstances required. That's the shift that matters when the ground keeps moving.

Start your Day 1. Set up your haversack. Capture your first scrap. An hour of preparation, then 30 days of consistent small actions. The challenge isn't impressive, but the cumulative effect is.

In the age of AI job displacement, the ground will keep shifting (that's what it does now). You now have a method for walking on it.

Glossary

Arc A focused period of deliberate practice where you test and develop scraps in real-world situations. Arcs convert theoretical knowledge into practical capability by creating opportunities to apply what you've collected. The process of building and testing scraps to develop a Minimum Viable Skill.

Clustering The pattern that emerges when three or more scraps point in the same direction, signalling a potential capability worth developing. Clusters indicate where your natural curiosity and professional environment are converging.

Fragment Raw material noticed in the world - an article headline, a colleague's comment, a technique observed in a meeting. Most fragments pass without significance. A fragment becomes a scrap when you recognise potential value and choose to keep it.

Haversack Your portable collection system for capturing and organising scraps. Named after the canvas bags travellers carried for essential supplies. The format doesn't matter (notebook, app, folder); the habit of consistent capture does. Travels with you regardless of employer, industry, or role.

Integration Moment An opportunity to apply a scrap or developing skill within your existing work. Integration moments let you test capabilities in low-stakes situations before they become critical.

Minimum Viable Skill (MVS) The smallest usable version of a capability that creates immediate value in your current work. Unlike traditional skill development requiring complete mastery before application, an MVS gets you contributing while learning continues. Built through clustering scraps and running focused arcs.

Proof Piece Tangible evidence of capability - a completed project, documented outcome, or demonstrated result that shows rather than tells. Proof pieces counter algorithmic bias in hiring and make abstract skills concrete for employers.

Scrap A fragment you've selected for potential value. The moment you decide "this might be useful" and choose to save it, a fragment becomes a scrap. Scraps accumulate in your haversack until patterns emerge.

Temperance Learning A philosophy of balanced, sustainable professional development. Rejects both frantic upskilling that leads to burnout and paralysis that comes from feeling overwhelmed. Emphasises rhythm over panic, sufficiency over mastery, and continuous small adjustments over dramatic reinvention.

Notes and Sources

The research, reports, and legal developments that informed this book.

Throughout, I've drawn on employment statistics, academic studies, and legal cases. This section provides the details for anyone who wants to verify a source or explore a topic further.

From Chapter 2: The Myth of Mastery

AI and Economic Impact

Goldman Sachs. "The Potentially Large Effects of Artificial Intelligence on Economic Growth." Goldman Sachs Economics Research, March 2023. https://www.gspublishing.com/content/research/en/reports/2023/03/27/d64e052b-0f6e-45d7-967b-d7be35fabd16.html

Key finding: Up to 300 million full-time jobs globally are exposed to AI automation, particularly in administrative, legal, and basic technical roles.

The Talent Pipeline Crisis

Harvard Business Review. "Embracing Gen AI at Work." September–October 2024. https://hbr.org/2024/09/embracing-gen-ai-at-work

Research indicating AI could transform more than 40% of all work activity.

Walther, Cornelia C. "Is AI Pushing Us to Break the Talent Pipeline?" Knowledge at Wharton, Wharton School of the University of Pennsylvania, August 2025. https://knowledge.wharton.upenn.edu/article/is-ai-pushing-us-to-break-the-talent-pipeline/

Analysis of how AI could replace more than 50% of tasks performed by market research analysts and 67% of tasks for sales representatives, eliminating entry-level training grounds for future leaders.

Workforce Training Gaps

World Economic Forum. *Future of Jobs Report 2025*. Geneva: World Economic Forum, January 2025. https://www.weforum.org/publications/the-future-of-jobs-report-2025/

Survey of over 1,000 employers representing more than 14 million workers across 55 countries. Key finding: 60% of workers will require training before 2027, yet only half have access to adequate training opportunities.

Gen Z and Educational Value

Indeed and Harris Poll. "The Class of 2025: College Degrees in the AI Era." April 2025. https://www.highereddive.com/news/indeed-AI-training-gen-Z/745932/

Survey of 772 U.S. adult workers and job seekers. Key finding: 49% of Gen Z job seekers believe AI has specifically made their degrees less valuable in the job market.

From Chapter 4: The Machinery Behind the Shift

World Economic Forum Data

World Economic Forum. *Future of Jobs Report 2025*. Geneva: World Economic Forum, January 2025. https://www.weforum.org/publications/the-future-of-jobs-report-2025/

Survey scope: Over 1,000 employers representing more than 14 million workers across 55 countries.

Key findings referenced:

- 59% of workers will need training by 2030; 48% expected to receive it (Fig. 3.9, pp.46-47)
- 85% of employers plan to prioritise upskilling existing workforce (Fig. 4.4, p.52)
- 70% intend to hire staff who already possess new skills (Fig. 4.4, p.52)
- 40% explicitly plan to reduce workforce as certain skills become less relevant (Fig. 4.4, p.52)
- Fastest-growing and fastest-declining job roles (Chapter 3 of report)

Labour Market Signals: United States

U.S. Bureau of Labor Statistics. "Employment Situation Summary." September 2025. https://www.bls.gov/news.release/empsit.nr0.htm

August 2025 data showing employers added only 22,000 jobs. Annual benchmark revision (September 9, 2025) revealed 911,000 fewer jobs created between April 2024 and March 2025 than initially estimated.

Labour Market Signals: United Kingdom

TWM Solicitors. "Mass Dismissal Programmes Analysis 2024/2025." 2025. https://www.twmsolicitors.com/

Report showing proposed mass dismissal programmes rose by 5% in 2024/2025, reaching 3,715 programmes with 267,800 proposed dismissals. Manufacturing sector saw 12% increase; public administration, education, and health recorded 19% rise.

Labour Market Signals: Ireland

Department of Finance & Department of Enterprise, Trade and Employment. "AI and Employment Exposure in Ireland." 2024.

RTÉ News. "AI Job Postings Double Since 2023." 2025.

Irish Examiner. "Dublin Shows 71% of Employees in Highly Exposed Roles." 2024.

Combined analysis indicating 63% of Irish employment is exposed to AI transformation, with Dublin and Cork facing disproportionate impact.

Labour Market Signals: Asia-Pacific

Boston Consulting Group. "AI Adoption and Worker Sentiment in Asia-Pacific." July 2025.

Survey of over 4,500 employees across nine APAC markets. Key findings: 78% use AI at least weekly (vs. 72% global average); 53% fear job loss from AI (vs. 36% globally). Job displacement fears by market: Thailand (71%), South Korea (66%), Singapore (65%), Japan (40%).

Labour Market Signals: OECD Countries

Organisation for Economic Co-operation and Development. *OECD Employment Outlook 2023*. Paris: OECD Publishing, 2023.

Organisation for Economic Co-operation and Development. *OECD Employment Outlook 2025*. Paris: OECD Publishing, 2025.

Analysis indicating jobs with high automation risk (where more than 25 of 100 core skills are easily automatable) constitute approximately 27% of employment across OECD countries.

Global Layoff Tracking

Challenger, Gray & Christmas. "October 2025 Job Cuts Report." October 2025. https://www.challengergray.com/

153,074 job cuts announced in October 2025 (highest October total since 2003). Year-to-date cuts exceeding 1 million. AI explicitly cited in 31,039 October cuts; 48,414 AI-attributed layoffs year-to-date.

Expert Commentary on AI Displacement Claims

CNBC. "Analysis: Are Companies Using AI as Cover for Workforce Reductions?" 2025.

Includes commentary from Peter Cappelli, management professor at the Wharton School: "We invest significant time analysing companies genuinely attempting to implement AI, and there's scant evidence that it leads to job reductions anywhere near the scale being discussed."

Amazon Automation and Workforce Changes

Amazon. "Amazon Deploys Over 1 Million Robots." About Amazon, July 2025. https://www.aboutamazon.com/news/operations/amazon-million-robots-ai-foundation-model

CNBC. "Amazon Deploys Its 1 Millionth Robot in a Sign of More Job Automation." July 2, 2025. https://www.cnbc.com/2025/07/02/amazon-deploys-its-1-millionth-robot-in-a-sign-of-more-job-automation.html

Bloomberg. "Amazon to Cut 14,000 Jobs as Jassy Looks to Ease Bureaucracy." October 28, 2025.

https://www.bloomberg.com/news/articles/2025-10-28/amzn-amazon-to-cut-14-000-jobs-across-corporate-workforce

Fortune. "Everyone Thinks AI Is Replacing Factory Workers, but Amazon's Layoffs Show It's Coming for Middle Management First." October 29, 2025. https://fortune.com/2025/10/29/amazon-layoffs-ai-middle-managers-robots-factory-workers/

From Chapter 13: Proof Beats Theory

Mobley v. Workday, Inc.

Mobley v. Workday, Inc., Case No. 3:23-cv-00770-RFL, U.S. District Court, Northern District of California. https://www.courtlistener.com/docket/66831340/mobley-v-workday-inc/

Case timeline:

- February 21, 2023: Lawsuit filed by Derek Mobley
- July 12, 2024: Court denies Workday's motion to dismiss on "agent" theory
- May 16, 2025: Judge Rita Lin grants preliminary certification of collective action under Age Discrimination in Employment Act (ADEA)

Plaintiff alleges Workday's AI-powered applicant recommendation system discriminated on the basis of race, age, and disability. Workday represented that 1.1 billion applications were rejected using its software tools during the relevant period.

Legal Analysis and Commentary

Seyfarth Shaw LLP. "Mobley v. Workday: Court Holds AI Service Providers Could Be Directly Liable for Employment Discrimination Under 'Agent' Theory." July 2024. https://www.seyfarth.com/news-insights/mobley-v-workday-court-holds-ai-service-providers-could-be-directly-liable-for-employment-discrimination-under-agent-theory.html

Holland & Knight LLP. "Federal Court Allows Collective Action Lawsuit Over Alleged AI Hiring Bias." May 2025. https://www.hklaw.com/en/insights/publications/2025/05/federal-court-allows-collective-action-lawsuit-over-alleged

CDF Labor Law LLP. "Federal Court Grants Preliminary Certification in Landmark AI Hiring Bias Case." May 2025. https://www.callaborlaw.com/blog/federal-court-grants-preliminary-certification-in-landmark-ai-hiring-bias-case

EEOC Position on Algorithmic Hiring

U.S. Equal Employment Opportunity Commission. "EEOC Launches Initiative on Artificial Intelligence and Algorithmic Fairness." October 2021. https://www.eeoc.gov/newsroom/eeoc-launches-initiative-artificial-intelligence-and-algorithmic-fairness

U.S. Equal Employment Opportunity Commission. "The Americans with Disabilities Act and the Use of Software, Algorithms, and Artificial Intelligence to Assess Job Applicants and Employees." Technical Assistance Document, May 2022. https://www.eeoc.gov/laws/guidance/americans-disabilities-act-and-use-software-algorithms-and-artificial-intelligence

U.S. Equal Employment Opportunity Commission. "Select Issues: Assessing Adverse Impact in Software, Algorithms, and Artificial Intelligence Used in Employment Selection Procedures Under Title VII of the Civil Rights Act of 1964." Technical Assistance Document, May 2023.

U.S. Equal Employment Opportunity Commission. "Employment Discrimination and AI for Workers." Guidance Document, April 2024. https://www.eeoc.gov/sites/default/files/2024-04/20240429_Employment%20Discrimination%20and%20AI%20for%20Workers.pdf

Key EEOC position: Algorithmic hiring tools are not exempt from discrimination law, and vendors cannot avoid accountability simply by calling themselves third parties.

www.ingramcontent.com/pod-product-compliance
Lightning Source LLC
LaVergne TN
LVHW100301210926
848480LV00003B/984
9781919417417